# Then and Now

## Reading Old Journals
with Eyes of the Heart

Randall Mullins

*for our grandchildren*

**Owen David and Olivia Elizabeth**
**Henry James and Hadley Marie**

*May you come to know your deep kinship with people*
*in every land and with all creatures and all creation.*

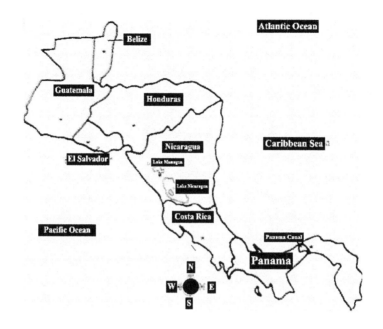

# CONTENTS

*"...so that, with the eyes of your heart enlightened, you may know the hope to which he has called you."*

Ephesians 1: 18

*"Listen to your life. See it for the fathomless mystery that it is. In the boredom and the pain of it no less than in excitement and gladness: touch, taste, smell your way to the holy and hidden heart of it because in the last analysis all moments are key moments and life itself is grace. What I started to do as a writer and preacher was more and more to draw on my own experience, not just as a source of plot, character and illustration, but as a source of truth."*

Frederick Buechner

# INTRODUCTION

The connection to Central America that changed my life began in a San Francisco courtroom in 1982. I was in San Francisco during a sabbatical and a friend invited me to go with him to a hearing at the court of what then was called the Immigration and Naturalization Service. A Salvadoran named Rene Guerra in a business suit who spoke very good English was there to make his case for what the INS called "Extended Voluntary Departure (EVD) Status," a category close to political asylum but not precisely the same. With an articulate lawyer, this man from El Salvador made a strong case that he should be allowed to stay in the United States because if he were to return to El Salvador he would be under constant surveillance and death threats from the government's military "death squads" which had been in the news often in the U.S. I was so naive then that I thought this case was a no-brainer, that "the land of the free and the home of the brave," and the nation with the words posted, "give me your tired, your poor longing to breathe free…" would promptly welcome this impressive man as a guest in our country and offer him protection for as long as he needed it. But the hard questioning of the immigration judge gave clear evidence that this would not an obvious case to him and that it was far from a done deal that Mr. Guerra would be granted EVD status.

I never learned what happened to Rene Guerra, but the judge's harsh words changed my life. Two years later, I took a month-long visit to Nicaragua and Honduras. A year after that, I headed for back for what I thought would be three-month visit. I stayed for three years and came home the adoptive father of two children.

I was among those who had only a very general knowledge of U.S. relations to Central America at the time. We had heard of the Monroe Doctrine, banana republics and the Panama Canal. We knew that Cuba had gone communist, of course, and since the Carter Administration El Salvador's civil war had been in the news. Most of us had heard the term "death squads" by the early 1980s. But until that immigration hearing in San Francisco, Central America had been a remote place in my sense of the world. I had much to learn.

When I returned to Seattle and to my work as Minister of Outreach at University Congregational United Church of Christ (UCC), a large, affluent and fairly liberal church, it seemed that Central Americans were everywhere and that the city had a growing number of people concerned about their welfare. Archbishop Oscar Romero of El Salvador had been assassinated by death squads while saying Mass in San Salvador two years before, in 1980. Seattle's Catholic and ecumenical community had among its leaders then Archbishop Raymond Hunthausen, who in the face of strong reprisals from the Vatican had taken a number of controversial stands, including his very public support to the victims of repression, including U.S.- funded violence and repression, in Central America. In 1979 the rebellion of the Sandinistas in Nicaragua had overthrown the Somoza dictatorship after two generations of brutal repression and mass murder. The local evidence of Central American realities was increasing all around.

In our University District neighborhood in Seattle, there were six mainstream Protestant churches who often cooperated in common missions, often through the Church Council of Greater Seattle, whose offices were also in the neighborhood. One of those churches, University Baptist Church, voted to become a "Sanctuary Church." They turned some of the rooms in their education building into an apartment and took in a family of Salvadoran refugees in open and public opposition to U.S. immigration policies which frequently sent refugees back to El Salvador where, as in the case of Rene Guerra, they faced danger and often death. This became national as well as local news. We were all invited to show our support in any way that we could. University Congregational UCC voted to stand in support of University Baptist.

Within weeks it seemed, my life had been transported into a new sense of connection to Central American people and realities. A doctor in the church offered free medical support to refugees. Others hired refugees to do home repair and other odd jobs. Activist lawyers in the area formed the Northwest Immigrant Rights Project. Along with many others, my former wife and I had a refugee live in our spare bedroom for a time. Church groups were traveling to Central America to see the realities there firsthand.

In January 1984, the national office of our denomination, the United Church of Christ, sent out a letter to churches that our national Office for Church in Society and our United Church Board for World Ministries would be sponsoring a delegation to visit Honduras and Nicaragua and invited people interested to apply. I was among eight from Seattle UCC congregations to be a part of that delegation.

That trip in March 1984 to Honduras and Nicaragua had a strong impact on me. The following stories are taken from journals I kept in Costa Rica, Nicaragua, and especially Honduras from 1984 to 1988. I returned to Estelí, Nicaragua in the summer of 1984 for a month-long experience of cultural immersion, political education and language study. Then in 1985 my former wife Kathy Williams and I decided to move to Central America for at least a full year. We stayed almost three.

Poverty and violence were widespread in most of Central America in the 1980s. As of this writing in 2020, both are much worse today. The added reality of climate change has resulted in rainfall insufficient for growing the corn and beans that have sustained the majority poor in Central America for centuries.

As this is being written, we are also in the midst of the Covid-19 pandemic, a new awakening to the centuries-old police violence against Black and Brown people in our country, and the ongoing brutal treatment of immigrants in "detention centers," which are really immigrant prisons.

The U.S. government's violence against immigrant children, including separating them from their parents, especially stands out in our country's willingness to engage in the most egregious crimes against humanity on our own soil. The Nicaraguan Revolution that began with much hope has collapsed and the situation in Honduras that was so desperate in the 1980s is much more desperate today. In most ways the severe problems of inequality and poverty, while widespread in the United States, is comparatively much greater in most of Latin America. Much of it is a result of U.S. domination and policy in the region.

The moral and political questions will be obvious but the primary purpose here is not extensive political analysis. They are simply the stories of a younger me trying to see more clearly what it means to be a stumbling follower of Jesus, a U.S. and global citizen and a more human being. I have deleted some parts where my unconscious colonialism, racism and general lack of formation were too obvious. Some will be in plain view here. I was far from fully formed then I am still learning how much I don't know and about how much I cannot yet see.

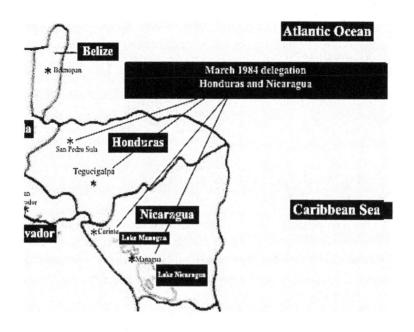

# CHAPTER 1
# HONDURAS AND NICARAGUA
## MARCH 1984

*2020 notes: Our 1984 United Church of Christ (UCC) delegation to
Honduras and Nicaragua included about 30 people from across the
country for seven days in Central America. At the time Central
America had become a place of much interest in the U.S. and across
the world. Leftist rebellions against repressive regimes brought out
fears of the spread of Communism. Church leaders in both Latin
America and the U.S. were very much a part of the conversation.
This delegation was an attempt by the UCC to have typical church
people see Central America first-hand and return to report on what
we had seen in our local communities. Among us there were pastors,
two former long-term foreign missionaries, two African Americans
and one Latino brother, leaders in national church agencies, and a
good balance of male and female. Our leaders were Dr. Patricia
Rumer who was then Latin America Secretary for the United Church*

*Board for World Ministries, and Rev. Gus Kuether, who had previously served for twenty years as a missionary in Honduras and who knew the country well. For most of us it was out first trip to a so-called Two-Thirds World country. We were an enthusiastic crowd. It was my first trip anywhere in Latin America. We met first in Miami for two days of orientation and training before boarding a flight to San Pedro Sula, Honduras. The following is from a journal kept during that trip.*

## Thursday March 1, 1984 Departure Day
*Flight from Seattle to Miami*

For the first time in my life, I decided to watch the in-flight movie. I think the title was "Running Brave." It was the true story of Native American athlete Billy Mills and how he left a sports program at Kansas University that was destroying his soul. He later went on to become an Olympic champion.

The movie was at once engrossing and difficult for me to watch, probably because it touched into some wounds to the soul that I sustained as a varsity athlete in high school and college.

Pat Ryland and I were freshman football players together in college until a shoulder injury forced him to give up football. Within a year he was a proud US Marine. I still have one of his first letters from boot camp. One line in it went something like this *"When I get home I'll be a tough sob, so you'd better tell everyone to get the f. out of the way."*

Patrick became a tail-gunner on a helicopter in Vietnam and was a proud Marine for nearly two years. The first service I ever attended in a Roman Catholic Church was his funeral.

He and I were raised on sports banquet speeches with "inspiring" lines such as "winning isn't everything: winning is the only thing," or "the reason America has never lost a war is because high school and college athletics have made our boys the strongest in the world."

Some old knot in me and maybe in my country unravels a little as I watch the movie. It is strange how my head can so clearly perceive that some attitude is dreadful and then see that it takes ten years for my heart (or my stomach) to understand it.

Somewhere over Missouri, I am sitting here wondering what else might start to unravel during my time in Honduras and Nicaragua. Maybe that's part of what this trip is about for me -- to do a little more unraveling of some personal and national knots that have remained tangled for a long time inside me.

Unraveling seems unlikely to happen without sitting in a very vulnerable posture. My head knows this. I wonder if my heart and my stomach does.

## Friday March 2, 1984
*Skyways Hotel, Miami*

The Skyways Motel is surrounded by freeways and the constant roar of jet engines. It has a kind of Greyhound bus smell. You really do know that it's clean, and you see the polite "for your protection" paper band on the toilet seat. But there's a certain something that feels tarnished beneath the gloss. Or is this simply a projection onto the hotel of some of the harder moments in my inner life?

One instantly senses the pervasive influence of Spanish-speaking cultures in Miami, or at least in this part of town. Airline ticket agents speak with an accent. Tourist brochures are in Spanish and English. Every hotel employee seems to be bilingual. And there is a high-quality Spanish language television station.

One feels keenly here the reasons why many are saying that we in the U.S. will either learn to better understand and integrate Latin American and other Spanish-speaking cultures into our national life, or we will know much pain and division.

*2020 note: Father Henri Nouwen, S.J. had become a popular spiritual teacher and writer for both Roman Catholics and Protestants in the 1970s. It attracted a lot of attention when he decided to shift his attention to Latin America and move to live and work in Peru for a year or two.*

Henri Nouwen has stated it better in the context of Christian faith. A priest, teacher, and writer, Nouwen recently spent time in Latin America to consider the possibility of continuing his ministry there. Here are some excerpts from his reflections on that time:

"My intuition has been that the spiritual destiny of North America is somehow intimately connected with the spiritual destiny of Latin America. . . and I even dare say that knowing God here cannot be separated from knowing God there. The Lord who became flesh wants the two parts of this American continent to live in peace and speak in one voice as a witness for God's presence in history.

"Today we see that the cord called Central America, which binds these two continents together, is beginning to fray, not simply because of economic, social, political, or military reasons, but because of spiritual reasons.

"When I moved to Latin America, I was teaching spirituality and prayers. But gradually I realized that I could not avoid the political, economic, and military mess. I saw then that our spiritual call takes place in the midst of ambiguity and that if I waited until I had a very clear, final view of how things really were before I started saying anything, I would never speak."

Today we will meet for the first time with all the members of the group. It may be easier to argue about international politics on this trip than it will be to see things in the context of Christian faith, the only real authority that we take with us to Central America.

## Friday, March 2, 1984
*Miami*

Rev. Gus Kuether stands a gentle six feet, four inches. Being six feet five myself it is comforting to have someone else around whose head moves about so high up in the air. Word has gotten around that he played a few seasons with the Baltimore Colts. For over twenty years, he served as a missionary pastor in Honduras through the United Church Board for World Ministries (UCBWM). He now lives in Illinois and works for one of the national offices of the United Church of Christ

His introduction today to life in Honduras was thorough and sobering. His concern for Honduras is clear, but it is clear that he does not feel that structural patterns in Honduras will change soon. Some cases in point:

The Evangelical and Reformed Church of Honduras, the United Church of Christ's partner denomination there, would be considered theologically conservative by US mainline Protestant standards. Yet in Honduras they have sometimes been excluded from what ecumenical activity there is among the denomination because they have been too "leftist."

Some 85-90% of the population is nominally Roman Catholic, but only 15% are practicing Catholics. As recently as the 1960s, priest-inspired violence against Protestants occurred. Protestant-Catholic relations are better now, but both groups are still cool about too much working together.

A new law in Honduras allows citizens to call authorities to report anyone they feel may be a "subversive." This has been known to apply to most anyone who has an alternative way of looking at things.

Most of Honduras' business interests are controlled either by people from the Middle East or from the United States. Although law requires that controlling interest in every business must be held by a Honduran, Gus feels that it is widely known that it is not a difficult to "buy" a Honduran in a way to satisfy this requirement.

Honduras is about the size of Tennessee with a population of about 4.5 million. Radio is the media which reaches the largest segment of the population. The country has a number of daily newspapers. Among the major ones are El Tiempo, La Tribuna, La Prensa and El Heraldo.

## Saturday, March 3, 1984
*Gran Hotel Sula, San Pedro Sula, Honduras*

We were definitely not "roughing it" on our first night in Honduras. This hotel has air-conditioning, red tablecloths in the dining room, a swimming pool, and a little balcony outside each room. The water is known to be safe, and the surroundings feel cool and clean.

I don't want to admit it, but it feels good to have this refuge in the midst of the most desperate poverty I have ever seen. It is difficult to see too much of it too soon.

Looking down from our room early in the morning, a man is asleep in the back of a parked pickup. On the streets most every bus stop bench seems to have a body under it. One had two. Just outside the front door of the hotel, one is surrounded by begging children.

One does not easily send them away. They have learned persistence from someone. I don't want to give support to begging as a way of life. I hope they will seek other alternatives. The image of a child's hand reaching out with eyes beseechingly at me is a haunting sight for me. Room prices here seem to be around $20.00 per night. I am told that it is far from the finest of San Pedro Sula's hotels. But it is good to know that one does not have to undergo an instant conversion to deprivation in order to see some of the life in Honduras as it really is.

## Saturday evening, March 3, 1984
*San Pedro Sula, Honduras*

> *2020 notes: The Evangelical and Reformed Church (E and R) in the U.S. had roots in Germany and merged with the Congregational Christian denomination in 1957 to become the United Church of Christ. The E and R Church of Honduras came into being earlier in the 1900s, a result of work by*

> *Caption: Group meeting by the pool, San Pedro Sula, Honduras*

> *E and R missionaries from the U.S. Beginning in the 1960s many U.S. denominations began to recognize the paternal and colonial nature of "foreign missions" supervised by North Americans. The E and R Church of Honduras is now what we call a "partner denomination" with the United Church of Christ. All the property formerly owned by the United Church of Christ has been turned over to the E and R Church of Honduras. Some financial support has continued, but the relationship is now one of two independent entities.*

The Rev. Omar Wills, 34, is articulate, warm, impressive to behold, and probably a person with more passion than he has space to express in Honduras. He speaks of a desire to study in the United States someday.

Omar is one of the leaders of the Evangelical and Reformed Church here. Presently, he is teaching at the Theological Institute, a training center for clergy. By our North American standards, it would span a high school to college academic level. But by Omar's standards of faithfulness in a setting bound by countless limitations, there is pervasive excellence.

He almost seems to be a minority of one here with his open theological perspective. We have not met any Honduran pastors who seem to be deeply involved with the struggles of the poor here. But then why is it that we should expect them to give up everything when so few of us in North America are willing to do so?

Omar shared one telling story of the life of the evangelical (which In Latin America is interchangeable with Protestant) church in Honduras. An evangelist from Oklahoma will be here in April to do a three-day revival in the local soccer stadium. For those who attend all three days, rice and beans will be given out, the amount to be determined by the size of each family. Those who do not manage to maintain perfect attendance will receive nothing. Like Omar, I find this to be a cruel and demonic operation, but I assume that the amount of hunger here will ensure that the Oklahoma brother will get his crowd. I didn't get his name. It's probably just as well.

Apparently this style of Christianity is common not only in Honduras, but throughout Latin America.

Omar is keenly sensitive to the desperate economic situation in Honduras and longs for a restructuring of the society. But he does not want the violence that has been a part of such struggles in other Latin American countries. Is he naive in this?

He believes that the poor here cannot speak up for their own dignity because they lack any kind of "critical consciousness." They simply have not been given access to any perspective other than "communism is bad."

I wonder what Omar's life will be like in 1994. I wonder what the Protestant church in Honduras will look like in 1994.

Our room is on the eighth floor of the hotel, one of the tallest buildings in the city. San Pedro Sula rests in the shadow of beautiful mountains nearby. Scattered streets lights dot the city for miles. The sound of a church bell mixes with the sounds of rock music somewhere on the street below. And in between both I think I heard a rooster crow.

Much is beautiful here. Much is ugly here.

11

In the presence of both there is a sense of being held more completely by a world that is a lot more real, even if a lot more tragic.

## Sunday morning, March 4, 1984
*Central Evangelical and Reformed Church, San Pedro Sula*

Daniel Gomez is apparently one of the key lay leaders in this historic central parish of Evangelical and Reformed Church of Honduras. He is around thirty, attractive, vigorous in his teaching, and obviously well-prepared to teach today's session.

About twenty-five men are present seated in rows. We are on one end of a long and narrow room with glassless windows at both ends. The air is hot and sticky with an occasional breeze making its way into the room. We can hear the rumble of the larger Women's Bible Study class meeting out in the sanctuary.

Daniel moves back and forth between blackboard and podium. The passage is from I Samuel 17, the stories of David and Jonathan. The men in the room, most of whom seem to be much older than Daniel, are quick to respond in taking turns reading the verses in the passage.

It is not difficult to sense much of what is happening here, but I could sure understand more if I could only speak Spanish.

There is much participation. At least half of those present attempted to answer questions at some point during the session.

The group seems to fully support Daniel's authority as the teacher. He probes and probes with his questions until he gets from someone the answer he is seeking. Once or twice the group does not come up with the answer he is seeking, and he answers his own question by turning and writing it on the board.

At the end of the session the board is filled with a neat list of virtues extracted from the David and Jonathan stories: sincerity, humility, love, lack of egoism, intersession, and strength.

Our group of four men are warmly welcomed as visitors, bit no spectacle is made of our presence.

The class ends with the collection of an offering.

*Sunday Worship Service*

After the men's class we joined the women of our delegation in the sanctuary for the worship service.

*Personal Flashback*

This church reminds me of the time when I went to church barefoot in the small country Baptist church where I went as a child in rural Tennessee. People kept cool then with open windows for breezes, fans given away by local funeral homes and one large ceiling fan in the middle of the room. During evening revival services, the children would sleep on folded quilts under the benches (they really weren't fancy enough to be called pews). During the revivals, there would often be a flower service. People would bring their freshly cut flowers and at a point in the service would move about the room giving flowers to others and sharing words of love with them while blind Miss Suty played hymns on the upright piano.

Today in Central Church in San Pedro Sula, the windows were open, electric fans kept the breezes moving, and children were everywhere. There was a time during one hymn when the people moved all over the sanctuary sharing warm greetings with each other.

There were theologies on the loose in both settings which I cannot abide, but much bad theology is bypassed when people speak their gentle words to each other and when cool breezes blow in the heat of life.

Rev. Jeremiah Wright, pastor of Trinity United Church of Christ in Chicago, was invited to preach on about ten hours' notice, including sleeping time. Dr. Wright is one of the outstanding preachers in our denomination in one of the outstanding congregations, Trinity United Church of Christ on Chicago's South Side. We are a predominantly white denomination, but Trinity UCC is one of the few churches in the UCC that can be called authentically African American. Rev. Gilberto Justiniano, a Puerto Rican Latino brother, also from Chicago, translated Dr. Wright's sermon line by line. The sermon combined the best of Black and Latino preaching. Every line in the sermon got double emphasis for anyone who understood even a little Spanish. It was powerful and very well received by the members of Central E and R Church.

The service included a lot of free singing and clapping. These people are not inhibited in their worship life, and it was very good for my soul.

*2020 note: Rev. Jeremiah Wright would later be in the news in 2008 as Barack Obama's former pastor in Chicago. Having gotten to know him as we traveled together, we could see what a distorted and unfair picture of him went out in out of context news bites. He is a man of great compassion and a very gifted pastor and preacher.*

**Sunday evening, March 4, 1984**
*San Pedro Sula, Honduras: A meeting with "refugees" from Nicaragua*

"Refugees" is in quotes because the men in this group were not typical refugees of the world. About ten of them were present. Our group faced theirs in the way the seating was arranged in a cavernous old auditorium in a local high school. The "face-off" of our seating arrangement was somewhat symbolic of the way the conversation began. It felt polite but a bit testy.

Before anyone in the group began to tell their stories, in Spanish only at first, we went through something of an interrogation by them—the only such experience we've had in our first few meetings here. "Who are you? What is your political perspective? Who will you see when you go to Nicaragua?" We could feel the political tensions now typical of Central America, especially on the topic of Nicaragua.

*Meeting refugees from Nicaragua*

After we went through this testing, the group was finally ready to speak of their stories. Some of us could not help but feel that we were being spoken to on the basis of who we were --that we might have heard a different story if we had been a different group of U.S. citizens.

All of these former residents of Nicaragua had undergone great suffering. There was no question about that. All who spoke had been businesspeople of a significant means before the event of the 1979 revolution forced them to leave Nicaragua. Now everyone of them seems to have a comfortable and even opulent life in the influential business community of San Pedro Sula. Would that all the world's refugees had it so well, materially at least.

Here are excerpts of their stories:

An urban architect who had been involved in building and moving houses in Managua was required by the Sandinistas to terminate his business because they said it was exploitive. He commented, "during the first year the Sandinistas did give out a lot of houses... The houses now being built are inferior, earthquake vulnerable, and inhuman to live in.

*"People in charge of the military have taken the better mansions.*

*"I am now selling clothes in Honduras, waiting for Reaganomics to stabilize the world economy so I can live better."*

A chemical engineer, specializing in medicine and nutrition-- (who is presently working in the same industry in Honduras) said: *"I first left Nicaragua because I was on a hit list. Later I returned because I had committed no crimes. But I left again because I knew they were looking to kill me.*

*"The Sandinistas have infiltrated all of Central and South America. It is only a matter of time. (here he seemed to assume) "until all nations have fallen to the Communists."*

*2020 notes: It was interesting and insightful to witness this fear of communists and communism which had filled my upbringing in the U.S. and to meet such affluent Nicaraguans who had to live in fear of their lives. I arrived in Central America with a strong bias in support of the Sandinista Revolution. I did not want to hear that they could be repressive. This was my first experience of learning of the strong opposition to the Nicaraguan Revolution by many Nicaraguans.*

A man who would not share his name or his business because he didn't want to place himself or his business in danger. His business is still operating in Nicaragua. He now lives in Houston, Texas. He was very outspoken, bright, and spoke perfect English (a bit of a surprise to us, for all the conversation up until he spoke had been by an interpreter. We wondered if he wanted to "listen in" for a few minutes to get us "sized up" before the spoke.)

*"The system in Nicaragua now is a brainwash,"* he said. *"For example, the Sandinistas want sixteen-year-olds to vote because they have had four years to brainwash them in the schools.*

*"When you go to Nicaragua, you are going to feel like you are in a police state.*

*"You, the U.S., are the greatest country in the whole world. If you do not fight the Sandinistas, you are opening the doors to communists in the whole god damned world."*

*"This (Nicaragua situation) is a war between two powers-- capitalism and communism.*

*"There was never hunger in Nicaragua as there is right now."*

It was an evening full of tension, nervous laughter, anger, and probably a lot of distrust. I do not question the suffering these people have gone through. But I would be reluctant to buy a used car from any of them.

There was an air of cynicism and even brutality among them that left me feeling very uncomfortable. Their faces were for me studies in distrust, skepticism, and fear.

## Monday, March 5, 1984
*In the Village of Las Minitas in Yoro, Honduras. Remembering my Mississippi Grandmother - Quilla Belle Mullins, 1896-1983*

Grandmother was 87 when she died last summer. Until old age began to give to her its good gifts of endings, I never knew her to be sick. She did have one problem—swollen fingernails, from long days of work with her hands that included picking cotton, working the vegetable and flower gardens, the quilting frame, canning in the kitchen and the list could go on.

She had lived through 87 winters, most of them on one farm, all of them on some farm. She planted and harvested and watched for the sun and rain and for company on Sundays. She picked berries by the gallon, canned fruit and made cakes by the dozen at Christmas time. She was a tireless letter writer — I still have a drawer full of them. As I had expected she lived less than a year after she was moved from her home, garden, trees and sky into a nursing home. Although it would have been difficult for her caregivers, I mourned the fact that she was not able to die close to the land that she loved.

The women and all the campesinos (country folks/farmers) live much closer to the earth than grandmother did, but the land was much kinder to her than it is to them. Their homes are adobe huts arranged around a grassless dirt "plaza." The children we meet do not seem to be seriously malnourished, but we are told this is a large problem here. The signs of desperate poverty surround us, and yet we see hope and possibility in their faces. Whatever their desperations may be, their warm welcome and sharing were boundless grace for me. I would love for my grandmother to have met them.

*We quickly learned that mangos could be found anywhere in Central America.*
Photo credit: "Muchacha con mangos - Girl with Mangos; Lempira, Honduras" by Lon&Queta, CC
license 2.0. See photo credits at end of book for full details.

When we drove into the village after a bouncy ride in two pickups
over four miles of agricultural roads, everyone was waiting to greet
us—some 125 men, women and children. We crowded into their
sweatbox of a one-room schoolhouse where they had been in a class
on the use of fertilizer. The Christian ecumenical organization, the

Christian Commission for Development (CCD), was a source of new hope for them. The teachers at the school shared with much pride their program to minister to the whole person, spiritually, intellectually, and physically.

*Kathy Williams being greeted at a home in Las Minitas.*

Apparently, this village life in which the poor live in villages and work someone else's field for a scant living, is the way that at least 60% of Honduras lives. But Honduras is also made of God at work in the hearts of these campesinos. I felt something of God today that I have never felt before. I left Las Minitas not nearly so much burdened by the suffering of the poor as I did, humbled and lifted by the faith and courage of the people. Would that I could do so well with all in me that is poverty stricken. I hope I will be privileged to share some life with them again.

*2020 comment: At the time of this visit, I had no idea that we would work nearly 3 years with CCD, most of it in service to people in rural villages just like this one.*

Grandmother, the woman of 87 winters, and the campesinos of Las Minitas, were together today and they joined in showing me how life could be lived with integrity from the land we walk on.

## March 5, 1984 Monday Evening
*San Pedro Sula: The Honduran "Brain Drain"*

I'm thinking back over the weekend and of the number of Hondurans we've met who want so badly to leave Honduras.

Sunday after church I was almost stunned in coming upon a very personable and attractive US Marine in uniform. The stunning part was that he was obviously a Honduran. I had not known that one does not need to be a U.S. citizen in order to carry a U.S. gun. U.S. citizenship, however, is almost automatic upon discharge. A Honduran U.S. Marine will never move up very high in the ranks, but that is not what matters. Enlistment is a ticket to get into the U.S.

This young man, now stationed in Los Angeles, was home to visit his family and to make plans for his wife to join him later in New Orleans.

This was the third person within two days who spoke to us of plans to move to the US and all three of them were obviously among the more gifted members of the community.

I am told that this urging could apply to almost any Third World nation. The most skilled Latin American doctors and dentists now practice in the United States. Leaders in business live life by U.S. standards here but many of them would like to live in the U.S.

Nations like Honduras suffer not only from poverty and underdevelopment. They also suffer because the people who grew up here and who would be most able to lead in the nation's progress, are often the first people to go and live elsewhere.

I'm wondering what kind of incentives would influence more talented Hondurans to seek training in their own country, and to live out their lives there. Someone, somewhere must be working on this.

*2020 notes: I learned over time that some Hondurans with the means to do so were able to travel back and forth to the U.S. Some go to visit or to attend college. Many go with hopes of living there. I came to believe that just as the U.S. protested against "taxation without representation" in colonial times in relation to England, Honduras had strong reasons to feel the same way in relation to the U.S. Being a poor nation very dependent on the U.S. it remains the truth that the U.S. government and U.S. companies are able to extract products from Honduras that have little benefit for the majority of Hondurans. One of Honduras' export crops is sugar. We were told that one decision about prices made by a remote individual in the U.S. Department of Agriculture could instantly put thousands of Honduran sugar cane workers out of work. I also came to believe that Honduras should really become a U.S. state. Then our federal government would at least have to provide services that it provides all states instead of just taking wealth away without giving anything back.*

*In the years from 2011-2020 we have seen massive immigration by poor Honduras to the U.S. This was not the case in 1984. The desperation of Hondurans in the 1980s has increased exponentially over the years, especially given the population increase there from 4.5 million in 1984 to over 9 million in 2020, the devastation in Honduras caused by hurricane Mitch in 1998, gang activity and global warming which has made it impossible to grow basic food crops, especially corn and beans.*

## Tuesday, March 6, 1984

*San Pedro Sula, Honduras: Prof. Anibal Delgado Fiallos--Dean of The Regional University Center Of The North, The Autonomous University Of Honduras*

An economist by training, Anibal Delgado Fiallos has been in university education for fifteen years. He is active in politics and an outspoken advocate of human rights. He is forty-seven years old, married, and has six children. His eldest daughter will graduate this year with a degree in chemical engineering.

The "autonomous" in the title seems to be important. The university in Honduras, although funded by the government, seems

21

to be among the freest institutions. Fiallos has been elected Dean three times. The controlling groups in the university are the students and the faculty.

He is a man with a stern but somehow kind face. He receives us in a formal but friendly way, and invites us into a conference room with a u-shaped table. We opt to endure the heat in order to be without the noise of the conditioner.

Conviction and knowledge in a broad area of subjects are apparent soon after he begins to speak:

*"We believe the university campus is the entire country,"* he said. *"The university must go where the people are. It has the role to turn out professionals who are technically capable, but at the same time sensitive to the changes that are needed for the good of the people. We are now prevented from doing this because of national budget cuts in education.*

*"We believe the struggle for peace is fundamental, because only in an atmosphere of peace can there be progress.*

*"We are not the enemy of any country. We believe the U.S. military is here to defend the economic and strategic interests of the United States.*

*"There is a difference between the government and political power. The military here is the real political power, and it carries out the purposes of the U.S. multinationals and the U.S. government.*

*"The economically powerful sections of the US, not the people, have related to us in ways that make us come out on the short end. Yet when our people protest their terrible life conditions, the response of our government is repression."*

*2020 notes: The three preceding paragraphs here are a good, concise description of what the relationship of the U.S. and Honduras has been for well over a century.*

When he began to speak of the history of Honduras, we could see that he became slightly tearful.

*"In the time of the Spanish conquistadors, there was much spilling of blood and innumerable riches were extracted from our country. Then, in the age of colonization, the resources of our work*

*and our country served to enrich Spain. Now it is the US whose practices make us come out on the short end."*

Finally, he gave hints of the risks he incurs by speaking out so freely against repression.

*"In El Salvador, I would be a good candidate for the death squads. Anyone who speaks out as I do must recognize that he could be killed at any time. In Honduras there are also many lists (of people seen as "threats" to the government). circulated. On these lists you will find my name."*

## Ash Wednesday, March 7, 1984
### *At the U.S. Embassy in Tegucigalpa, Honduras*

> *The devil took Jesus up to a high place and showed him all the Kingdoms of the world and said to him, "I will give you all of these if you will fall down and worship me." --Matthew 4:8-9*

Today the scripture was fulfilled before our eyes. The difference is that Jesus managed to say "no" to the devil's offer. The United States continues to say "yes" and bow down at many an altar of death. At least Satan had the integrity to call the offer what it really was-- unabashed control, power over all the nations. In the case of the United States in Honduras, there is a stiff and polite denial that what we are about there is the use of that country for our own purposes.

I am with others in our group outside the main entrance to the U.S. Embassy. The streets are full of guards and guard stations, all staffed with Honduras on the payroll of the US government. We are promptly told to put our cameras away. Before we enter the office building where we are to meet, all cameras and tape recorders are taken up. (This would happen only once more on our trip--at the U.S. Embassy in Managua.)

The sliding steel door finally allows us in--a cautious single file. Our "hostess" made repeated attempts to apologize for all the security. *"This place has been fired on a number of times, you know. We just have to be careful."* Her attempts to cover prison-like security with down-home hospitality never quite succeeded. We are ushered to a basement room and hear first that the ambassador will not be meeting with us. Then we are greeted by Mr. Chris Arcos, the

23

embassy's public affairs officer, the stiffest of all the stiff faces we encountered there. He explained that the Ambassador would soon be in, but would be able to meet with us for only a few minutes because of his tight schedule. Then there's yet another apology for all the security.

Ambassador John Negroponte finally entered. He has all the charm required by the power brokers of this era.

*2020 notes: John Negroponte was U.S. ambassador to Honduras from 1981-85 and is assumed by many to have been one of the chief architects of the massive increase in U.S. military presence during that time as well as one of the key people in using Honduras as a stage to promote and support the "Contras" who were fighting in Nicaragua and trying to overthrow the Sandinista government. He would later serve as U.S. Ambassador to the UN, as Assistant Secretary of State under Condoleezza Rice and as head of National Intelligence. Some felt he was overqualified for the position of Ambassador to Honduras and that he was persuaded to take the post by President Reagan in order to preside during a crucial time in the Reagan administration's determination to overthrow the Sandinista government.*

Arcos introduces him. The ambassador moves from greetings into a speech, but stops to ask us how long we can stay. When we say we are free for the next two hours, the Ambassador proceeds as if there is no rush at all. Arcos breaks in to say to the ambassador that he has explained to us about the Ambassador's schedule and that he is able to stay for only a few minutes. There was a stiff exchange of glances between them. Given that the Ambassador did not seem rushed at all, I suspected that this was the first he had heard of his "tight schedule."

A number of times we heard from native Hondurans that their country is run by the "Holy Trinity" of Ambassador Negroponte, General Gustavo Alvarez, and Honduran President Suazo.

A few comparisons of Negroponte's comments with others we heard from native Hondurans will help to explain why many in our group left with mixed feelings, if not deeply troubled.

Negroponte: *"If anything looks Marxist we must be prepared to defend against it--Nicaragua is one of the most heavily militarized nations in the world."*

On the day before we had met with the ambassador we had an hour with Dr. Carlos Roberto Reina, former professor of constitutional law in Honduras and now a leader in democratic reform and candidate for president in a branch of the Liberal Party of Honduras. It is helpful to compare his comments to those of Ambassador Negroponte. *"Nicaragua is not planning to invade Honduras. It is the other way around.... the threat from Nicaragua is not a military threat, but an ideological threat, and the way to defeat it is by a better idea--democracy."*

Negroponte: *"...we have encouraged the Honduran government to focus on economic development and not the military."*

Reina: *"Honduras paid $4 million just for fuel during the Big Pine military exercises. (This was a joint military operation with U.S. and Honduran troops working together). There is not a fraction of that amount for schools in all of Honduras.*

*"The U.S. has put its eyes on Nicaragua, its hands on El Salvador and its feet in Honduras, flattening us."*

Without quoting any statistics, a press statement by Negroponte on the issue of human rights did acknowledge *"arbitrary arrests and credible allegations of some disappearances,"* but went on to say *"there is no indication that the infrequent human rights violations that do occur are part of deliberate government policy."*

Reina had confirmed the statistics of CODEH, the Committee for the Defense of Human Rights in Honduras: since 1982 eighty persons have disappeared, three clandestine graveyards have been found, and fifty-one political killings were reported in the first six months of 1983.

*2020 notes: Carlos Roberto Reina did not have much of a chance of being elected president given the political realities of the mid-1980s. But he was elected president later and served from 1993-97. As a young activist he survived time as a political prisoner under a Honduran dictator and the bombing of his home in 1996. Unlike most recent Honduran presidents who accepted and obeyed the rule of the military, Reina was able to transfer the power of the military* *into civilian leadership and abolished compulsory military service. During his 1993 campaign, he said that he was running to "remove the stain of being the base for 12,000 Nicaraguan Contra terrorists who waged war to overthrow the democratically-elected government of Nicaragua." He called for a "moral revolution" in Honduras), reduced the military budget from $52 million to $29 million and disbanded the notorious B-316 battalion, known for its terrorism against Hondurans. It seemed so clear that this was a Honduran leader who fully represented the best of professed United States values, yet he received very little support from the United State, especially during the 1980s.*

At one point in the question-and-answer session with our group, Ambassador Negroponte was quick to latch on to a metaphor that surfaced in the conversation to describe present US policy toward Nicaragua, *"if it feels like a duck (or a communist) it must be a duck."* One almost got the feeling that the ambassador felt it urgent to get rid of communists with a "when in doubt, shoot," attitude.

I know that foreign policy is based on self-interest long before it is concerned with morality. But today I saw a painful glimpse of my country's attempts to control all the kingdoms of the world, at the expense of its national soul. And I could not see any national self-interest in policies that were both cruel and undemocratic.

*2020 comment: In April 1984, soon after our trip, General Alvarez resigned as head of all Honduran armed forces. While some felt that this could result in improved democracy in Honduras, others have seen it as just more evidence that the military is in control. Apparently, Alvarez was pressured to resign from higher-ups within the military rather than by independent voices in the civilian government because of human rights violations such as those noted above.*

## Wednesday, March 7, 1984
*Tegucigalpa: The Funny Van with the Tinted Window*

Walking from the US Embassy here to the nearby office of a church agency, we passed an unmarked van with tinted windows. One in our group noticed that we were being photographed.

Although tempted to walk up and give that seemingly clandestine photographer my address and ask him to send me a copy of the picture, I was persuaded by my companions to let it be. I did return the gesture and take his picture. I now own a snapshot of a tinted-window van with a lens-wide opening in the driver's side window. It is strange to go from a country in which so many freedoms are sacred into a place where clandestine actions against its own citizens are part of the order of things. It was more than strange--it was painful to have good reason to wonder if my own government was related to this very strange and disheartening incident.

## Wednesday evening, March 7, 1984
*Tegucigalpa: Excerpts from a Talk By Oscar Puerto, Vice-President Of The Committee for the Defense of Human Rights in Honduras (CODEH)*

"*Four million people live in Honduras. 68% are peasants. Only 22% live in larger cities.*

"*Of the 220,000 hectares (1 hectare equals 2.5 acres) of land owned by transnational corporations here, only 35% is cultivated.*

"*In 1963, the bloodiest coup in Honduran history was used by the military to liquidate a strong campesino and labor movement.*

"*In 1965, a new campesino organization set up the first campesino cooperative in the country. They now have a factory to make oil from crops and have constructed their own subdivision, all in the department (state) of Yoro. This was a proud moment because it demonstrated the capacity of the Honduran campesino. It also showed that we could handle the banana industry, fi it were ever allowed.*

"*From 1962-83, with short exceptions, all the governments of Honduras have been military governments. Hondurans have not had the opportunity to elect their own government. Our governors have come out of our military cartels.*

"*The present U.S. government serves the interests of the United States and is against the interests of the Honduran people.*

"*Now Honduras is a military base. You North American citizens knew about this before we Hondurans did. It has touched all sectors of the people.*"

*2020 notes: The word "American." It became clear after only a few conversations that we were not being referred to as Americans. Most often we were called North Americans ("norteamericanos'). I came to believe, as many in Central America also did, that using the word American to refer to U.S. citizens was an expression of colonialism. In our usual usage referring to people in the Western Hemisphere, there are Canadians, Mexicans, South Americans, Central Americans and finally, "Americans." It almost seems like this means the "real Americans" are only those who are U.S. citizens. I don't believe this will change, but in most of the following I have tried to avoid the word American except when quoting someone else. Spanish has another word for referring to a U.S. citizen, "estdounidense," (United Statesian) but I seldom saw or heard it used except on legal forms. There are many people who do not think of us as the only authentic "Americans." Some Native American writers use the term "U.S. Americans."*

## Economics in Honduras

*More comments by Oscar Puerto:*

*"The Honduran Progress Association (APROH) has the purpose of controlling all the forces of the country, those establishing a totalitarian state. They now control everything that has to do with organization in Honduras.*

*"Industry, banking, and commerce in Honduras are owned by the Arabs.*

*"APROH is closely linked with the Unification Church. Much financing of APROH has come from this church.*

*"In Honduras, the sons of the rich do not do military service. It is done by campesinos and the laborers.*

*"Per capita income in Honduras is $430.00 annually. The majority live on $40/month.*

*"There are 40 hospitals. 26 of these are private.*

28

*"There are only 1200 doctors and all of them are in the cities. This is one doctor for every 10,000 people."*

*2020 notes: In 1988 after we had moved to Tegucigalpa, I would serve as a companion and driver for Oscar Puerto on an evening when he was speaking to a visiting delegation. He was not someone I got to know well, but during his talk he made it clear that one purpose of my accompanying him for the evening was for his own security. He apparently lived his life assuming that he was a target for assassination. But with a U.S. citizen with him, the likelihood of his being captured or killed was very low. Shots had been fired into CODEH's offices in Tegucigalpa and two of their leaders were killed in San Pedro Sula in January 1988.*

## Wednesday, March 7, 1984
*Tegucigalpa, Honduras*

Rev. Gilberto Justiniano, a pastor from Chicago traveling with us, has a large heart to go with his very helpful experiences in having grown up in Chicago's Puerto Rican community. A few minutes before our speaker was to arrive he stood up and suggested that it might be good if we would just stand up, walk around and hug each other.

My defenses and cynicism quickly rose. I am against contrived intimacy. I do not like it when people feel touching as an intrusion rather than as an expression of affection.

But while I sat there a few seconds grinding away inside my cynicism, I notice that the rest of the group was complying.

I guess the social pressure got to me. I managed to get up, hug, and be hugged. The room was filled with joy. I realized what a subtle loneliness can set in in just a few days away from the friends that one can touch. I was very grateful to have some new friends to touch.

It was not contrived at all. Thank you, Gilberto.

## Thursday morning, March 8, 1984
*Arrival at Sandino Airport, Managua, Nicaragua*

Unlike the worn and ragged feel of both airports in Honduras, this one has a clean feeling. It is even shiny and looks modern.

One of the first things I saw upon arriving at this airport was a cleaning employee stepping out of his way to pick up a small piece of litter. Was this evidence of a new sense of dignity in this country or is it just a subjective urging within me that wants so badly to find that the marks of the spiritual, including material, progress in this nation are indeed real.

*Hotel Estrella (Spanish for star)*

The tiny lobby area has a red brick floor. I notice that one of the bricks is loose. A color television plays in the adjoining area of the lobby. The hotel is under ten years old. it has a kind of motel design, two floors with outdoor sidewalks, the kind you'd see on a lot of U.S. interstate highways. But there's a pool here, and a rather nice restaurant. When I mentioned the name of Hotel Estella later to a pastor, he commented on what an expensive hotel it was. For us, it seemed a low-grade hotel. In Nicaragua, it was an expensive one.

**Thursday afternoon, March 8, 1984**
*Beside the pool at the Hotel Estrella, Managua*

A welcome by Sixto Ulloa Dona, Coordinator of National and International Affairs for the Evangelical Committee for Aid and Development (CEPAD), an agency representing over 40 Christian denominations in Nicaragua

A busy but soft demeanor about him, Sixto is dressed in a sport shirt. His welcome was warm and energetic. His words for us were clear, respectful and firm:

*"A few years ago, after your missionaries came here and taught us not to drink and not to smoke Then some of us traveled to the U.S. We stayed in pastors' homes and swam in the swimming pools of some pastors' homes. We also saw the pastor's wife in a bikini, and our reaction was. 'We sure like your theology.'*

The group roars with laughter. There is much more to the missionary heritage in Nicaragua than this story, but Sixto's charm and wit moves us into realizing the hypocrisy of much of that heritage.

*"I think many U.S. denominations still think like multi-national corporations -- Latin America is the land of the conquered. All the denominations that came here taught basically the same thing-- a list of don'ts: don't smoke, don't drink, and don't get involved in any politics which threatens the power structure.*

*"But about twenty years ago, out of the very seeds planted by the missionaries, we began to question. We now believe in a Gospel that is prophetic, free, for the people, and for the poor. Injustice needs to be stopped and we demand justice.*

*"During the time of Somoza, Christians representing our churches went to Somoza to protest that fifty-four Christians had been burned alive. Those who went did so in fear.*

*"Somoza never had a literacy campaign. The Sandinistas had a very successful one. When the U.S. sent money here for aid after the 1972 earthquake, Somoza sent it to a bank in Switzerland.*

*"Now with a political change here in Nicaragua, we Christians participate. Here something happens that does not happen in Cuba--the Church participates in the government. Here there is freedom of worship ... tons of Bibles enter monthly. No one from the Sandinista government is questioning why the churches are gathering.*

*2020 note: The free participation of churches in the political life of the country was one of the clearest aspects that set Nicaragua apart from Cuba, a comparison that was constantly made.*

*"While you are here, we want you to talk to those who are for the government and those who are against it. Ask any question you wish.*

*"We distinguish between the government/imperialism of the United States and the people.*

*"We feel that in being here you are sharing the beatitudes (Matthew, Chapter 5) with Nicaragua."*

*Thatched roof under construction*

Sixto Ulloa's words had extra significance because he was one of us, a product of more progressive Christian denominations, such as ours, which had long histories in sending foreign missionaries to Nicaragua.

### Friday morning, March 9, 1984

*U.S. Embassy in, Managua, Nicaragua:    Ambassador Anthony Quainton*

Conversation on the bus before we arrived includes some hearsay that Quainton will be leaving Nicaragua because Henry Kissinger feels he is too complimentary of what the Sandinistas have accomplished in housing, literacy, and health care.

The U.S. Embassy in Managua is different than the one in Tegucigalpa. Security is apparent, but not with the same intensity. The grounds are surrounded by an iron fence, but the bus is allowed to drive inside the gate.

That gate, we are told, is a weekly gathering place each Thursday for Americans who live in Managua. They come to demonstrate against U.S. policy. At about the time of the Grenada Invasion, one placard read, "Mr. Reagan, please do not come and rescue us."

We are ushered into a conference room. "Tony" Quainton enters in an informal manner. Anything pretentious seems minimal. He is dressed in a Guayabara white shirt, one of those short-sleeved, shirt-tail-out type shirts that are an option for "dress-up" in the heat of Central America. He greets us and starts by asking us what we want to know. When we ask him for some introductory remarks, he notes early how many U.S. church groups have traveled to Managua, every one of them questioning U.S. policy toward Nicaragua. He mentions no groups that have traveled to Nicaragua to support present U.S. policy.

Nevertheless, his line is basically that of the administration, but with such a different feel than at the embassy back in Honduras. He points out that there are twice as many in the Nicaraguan military now as there were under Somoza, but does not mention the difference in technology between its weaponry and the weaponry being provided the anti-government Contras by the United States. Nor does he mention how many Nicaraguans were killed or tortured under Somoza.

The atmosphere here is very different than the atmosphere at the U.S. Embassy in Tegucigalpa. Quainton comments, *"I have not felt any hostility toward me as an American."*

Quainton makes a sound academic case for current administration policy. He is not very convincing and is generally "not free to comment" on issues which we feel are most central (e.g., U.S. covert aid to the Contras). One can't help but wonder if he's more tied to his diplomatic career than he is to getting all the truth out.

He promises to meet with some of us again in Seattle. As ambassadors come and go in this administration, he is not the most discouraging. Trouble is he is going instead of coming. He will leave his post in Nicaragua in May.

As we departed, the ambassador shared with us a longer paper he had written entitled, *The Nicaraguan Revolution: Marxism, Nationalism and Christianity.*

Here are quotes from that paper:

*"None of the Central American Republics has a history of sustained democracy. Turmoil, coups and civil wars have been the*

*order of the day. Such continues to be the reality in the region except in tranquil Costa Rica with its forty years of continuous democracy.*

*"Few political observers watching Central America in the 1970s would have predicted the complexity of the Sandinista Revolution. A few asserted that Nicaragua would become a carbon copy of Cuba with all of its totalitarian features. Others hoped that a Fabian socialist system might emerge. The reality is neither fish nor fowl but a complex mixture of Marxism-Leninism, Christian Socialism, and fervent anti-American nationalism. These ingredients are not static and the future here depends on how the Revolution evolves.*

*"Come with me for a minute to the suite of offices of one of the nine commandants of the Revolution, Tomas Borge Martinez, Minister of the Interior and Head of State Security and the Sandinista Police. In one of the three rooms of his suite, next to the drinks, is his desk. On it are two books: the Bible and the Fundamentals of Marxism-Leninism. On the wall is the largest collection of crucifixes in Nicaragua. They come in all sizes and shapes, from all corners of the world.*

*"Come with me to a mass demonstration. There are, perhaps, sixty to one hundred thousand people present. The crowd, echoing the epistle to the Hebrews, chants: "Sandino yesterday, Sandino today, Sandino forever." The nine commandants are seated on the platform. there is a tenth chair — and empty chair— for Carlos Fonseca Amador, one of the three founders of the Sandinista Front for National Liberation who had died in the fighting in 1976. When his name is mentioned the crowd shouts "presente!" (he is present!) Nearby, his tomb, with its eternal flame, proclaims him to be one who will never die.*

*"If we drive around Managua we will see many billboards, one of them warning, 'Counterrevolutionary: the eyes of the Revolution are watching you 24 hours a day.'*

*Another one depicts Augusto Cesar Sandino, military leader of the Nicaraguan struggle against the U.S. Marines in the 1920s and 30s and after whom the Sandinistas are named.*

*"The Revolution uses Christian forms and proclaims itself to be inspired by the Gospel. It insists there is no contradiction between Christianity and the Revolution. There is no doubt that Christianity*

*and Marxism infuse the Revolution, but the latter is more important than the former ... Class struggle, nationalization and confiscation are necessary phenomena if (the revolution is to be complete).*

*"Many Nicaraguans feel that the Revolution has lost its nationalistic focus. Eden Pastora, one of the original Sandinista commandantes, has taken up arms on exactly that issue. He believes that the Sandinista leadership has sold out to the Soviet bloc and replaced Somoza's dependency on the United States with a new dependency on Cuba.*

*"But what about Christianity, the third ideological element of the Nicaraguan Revolution? No other Marxist revolution has ever explicitly emphasized its Christian origins, nor talked so much about the compatibility between its values and the values of the church.*

*"There is no doubt that for the Archbishop of Nicaragua and for many Catholics in the country, the revolution is seen as moving toward a materialistic and atheistic state in which religion will be marginalized.*

*"The interaction of Christianity and the Revolution does not take place only at the level of ideological competition between the nine commandantes and the established Catholic Church, especially the Nicaraguan Catholic Bishops Conference. Revolutionary structures are permeated with practicing Christians. Four Catholic priests hold high positions in the government and/or the party: The Foreign Minister, the Minister of Culture, The Ambassador to the OAS, and the Vice Chief of the Sandinista Youth Organization. Many of these Christians have been deeply influenced by Liberation Theology. Some affirm a compatibility between Marxism and Christianity. All would insist on a "preferential option for the poor" as a basic Christian and Revolutionary goal.*

*"Christian student groups at the Jesuit-run Central American University provided grist for the revolutionary mill. At least one of the nine commandantes, Luis Carrion, entered the Sandinista (FSLN) Movement through a radical Catholic student group. Others came under the influence of Father Ernesto Cardenal, now the Minister of Culture, who in the mid-60s formed a small community on the island of Solentiname, to which were attracted not only artists and poets,*

*but also those who saw the possibility of convergence between Christianity and revolutionary change.*

*"Nicaragua, in its way, is almost as religious as Poland. The Revolutionary leadership recognizes the perils of confrontation with the hierarchical church. Nonetheless it has not hesitated to challenge the church, indeed the Pope himself, when it sees Revolutionary values challenged or Revolutionary programs thwarted.*

*2020 notes: Before founding the community on Solentiname, Ernesto Cardenal had been a novice at the Catholic Abbey of Our Lady of Gethsemani in Kentucky and was a novice there when well-known author and priest Thomas Merton was novice master. Merton's writings revealed that he had considered moving to Solentiname himself after Cardenal had begun the community. Polish Pope John Paul II, was firmly against what the priests were about as part of the Revolution. He made a visit to Nicaragua to bless the "faithful" there (i.e. those who were loyal to the traditional Catholic structure but not the Revolution). and to reprimand priests who were involved in the Revolution When his jet landed in Managua Father Ernesto Cardenal was there to greet him. Cardenal kneeled to kiss his ring as is the custom to show reverence to the Pope, but the Pope instead shook his finger at Cardenal and told him he had to get his politics in line with the church. It became a well-known piece of news footage in the early 1980s. Cardenal never departed from his commitment to the Revolution.*

*His brother, Jesuit Father Fernando Cardenal, served as the Minister of Education in the Sandinista government. He led a massive literacy campaign that reduced illiteracy in Nicaragua from over 50% to under 15%. When his priesthood was suspended by Pope John Paul II, he said he had to choose between the voice of the Pope and the voice of Jesus. He was later reinstated to the Jesuit order. He resigned from his government post when he felt that the Sandinistas had abandoned the poor.*

*"Liberation Theology," a strong movement in the Catholic Church which began in South American in the 1960s, had become well-known among U.S. Catholics and many Protestants. For many of us it became an important restoration of the New Testament's obvious*

*priority for the poor, the "least of these," as primary in Christian practice. I had taken a class on Liberation Theology in seminary in 1976.*

*Ambassador Quainton was a respected moderate in relation to all that was going on in Nicaragua. Apparently, the Reagan administration wanted someone in the post who was not so moderate. He was replaced as Ambassador to Nicaragua within two months after our visit with him. I disagreed with him on some points but had great respect for his broad knowledge of Central America.*

*Both Pope John Paul II and his staunch ally President Ronald Reagan stood in firm solidarity in their conviction that the Sandinista Revolution must be opposed and/or destroyed in every possible way. I felt then, and still feel today, that U.S. unwillingness to engage with governments whose systems are very different from our own has brought tragedy after tragedy to the citizens of other countries as well as to the soul of our own country. It appeared in the 1980s that Great Britain, France and a number of other European allies had no trouble having diplomatic relations with Nicaragua. There were a number of cases in which our allies showed active support. It was especially hypocritical to me that even a strong moderate like Anthony Quainton could speak so forthrightly about the flaws of the Sandinistas without mentioning the long history of U.S. support for the Somoza dictatorship there and the many other instances of U.S. domination and repression.*

### Friday afternoon, March 9, 1984

*The Offices of La Prensa Newspaper Managua: A visit with Jaime Chamorro, General Manager and Secretary of the Board of*

*Directors, La Prensa Newspaper*

There is censorship in Nicaragua. Let there be no question about that. The Sandinista government apparently reasons that with the country under constant attack by U.S.-supported Contras, censoring opposition papers such as La Prensa was justified. Could their reality be similar to the U.S. reality during World War II when many U.S. papers loyal to our cause were very willing to respond to government requests to censor articles that might be a threat to national security? It is not easy to compare, but security is certainly an issue for this country.

La Prensa is the one opposition paper among the three large papers in Managua. Each week the Sandinista representative comes and clips out articles that will not be allowed. A bulletin board on the front door of the newspaper's offices displays them.

I do not wish to defend or criticize the censorship. I do not honestly know if it is necessary or not to "maintain security in a time of emergency," as the Sandinista government seems to be contending at present.

I do have some concerns to see this censorship within perspective.

Today we also met with two human rights leaders from Guatemala, another U.S. "ally." Their word was that some fifty Guatemalan journalists have been assassinated by the government, and that those who survive are afraid to publish. Those who died could have been killed by U.S-supplied weapons, as have many others in Guatemala.

(The meaning of press censorship seems to be a relative term among Central American countries.)

I am concerned about basic freedoms in Nicaragua. I am not convinced that human rights there could never take a turn for the worse.

*2020 note: Especially during the last ten years, 2010-2020, human rights have certainly taken a turn for the worse, and many of them a result of the abuses of power by Daniel Ortega, president and one of the key leaders of the Sandinistas in the 1980s*

But I am thinking about a certain scripture that has to do with "getting rid of the log in one's own eye before attending to the splinter in the eye of the neighbor." If we are really concerned about censorship and freedom of the press in Central America, then we have work to do first in Guatemala and El Salvador-- among our allies.

**Saturday, March 10, 1984**

*Corinto, Nicaragua: The CIA in Nicaragua*

Today we got an up-close introduction to the work of the Central Intelligence Agency in Nicaragua. While the primary means for the United States to attempt an overthrow of the Sandinista government is through training and funding of the Contras, we learned today that this policy also includes attacks carried out by the CIA. We visited the small city of Corinto (Corinth) on the Pacific coast about 75 miles northwest of Managua. Corinto is Nicaragua's largest port and an entry point for the import of oil, so crucial to every aspect of the lives of Nicaraguans. We met with leaders from the government who told us how CIA gunboats known called Piranhas fired on and destroyed the crucial tanks for holding oil in Corinth. Piranhas, also known as Q boats, were heavily armed and disguised as fishing boats.

Our group is made up of a spectrum of people from moderate Republicans more inclined to give every benefit of doubts to U.S. policies and others of us who came with a strong sense of the wrongdoing of the United States throughout Central America. But there seemed to be no disagreements among us about how wrong these U.S. attacks at the port of Corinto were.

One of the officials speaking to us had a name for the CIA

with a distinct pronunciation. He referred to it as "La SEE-ya." We also heard this distinct pronunciation from others. It was for me an awakening moment of how much Nicaraguan knew about the CIA that I knew nothing about.

*One of the oil tanks bombed by the CIA in Corinto*

The time at Corinto today was a harsh awakening for me and I think for all of us.

*2020 notes: CIA attacks on Nicaraguan harbors had been front page news but it soon faded from public view. In September 1983 it was agreed by the CIA and the Senate Intelligence Committee that the U.S. could support the Contras but not conduct any paramilitary operations of its own. In spite of this agreement, at both Atlantic and Pacific Coast Nicaraguan ports, attacks continued to be carried out with a CIA mother ship moving back and forth through the Panama Canal to provide all weaponry needed. Included were shelling of oil tanks and mining of ships in the harbors. It was widely reported that dozens of merchant ships belonging to six nations were mined. In spite of resistance across the U.S. the harbor attacks did not bring U.S. attempts to overthrow the Nicaraguan government to an end. But in 1986 the highly illegal Iran-Contra affair became public and for two years remained a public scandal for the U.S.*

*The Pledge of Resistance: This movement across the U.S. in the late 1980s to oppose U.S. actions in Nicaragua remained strong. One aspect of it was the "Pledge of Resistance." Thousands from cities across the country signed a public pledge that if the U.S. were to directly invade Nicaragua to overthrow the government, everyone who had signed the pledge would fill the streets in civil disobedience of such U.S. actions. Many believed this movement served as a strong deterrent to more U.S. atrocities than those which did occur.*

*Front porch in Corinto*

## Sunday morning, March 11, 1984

*Worship at First Baptist Church, Managua*

Everything at church today felt so familiar. The hymns sung were Spanish versions of the hymns sung throughout my childhood in Baptist churches. Even though it was Nicaragua there was something very recognizable in the Baptist culture there.

Two leaders who met with us after the service were especially impressive. The pastor, Rev. Gustavo Parajón, was also a medical doctor who had been educated at a number of U.S. universities. He, of course, spoke perfect English. It was immediately clear that he knew a lot more about U.S. culture than we knew about life in Nicaragua.

Dr. Parajón had been among the founders of CEPAD, (Evangelical Committee for Aid and Development) which grew to include over 40 Protestant denominations in its country-wide relief and development work. It had begun in response to the devastating Nicaragua earthquake of 1972.

Rev. Gilberto Aguirre, the Executive Director of CEPAD, was also present. Both of them made it very clear that they had many disagreements with the Sandinista government and showed no hesitations in speaking of them openly. They also spoke of ways in which the Sandinistas had been supportive of CEPAD's work. It was very clear that many Protestant and Evangelical churches felt support by the Sandinista government that had never been possible under the Somoza dictatorship.

*2020 notes: During the Sandinista Revolution and the war in the 1980s, CEPAD was the intermediary between the evangelical churches and the government, and won the attention of Nicaraguan President Daniel Ortega, who appointed Parajón a member of the National Reconciliation Commission, together with Cardinal Miguel Obando y Bravo, former Roman Catholic Archbishop of Managua.*

This appointment led to misrepresentation in some circles that CEPAD was a communist organization working in tandem with the Soviet-backed government. As a result, CEPAD's clinics became targets for attacks from Contra rebels who sought to overthrow the government, placing doctors, nurses and patients at risk. An intervention by Eastern Baptist Theological Seminary (now Palmer Theological Seminary) professor and author, Ron Sider, who organized visits by conservative leaders from the USA to the sites served by the organization, helped to dispel the accusation. CEPAD continues its ministry of reconciliation.

*Statue of St. Francis in front of the Church of Santa Maria de los Angeles, Managua*

## Sunday evening, March 11, 1984
*The 5:30 mass at the Church of Santa Maria de Los Angeles, Managua*

> *"Daddy, what will we do if the US Marines come and invade us?"*
> *"I'll tell you what I'll do, I'll take you and mama and put you in a safe place, and then I'll go and kill Marines one each day, every day."*

These were the words in story told by a lay member on this parish after his young son had asked the above question. The words were shocking and not easy to hear for this North American trying to be devoted to nonviolence. His testimony was one of two requested by Father Uriel Molina, the well-known pastor here, following his own sermon. Father Molina is obviously a priest of the revolution here, a spokesperson for Liberation Theology and God's "preferential option for the poor."

I cannot condone those words of determination to the point of violence and killing, spoken in the context of Christian Worship. And yet within the perspective of all I have seen here, I must say that I hear with some understanding. I hear them with more understanding than when I heard the news of My Lai or when I woke up to the brutality of Bull Connor in Birmingham.

Would words of the necessity to resort to violence here be so necessary if it had not been for the history of U.S. influence? I do not know the answer to this. I do find that I cannot see this man as lacking compassion. Nor can I quickly flail at him the Gandhian ideals that violence only begets more violence. So much that we have seen here and in Honduras suggests that the systematic destruction of the present Nicaraguan government is quietly underway, and that a more overt effort to overthrow it would ensue if only the U.S. Congress and public would allow it.

Although they were hard words for this North American to hear, but they were words that touched in me more of the tragedy of my country's presence here than my belief that all war is obsolete. One does not forget such words especially if they are spoken in the context of Christian worship. And yet the words are not what I will remember most about this remarkable worship experience.

*2020 notes: The harshness of these violent words were shocking to me. It was more evidence that the Sandinista Revolution had been committed to overthrowing the dictatorship by any means necessary. While I could not and cannot support violence as either the most moral or most effective form of resistance, I could not make harsh judgments of even these violent words spoken in church when I compared it to the decades of harsh violence against Nicaraguans that the U.S. had either directly committed or supported through the Somoza generations.*

*Father Miguel D'Escoto, a Maryknoll priest who became Nicaragua's Foreign Minister, spoke our often for nonviolence, and while serving as Foreign Minister, went on a 30 day fast to denounce the policies of Ronald Reagan. Later in his career Father D'Escoto became a trusted diplomat among Latin American countries and in the United Nations. He seemed to believe that the Sandinista Revolution had no choice but to resort to violence to end the vicious dictatorship.*

During his sermon, Father Molina invited all the children to come and sit beside him on the platform. When it came time to "pass the peace," the children were the leaders--bare-chested, barefoot, they moved about the church embracing natives and strangers alike.

Nicaragua's future embraced me more with love than with violence. Barefoot faith, naked in its poverty, and boundless in its possibility, sent me away with a heart unraveled a little by a compassion I have never known before.

A bare-chested, barefoot seven-year--old walked right up and embraced me with no hesitation, this U.S. citizen whose tax dollars may someday be used to kill him (and may already have been used to kill someone who loves him).

This was the miracle of Los Angeles church, and the miracle that will stir in me for a long time to come.

There was much more to Los Angeles church--space allows only the following snapshots:

--the platform filled with youth with guitars and other instruments, filling the Mass with their enthusiasm and their excellent music.

--the presence of dozens of Europeans and North Americans. This Mass has become a stopping place for the hundreds of foreigners who come through Managua each week, wanting to offer support for the Revolution.

--the murals all around the room, telling the story of Nicaragua's struggle for freedom and the central mural high above the altar of Christ on the cross, and oppressive earthly powers being put to shame by this power.

--the sermon of Father Molina, reminding hits people of the Exodus story, and how, when the children of Israel had gotten out of

Egypt, many became discouraged and wanted to return to the security of Pharaoh.

--the dirt streets, the tiny huts, and the dusty surface on everything.

the utter and complete immersion of this parish to the life of the barrio.

--the children holding hands in a circle around the communion table with Father Molina, just before the sharing of the bread and cup.

--the priests sharing the cup with a Protestant North American pastor assisting in the service.

The snapshots and stories could continue forever. I hope they will in this most special parish for the people.

**Monday, March 12, 1984**
*Managua, Nicaragua: Flashback to 1961, Westwood High School, Memphis, Tennessee*

*"If niggers try to get into this school, one thing we can do is to boycott them, treat them like the nobodies they are."*

*"Can you imagine having to sit on the same commode that a nigger has used?"*

In the eighth grade, our school days began with the national anthem on the intercom, the pledge to the flag, and the Lord's Prayer.

At "third period," the class was "health." As I look back now I would have to call it "racism for youth." This teacher, who was also my basketball coach and my strongest role model at the time, spent major portions of class time teaching us how we might resist integration if it should happen to us. There was enthusiastic support for all that he said. I never heard a dissenting opinion to his racism, save for one widely condemned comment by another teacher who suggested that the black schools in the area were inferior. My upbringing was soaked in overt racism.

In my high school, American history, a few years later, I do not remember one point that questioned the policies of the United States. Racism continued as the context for the study.

Finally, in my good Presbyterian college, the seeds of healthy dissent and dialogue were planted. And yet even there, it was only the heavy surgery of the 1960s that opened up the poison of deeply embedded values that could tolerate no alternatives. Its own racism was very clear. Racism became a part of my DNA before I was born, but I would not know this for a long time.

Today, some in our group visited a private school in Managua. They were saddened by what seemed to be pervasive Sandinista propaganda being given to the children. Perhaps it is sad. Perhaps the people here who are so devoted to their revolution would do well to teach the children that the capitalism and dictatorships which oppressed their ancestors were not all bad. Perhaps the children should not be so heavily convinced that the U.S. government is attempting to overthrow their country. Or perhaps not.

I have had to unlearn a lot of the racist, anti-communist propaganda of my early education. I also know that my education in the Southern United States had more overt prejudices built in than that of other regions of the country. And I know that racism in the US, whether covert or overt, is not limited to the south.

Should Black children in the United States be told that slavery was not all bad?

The children I have met here in Nicaragua, in the streets and in the churches, have not been taught to hate "gringos." Someone has taught them to love us and accept us as friends.

*2020 notes: As I have reread things I wrote over 35 years ago I feel some appreciation for my earnest desire to see the truth of Nicaraguan reality for what they were. I did not want to find so many flaws in the Sandinista Revolution but they were certainly present. I also feel some embarrassment at the ways my unconscious racism and colonialist mindset showed up in my writing.*

*Chickens on their way to the market.*

## Monday, March 12, 1984

*At the Moravian Church in Managua: The Miskito problem in Nicaragua--Signs of Reconciliation*

One of the areas where the Sandinista government has had severe criticism is in its treatment of the Miskito Indian population on the Atlantic coast. "Miskitia," as the area is called, is a culture all to itself and very remote from most of the Nicaragua population. Miskito people live on both sides of the Rio Coco the boundary between Honduras and Nicaragua. Even though some are Nicaraguan citizens and some are Honduran, apparently, their day to day lives include a lot of intermingling both economically and socially, that has nothing to do with what country one belongs to.

It seemed clear to many that the Miskitos were virtually another country. They felt no need for a revolution and seemed satisfied when they were left along to carry on their lives in their own way. While the rest of Nicaragua was Roman Catholic, the one church that had become primary for Miskitos was the Moravian Church. They had not been included in the plans during the years building up to the Sandinista revolution. When the Sandinista went into Miskito region to export the revolution they apparently had little understanding of Miskito culture and were lacking in cultural sensitivity. The Miskitos rebelled and became known as people opposing the Revolution. When President Reagan learned of this around in the early 80s, he promptly moved to make them his allies against the Sandinistas. Many Miskitos became operatives of the CIA.

*captions: Rev. Fernando Colomer (left) and Rev. Norman Bent (center), The Moravian Church of Managua (right), 1984.*

*2020 notes: Sandinista leaders would later acknowledge mistakes they had made in relating to the Miskito people. Tomas Borge, who was in charge of negotiations with the Miskitos on behalf of the Sandinista government, said the following at their successful conclusion: "We are capable of demonstrating to the world that we are able to overcome our own mistakes...that we have the modesty to enrich our knowledge of reality. Practice has shown us that it is scientifically incorrect to reduce social reality to class distinctions. We therefore recognize that ethnic diversity is among the moving forces of the revolution."*

The Rev. Fernando Colomer and the Rev. Norman Bent are Miskito Indians. They are also committed and articulate Christians and pastors in the Moravian Church, the predominant Protestant presence among the Indigenous people in Nicaragua's remote Atlantic community on the east coast at Nicaragua.

Both of them wear healing faces which blend the rewards of compassion with the strains of suffering.

And both of then tell stories from inside the Miskito community that seem to have received scant hearing in North America. North American news widely reported that Sandinista treatment of the Miskito people was among the Sandinistas greatest failures.

We were received by them so warmly that it would seem strange not to refer to them by their first names. However, if I were to speak only out of the immense respect that I now have for them, no title or prefix would be adequate.

Norman Bent's ethnic heritage is both African and Miskito. He wears a bright red knit shirt and seems like someone who would be at home in any North American middle-class environment. He is sensitive, cheerful and his gifts of leadership become quickly apparent. It is very clear that he represents a unique cultural community within Nicaragua, and that he knows how to relate to U.S. citizens.

He is also the pastor of the Moravian Church of Managua in whose sanctuary we are meeting. The building is yet another "breezeway brick" structure, like so many in Central America. Brick patterns are artistically arranged so that air can circulate through the building at all times.

We arrange the sanctuary's folding chairs into a circle. Within a short time members of our group find themselves with children in their arms. This is not only a church. It is also a refugee center. The small courtyard surrounding the sanctuary is crowded with huts and unfinished buildings which house seventy-five Miskito Indians, refugees in Managua from the Atlantic Coast. There is a steady movement of Miskito people in and out of our meeting.

Fernando's facial features seem more fully Miskito. One senses in his presence something of the beauty of Miskito culture. But one can also see quickly that he is a person with a mind very awake to political realities, durable compassion, and political savvy, all borne of his commitment to his people and to his church.

He is also a superintendent in the Moravian church. The majority of his years have been spent in the remote Atlantic regions. He first came to Managua by order of the Sandinista government. He was held in jail for six days (for which the Sandinistas later apologized to him). Until the Sandinista government declared an amnesty toward the Miskitos on December 1, 1983, many had been brought to Managua and jailed. Some family members followed along, thus there developed the Miskito refugee community in Managua.

Upon his release from jail, Fernando saw the need for a ministry with the Miskitos in Managua and so has remained here to work with the church's refugee program.

Their approach to solving the Miskito problem in Nicaragua is not one that we hear much about in the US. It is one that deserves more attention. Comments by both of them here follow. Comments by both men included the following. U.S. Media Coverage of the Miskito Situation: *"Some of the most prestigious U.S. papers are misrepresenting the situation here."*

Sandinista Treatment of Miskitos: *"The Sandinistas have made mistakes in managing the Miskito situation, and they have admitted these mistakes. On December 1, 1983, there was a public declaration of amnesty by the Sandinista government toward the Miskitos. Some of those who had been jailed in Managua returned to the east coast. Some remained in Managua."*

*"During my six-day stay in jail, I was treated humanely. I had a room with a bed and three meals every day." (Fernando) People here are human, willing to forgive."*

Repatriation of Miskitos: *"The Miskitos now outside Nicaragua desire to return, but they have many fears. Repatriation will not happen overnight."*

*"The struggle of the Nicaraguan Indian is for Indian Identity. It is not anti-Sandinista. We will not become another political party."*

*"It will take much longer to incorporate all the east coast ethnic groups into the revolution. The culture is very different. And out of hundreds of villages, the national media reaches only a few."*

*"In the Atlantic coast region there is no real Nicaragua-Honduras border for the Indians. Although the Coco River is two hundred meters wide, Indians on both sides have always moved freely back and forth across the river."*

U.S. Policy As It Affects Nicaraguan Indians:

*"Our people will continue to suffer until your government changes its policy. Up to five thousand Nicaraguan Indians are presently employed by the CIA."*

*"The reconciliation of Indigenous people depends upon how much the U.S. State Department wants it to happen."*

*"Capitalism controlled by a military dictatorship has no future here. Nor will the Eastern Bloc nations have a dominant influence."*

Fernando Colomer and Norman Bent believe that their work, far above any other concern, is that of reconciliation of disagreements within their own Moravian church, of opposing forces with the Atlantic coast Indian cultures and reconciliation of the unique and remote Atlantic coast peoples with the best that is in Nicaragua's ongoing revolution.

Norman Bent tells of one experience which helps to explain why both of them feel that there is hope for reconciliation even if it may come slowly.

*"Over a year after I had been released from jail, I received word that a Sandinista commandante had been trying to locate me. Later I learned that upon finding out my whereabouts, the commandante did not have the courage to face me. He was the one who had made the decision to put me in jail, a mistake that I had already come to understand and accept.*

*"Later the commandante did find me. He apologized to me and asked me if he was forgiven for his mistake. I replied that I had already forgiven him at the time of my release from jail. That Sandinista commandante and I then embraced each other with tears in our eyes."*

I doubt if anyone who heard this story would want to contend that it is reflective of all the forces operating among the indigenous people of Nicaragua. But most all of us I felt that it was an important part of the story, and one that deserves a much wider hearing among the people of the United States, especially those who claim the Judeo-Christian tradition as their spiritual home.

*2020 notes: It was never possible for me to get anywhere near what I felt like was a thorough understanding to the relationship of the Sandinista or the Honduran government to the Miskito people. What did seem clear was that when the Reagan administration learned of opposition of the Miskitos to the Revolution it acted fast to claim the Miskitos as allies in fighting the revolution and showed no more cultural sensitivity than the Sandinistas had shown in the beginning. I never found any valid reason for the U.S. to intervene so strongly in the conflicts between the Sandinistas and the Miskitos.*

*A "study tour" such as we were on does not qualify one to speak as if one is any kind of authority on any aspect of Central American life. But it does give the authority to say "here is what I saw and*

*heard" and "here are the questions it raised in me." And it plants
important seeds for the future. After just that one hour with Revs.
Norman Bent and Fernando Colomer, I would never forget the
place of Miskito people in the history of Central America.*

## March 12, 1984
*Managua: Flashback*

I am remembering the Nicaraguan refugees we talked to last week
in San Pedro Sula when one said "Nicaragua is now a police state." I
must say that I do that I do not feel like I am in a police state. As a
matter of fact, after two days moving about here in Managua, I feel a
lot less paranoia than I did at certain times in two Honduran cities.

It seems clear to me that literacy, heath care, and housing have
improved immensely since the revolution. Although some poor
people we've talked to have spoken of the difficulty of getting food,
I believe this government has concern for the needs of the people that
the Somoza regime never had.

## Thursday, March 15, 1984
*Sandy Springs Motel, Miami Beach*

The trip is over. We are staying here for a few days of recollection
and rest.

There is a plastic emptiness and loneliness about Miami Beach.
The sun is warm but not hot enough yet to make it feel great to be in
the water. The ocean is beautiful. But coming back to hotels reaching
into infinity, an asphalt backdrop for everything, and seeing hundreds
of faces that we never meet is a stunning change from the places
where we have been.

Today we sat down for a sandwich in the motel diner. The
waitress who was also the cook who was the cashier came and
apologized that almost nothing on the menu was available. She did
the best she could to serve one table whose unprivate conversation
had to do with a choice between poker or sun for the afternoon.
Nothing wrong with that.

Ten feet away at the bar, a lonely man bordering on drunkenness
tries to work his way into their conversation. A town near Boston is

mentioned. He mentions cynically and sadly that this is the town where he has to send his monthly alimony checks to his "ex."

Miami's papers and apparently the national news are full of stories of community unrest in Miami following the acquittal of a policeman in a manslaughter trial. Events here seem to be touching the tenderest nerves among Miami's racial groups. Incidents of violence are reported in some parts of the city. For the first time since we left Seattle, I feel that there is some danger to be concerned about. We are careful not to go into the parts of Miami where there might be trouble.

Dangers to the lives of the people of Miami are no greater than are the dangers in Honduras or Nicaragua to the people who live there. In many cases, they are less so.

But I conclude quickly from our trip that to project all the world's dangers or evils to some other place in the world is a tragic mistake. And for me, this includes dangers to the spirit as well as the dangers of bodily harm.

### Friday, April 13, 1984
*Press Conference in Seattle*

*Seattle Post-Intelligencer article, April 14, 1984*

During our opening orientation on March 2 in Miami before we left for Honduras, we were given an excellent workshop by the Office for Church and Society of the United Church of Christ on how to communicate effectively with the media and how to hold a press conference. None of the six of us from Seattle who were part of the delegation had extensive experience in arranging press conferences, but we were willing to give it a try.

The good response by local media was helped by the fact that Central America was very much on the minds of many people throughout the Seattle area and by John McCoy, a reporter for the Seattle Post-intelligencer, one of two major Seattle daily papers, who was Roman Catholic and had a strong personal interest in Central America. We were the main story on their Saturday religion page. McCoy's angle was that we were all typical middle-class U.S. Americans, most of whom might be expected ordinarily to be strong supporters of U.S. policy, but who brought back hard questions and criticisms based on what they had seen. The coverage in the P-I and in other local publication provided motivation for us to continue to work on behalf of U.S. policies in Central America.

Excerpts from the article included:

*"They are white, Anglo-Saxon Protestants, respectable, middle-class members of the United Church of Christ. Yet they and thousands of others U.S. church people who have recently visited Central America say they are outraged by what the United States is doing in Nicaragua and Honduras.*

*Kathryn Williams, vice president of a Seattle mortgage banking firm and a self-described "strong Republican," said she would have problems voting for President Reagan again if the present U.S. policy toward Nicaragua continues.*

*"There is a socialist government, yet 75% of the gross national product is in private hands," she said. "It's far from a perfect democracy, but it's not our role to interfere."*

*The group met with Ambassador to Honduras John Negroponte and reported, "Ambassador Negroponte and his staff made several statements which reduced the problems of Central America to a black and white struggle of communism versus democracy." Mullins said.*

*"None of the Honduran leaders with whom we met felt that this was the central issue."*

UN OBISPO MORIRA PERO LA IGLESIA DE DIOS QUE ES EL PUEBLO NO PERECERA JAMAS"

*Mons. Romero*

*"A bishop may die, but the Church of God which is the people will never perish."*

*2020 Notes: St. Oscar Romero, Archbishop of San Salvador, 1917-1980.*

*More than any other leader, Archbishop Oscar Romero was the voice of truth and justice for all the people of Central America. While his devotion to the poor earned him reverence and admiration by the Marxist Christian priests of Latin America, Romero was in fact a conservative Catholic. The Church's "preferential option for the poor" was not limited to the proponents of Liberation Theology. When he became Archbishop in 1977, many priests devoted to Liberation Theology were not pleased with the choice. That would change.*

*When a repressive Salvadoran government came to power in El Salvador in 1979, Archbishop Romero went to the Vatican and requested a condemnation of the regime. Pope John Paul II refused and told him to go back and focus his work on the unity of the church.*

*In February 1980 he wrote a letter to President Carter telling him that military aid to the Salvadoran government would surely add to the repression and suffering of the people. Carter did not respond but had Secretary of State Cyrus Vance respond with a mixed message saying the U.S. would not support repression but would take its guidance from the government.*

*Romero's Sunday sermons on the radio became the most listened-to radio program in El Salvador and many said it was also the most dependable source of information about what was going on throughout the country. In a speech after receiving an honorary degree in Belgium in January 1980, he said that 50 priests had been threatened, seven had been killed, and the Church's radio studio had been bombed.*

*Romero spoke out continuously against poverty, injustice, assassinations and torture amid a growing war between left-wing and right-wing forces. In his most-remembered sermon on the day before he was assassinated, he said, "I would like to make a special appeal to the men of the army, and specifically to the ranks of the National Guard, the police and the military. Brothers, you come from our own people. You are killing your own brother peasants. Any human order to kill must be subordinate to the law of God which says, 'Thou shalt not kill. In the name of God, in the name of this suffering people whose cries rise to heaven more loudly each day, I implore you, I beg you, I order you in the name of God: Stop the repression!" The above photo was a billboard in Nicaragua where Romero was deeply revered as a man committed to justice and as a martyr.*

*Pope Francis made Archbishop Romero a saint on October 14, 2018.*

# CHAPTER 2
# JULY-AUGUST 1984
# FIVE WEEKS IN ESTELÍ, NICARAGUA

*2020 notes: Especially after the March 1984 trip to Honduras and Nicaragua, Central America became a central focus in my life. I was fortunate then to be working as Minister of Outreach at University UCC in Seattle. My work on Central America issues fit well with my position there, and many members of the church were also interested. I also began to think seriously about the possibility of living in Central America.*

*In August of 1984, the church agreed to my request for a six-week leave of absence without pay to be a part of Nuevo Instituto de Centroamérica de Central America (the New Institute of Central America) or NICA. NICA was founded by a group in Massachusetts, including theologian Harvey Cox, who saw potential for important learning in Nicaragua by anyone willing to go and live there for five weeks as guests of local people and students of the Revolution. The program was unique in that its invitation was not to go and evaluate life in Nicaragua since the overthrow of the Somoza dictatorship. The intention was that U.S. citizens would simply go to listen and learn.*

*In 1984, the successes of the Sandinista Revolution were very apparent, even as U.S. efforts to overthrow the government remained constant. NICA made Estelí, a smaller city located about 70 miles north of Managua the capital, the place where its work would be carried out. It was an important city in the story of the 1979 Revolution. The final battle to overthrow Somoza took place in Estelí. Stories still circulated about how the people, including women and children, dug up bricks from the streets to build barricades for protection during the fighting. Every house had someone with a personal connection to the Revolution.*

*There was also a strong sense of pride about a number of achievements among the people that had never happened under two generations of the Somozas. One of them was a literacy program in rural villages the resulted in a massive increase in the literacy rate for the country as a whole. Young adults who could read often working beside teachers sent from Cuba went into the mountains among remote villages where illiteracy was the highest. The people we met who had been a part of this spoke of their experiences with great pride.*

*NICA's program had three primary parts: living with a local family (cultural immersion), language study in the morning hours, and political seminars or work groups in the afternoons. The program had no affiliation with any religious group, although a number of the participants did. A percentage of our tuition payment went to pay the families we lived with for room and board, so it had a direct economic impact on the people there who needed it most.*

*I flew to Nicaragua from Houston, Texas with a layover in San Salvador, El Salvador. I had most of a day to explore the city. Not knowing anyone there, I stayed close to the downtown area. I visited the cathedral and wanted to visit the hospital chapel where Archbishop Oscar Romero had been assassinated, but time did not allow. It was a brief visit but it was good to at least make contact with the country some of whose people had become friends in Seattle.*

*The NICA staff met us at the Managua airport and we traveled by bus to a retreat center outside the city for a day of orientation.*

## Saturday, July 21, 1984

*Arrival & Orientation, 7 a.m. at a Conference Center near Managua*

I am sitting at one of the tables in the large, open air dining room under a thatched roof. It is a beautiful place to begin our time here. We are ten to a room with running water. Farming people (campesinos) walk in the distance to work in the fields. It appears that others have been working there for hours.

Earlier while sitting under a tree here, the morning was cool and quiet. I was surrounded by swarms of bugs. They don't seem to bite and they are quiet--my kind of bugs.

There are about forty of us here - more than I expected. A good crowd of sensitive, involved people.

Dinner last night was rice with a good sautéed vegetable sauce on top, a sliced tomato, slaw, a small portion of sliced beef, bread, and an odd coffee drink. The food was fine. The drink was, well, let's say different. This morning I feel a slight hunger that I suspect the poor of Nicaragua would not feel as hunger. I seem to keep my body so full so much of the time.

There are four or five pastors and two seminarians here. It is not a "church crowd," which is some relief to me.

Last night we were taught chants of the Sandinista revolution. Some of these were ok. Others I would not say. It is the same problem I have standing up for the national anthem back in the U.S.— the same problem I have with how US forbears came to the new world to establish a "city on a hill." Some chants seem to imply a worship devotion to nation whether its way are good or evil, just as the assumptions surrounding standing for our own national anthem seem to be. I need to be as clear as I can that my first devotion is to the way of Jesus, especially to myself.

## Saturday, July 21, 1984 at 5 p.m.

*Nuevo Instituto de Centroamérica, (New Institute of Central America) referred to as NICA*

Points from the Orientation:

NICA's purpose and other key points were stated clearly for us:

1. NICA seeks to strengthen the non-intervention movement in the US.

"Not for us to decide whether the Sandinistas are doing good. We are here non-judgmentally. Nothing the Sandinistas could do can justify a full-scale war here by the US."

2. Sandinistas are not recruiting members worldwide.

3. President Daniel Ortega has stated publicly his Nicaragua's support for the PEOPLE of the United States, even if the U.S. government is working to overthrow the government here.

4. No one will be excluded from exploring on their own.

5. Because of the dangers of attacks by the Contras north of Estelí, no one should travel north with members of host families.

6. The role of Cuba and the USSR is important and controversial. An important part of our learning will be to understand this.

7. It is not our responsibility to "debate" with Nicaraguans about their revolution.

8. Please use good judgment in offering gifts to families.

9. No photos are allowed around anything related to the military.

10. Gifts- to families- use judgment.

11. While living with your family, be willing to sacrifice, be flexible and humble.

12. Some households have many children. The average age in Nicaragua is 15.

13. There won't be any toilet paper in the latrines. Be ready to use alternatives.

14. If the food does not agree with you and you need to decline be as kind as possible. Most will have seen gringos who could not stomach the food well.

15. Families go to bed between 9 and 10:30, usually closer to 9.

16. Not good to walk alone at night. Be home early.

17. Fruits and vegetables are not common in the diet here. You will see a lot of beans, rice, plantains, and corn tortillas. Buying fruit in the market is a good idea.

18. Laundry - do your own or maybe your family will do it for you. Be flexible on this. If family does it, it could take a week to get it back. It has to be washed by hand in the creek.

19. Remember that there "adios" means both hello and good-by.

20. Don't speak English when Spanish-only speakers are around.

21. You may eat alone much of the time. Let family know when you will miss a meal.

22. You may hear shooting in the night. This is not a problem.

23. Bringing your family a bag of fruit form the market is a good idea.

24. If you are a jogger, running early in the morning, 5:30-6 is best. Wearing shorts is ok.

25. Don't sprawl on the furniture.

26. All visits should be in the front room. Don't invite friends to your home without permission.

27. Memorize the address for where you live and directions for how to get there.

U.S. Interventions in Nicaragua go back to the 1850s when a Tennessean named William Walker went to Nicaragua to set himself up as President and was actually recognized as the president by the U.S. government at the time. Walker's reign lasted only two years, but gained enough credibility that his presidency there was recognized by the U.S. government at the time. Interventions by the U.S. would continue until the 1930s when the two-generation dictatorship of the Somoza family came into power with their brutal and dreaded National Guard ("La Guardia"). U.S. president Franklin Roosevelt was quoted as saying about the first Somoza, "he's a son of a bitch, but he's our son of a bitch."

The historic hero of rebellions against U.S. ("yanqui") interventions was Augusto Cesar Sandino and his "crazy little army" of 29 men from 1927 until 1933 he was killed by Somoza's National Guard. The current Sandinista government is named after Sandino.

Since the 1800s, there have been efforts to build an intercoastal canal. An early plan was to have the canal go through Nicaragua, connecting with Lake Nicaragua in the middle, building connecting canals on both sides. Most U.S. interventions had something to do with being sure that no one but the United States would build such a canal.

In 1961 Carlos Fonseca left the Liberal Party of Nicaragua and founded the Sandinista National Liberation Front (FSLN) which set out to oppose the Somoza dictatorship and U.S. interventions. The FSLN became aligned with Cuba and other movements for national liberation in Latin America. The spirit of the people has long included an anti-U.S. Intervention and anti-imperialist element.

*Throughout Nicaragua murals and billboards reflected the passion of the Revolution and the history of U.S. support of the Somoza dictatorship. In this mural Augusto Sandino is in front on the right and Carlos Fonseca, founder of the Sandinista party and martyr to many, is in front on the left.*

## Sunday, July 22, 1984
*Arrival in Estelí*

We arrived in Estelí by bus this afternoon from Managua and we were unloaded into a joyful, welcome fiesta with lots of good food and music. All the host families of about 35 of us were there so it was quite a crowd. I immediately loved the fried corn tortillas with cheese on them that were being passed around. We did a playful ritual in which each person or couple met the family that we were to stay with. It was all a very joyful time and a wonderful welcome to Estelí.

*Welcome to Estelí fiesta*

Estelí is pronounced with the accent on the final syllable (s-tay-LEE). I began to notice that people in this part of Nicaragua do not pronounce the letter "s", so the local pronunciation sounds more like "eh-tay-LEE."

I learned that I would be staying with the family of Silvia Diaz. I also learned that this is a large family. I counted about 15 from the family who were there to meet me. When I found my suitcase, a smiling teenage boy took it from me, put it on his shoulder and walked proudly home with it, for over a mile to Silvia's house.

We arrived at the house which was on a street where the houses were built wall to wall on an unpaved street. There was a mud puddle just a few feet from the front door. We walked into a large dirt-floor living room with a few simple chairs and a treadle sewing machine on one side of the room. After I tried to visit awhile with my very minimal Spanish. They showed me to my room which has a small cot in it, a simple homemade table where I could place by suitcase and a stool to sit on. Plenty of room for all I brought with me.

I am tired and ready for sleep. I sit here amazed that I am having this experience.

## Monday, July 23, 1984
*6:30 a.m.*

My first morning in Estelí is already lively. Roosters, birds, radios and children fill the air with sounds that began at 4:30 a.m.

My home seems to be just what I need. The floor is dirt. There was only one chair in the living room but Silvia borrowed another one from the house next door. There is a fine outdoor latrine and an outdoor stall where one can take a dip and pour bath.

Since I have my own room, I calculate from the number of people I have seen so far who live here that I must be the only person who has a bed to himself. There is just enough floor space for me to do some simple yoga stretches. I can hear a pig speaking up through the cardboard which is my west wall. He seems very close.

I have made my first trip to an outdoor latrine since I was a child on our farm in Mississippi before we had indoor plumbing there. I was afraid this might be very difficult for me, but I made it just fine so far.

There does seems to be a high tolerance for manure in this part of town. Horses and pigs leave hearty deposits on the street out front. The mud hole out front seems to be a bathing place for neighborhood piglets.

The house is nicely arranged space-wise. The entry from the street is into the living room. A movable partition divides this into two rooms to make a small bedroom but is taken down in the daytime. There are two married couples who live here, so it is not clear just where everyone sleeps.

The living room opens into a courtyard in the back which has flowers and a fruit tree whose fruit I do not recognize. Along one side of the courtyard there are four very small sleeping rooms, mine being the first one. At the end of the sleeping rooms is the kitchen, an outdoor adobe stove with a fire going much of the day.

*The front door at Silvia's house*

## Noon hour

The kitchen area is full of women and activity. The open wood stove is hot. Silvia's adult daughter Rosa Maria is chopping away at "stove wood" (as we would have called it back in Mississippi) with a machete, a chopping tool I had never seen before coming to Central America. Flies are everywhere. This also reminds me of my childhood. I am feeling happy to be here, very happy and grateful. I suspect I am a bit caught upon the initial romance and adventure of it all.

*New housing construction in Estelí. More housing was one of the promises of the Revolution.*

### 3:30 p.m. Estelí Library

I have some time to explore the town this afternoon. This library is as private a place as I have so far found in Estelí, except maybe for the cathedral. The library is one room. All books are behind a counter, available, I assume, only through the person on duty. Books, no doubt, are rare and difficult to come by in Nicaragua.

The room is clean and cool. There are only five of us in here -- three children, one youth, and myself. One would think it would be filled given its silence away from heat and loud streets. And yet one can tell that even the poorest of houses here is home -- the place where nurture happens most completely and love is sustained.

I am certainly a beginner in Spanish, but I am becoming bolder to initiate a conversation on the street with my fifty-word Spanish vocabulary. In so many ways here in Estelí, on can feel a town ready to open its heart to strangers.

Nuevo Insituto de Centroamerica (NICA) certainly considers itself to be a solidarity organization. Its position is that no North American has the reason to come to Nicaragua as a judge of the revolution here. They are certainly very supportive of what is happening. At first I simply would not join in with the Sandinista chants that we were taught. It seemed too inauthentic for me. Or maybe it was because so many of them have "anti-yanqui" phrases, or maybe from having been taught all my life that such chants were things that "good Americans" never said. I did soften some last night when it was the very poor people of Estelí who were leading the chants. It felt more natural to join in or at least to try them out, to see what it feels like to raise my voice in support of a Christian Socialist revolution. These may be among the poor here many who are not supportive of the revolution. But there is much evidence to suggest that a large majority of the poor in Estelí have the feeling that their government cares about them. We will be learning more.

On Sunday during our opening invitation, Hans Gutierrez, the Director of Economic Planning for the country, gave a convincing talk. At the end he went around and shook hands with each of the fifty-plus people present. I felt in him a depth of compassion and commitment to a cause that he believes in which is very different from the feeling one gets in the presence of either of the US Ambassadors with whom I have met here.

The Sandinista hymn has a stanza in it which goes: "Los hijos de Sandino ni se venden ni se rinden. Luchamos contra el yanqui, enemigo de la humanidad." (The children of Sandino never sell themselves nor betray each other. We fight against the Yankee, the enemy of humanity). I cannot say that it warms the residue left from an old-style patriotic heart to be called a "Yankee and enemy of all humanity." And yet there is plenty of evidence of why Nicaraguans would feel like this. Furthermore, the compelling and interesting corollary to the hymn is that we are constantly greeted as friends here. My tax money yet supports the killing which is still initiated and supported by our government. At the economic gut level of the half-century plus of the US-Nicaraguan tragedy, I am from the land of the enemy, and yet I find myself being loved and welcomed constantly here. The people here clear make a distinction between the people of the U.S. and the government and policies of the U.S.

It is sobering to hear an anthem sung so passionately that refers to my country as "the enemy of humanity." But it is not difficult to see why such words have appeared.

There are moments when I fear the kind of repression that could result from the intense nationalism here. I also have moments when I long for more Nicaraguans to have the kind of emphasis on individual freedom that we enjoy in the United States. Yet it never takes very long for me to return to the heart of what is going on. A poor country whose people have never enjoyed hope now has hope. A people who have lived at the mercy of US economic control now has a pride about itself that it was never before allowed to feel. The needs of the larger community now come before the needs of any individual or a powerful few. A party which had no experience in the administration of a nation has made extensive gains in areas that matter to the poor masses-- and they have done so while also having to defend the country on many fronts from attacks funded and sometimes activated by the United States.

My patriotic residue does not hold up very long. If I'm lucky here I will not have to look at ripped-open bodies from a nearby Contra attack or see a health center bombed by US weapons. To love my country cannot mean feeling anything but outrage at what the US is doing here.

One former priest who has worked in Nicaragua for many years remarked, "the brutality of the Reagan administration is the stone on which this revolution is being sharpened." Perhaps so.

*2020 notes: Looking back at these notes I sense a strain in my words here as I tried to remain loyal to the Sandinista revolution, to give the benefit of the doubt to the Revolution, given the history of U.S. support for repression here and our outright violence. But it was becoming clear that the Sandinista zealots could be as repressive as any U.S. policies, although with only a minuscule percentage of the destructive power. The highest values of the Revolution were compromised often. Those who continued to stand for those values were often pushed aside.*

*As I write this in August 2020 Daniel Ortega, who was the beloved and respected first president of Nicaragua after Somoza's forces were defeated, has become a harsh and brutal leader, with some dictator characteristics of his own after over ten years of sharing power with his wife. The democratic reforms of the 1980s and the strong policies of justice and compassion for the poor did not survive.*

*No matter what became of Daniel Ortega and other Sandinista leaders of the 1980s, I remain convinced that if the U.S. had wanted to find a policy based in democracy rather than domination and fear of communism, it could have. We had and we still have the influence and the diplomatic expertise to choose a better way. For example, I note the simple step taken by President Obama to open some new doors in our relationship with Cuba. Doors that get opened can be shut again so quickly when people come to power whose priorities do not include democracy and justice.*

*One glaring example of this and a connection of U.S. policies in the 1980s to those of 2020 is the case of Elliott Abrams. He is best known for his involvement in the Iran-Contra scandal during the Reagan administration, which led to his conviction in 1991 on two misdemeanor counts of unlawfully withholding information from Congress. He was later pardoned by George H.W. Bush. While almost no one is watching now, Elliott Abrams, convicted of federal crimes, has been appointed by the Trump administration as a special envoy to lead in shaping U.S. policy and decisions in relation to Venezuela.*

*In 1967 Dr. Martin Luther King, Jr. said "the greatest purveyor of violence in the world" (is) "my own country." This has certainly been true in U.S. policy toward Latin America.*

## Wednesday, July 25, 1984

Today in Estelí, the roosters began to crow at 4 am. By 6 am, the town is busy. The shops are starting to open. The shoe-shine boys are headed to the park with their stools and wooden boxes. Women will build open fires on the streets to roast corn. It sells for 25 centavos. Others will sit with large baskets of mangos, slicing them into small plastic bags to sell for 10 centavos.

The Revolution in the sense of overthrowing the Somoza dictatorship is over and won. But the war goes on. The Reagan administration has seen to that.

And on every street, people will wonder and talk with each other about who died in the fighting this week and they will ask the questions that Nicaraguans have been asking since the 1830s -- when will the United States leave us alone?

### Thursday, July 26, 1984

Our daily routine here is Spanish class in the mornings (with many of the practice phrases being on the themes of the Revolution. So even Spanish class includes some attempted indoctrination), seminars or work projects in the afternoon, with most evenings and weekend free for exploration.

### Saturday, July 28, 1984

With the patient help of Silvia's daughter Rosa Maria, I think I have learned the names of everyone who lives here.

Silvia's children are: Rosa Maria, 28, Luis, 21, William, 18 (currently studying in Bulgaria), Donald, 15, Jorge, 9 and Nelson, 8.

Rosa Maria is married to Francisco Briones and they have four children: Armando, 10, Jony, 5, Silvia, 4 and Yessenia, 3.

Luis is married to Carmin, and they have 2 children, Amye and Carmin. They live in a house nearby but they are all here much of the time. This seems to be central headquarters for the extended family.

Three young people are from villages north of Estelí that have no schools, so they are staying here to go to school in Estelí: Eugenio Rodriguiz, 16, and Silvia's nieces, Elsa Maria Herrera, 16 and Elba Herrera, 13.

I believe the total is 14 with more who live here much of the time.

In the Hebrew Bible the prophet Isaiah admonishes us to "receive the homeless poor into your home." I have never been able to do that in my life but it seems that here in Nicaragua everyone does this, or something close.

### Sunday, July 29, 1984
*Silvia's Story*

Having been here a week or two now I have been able to get sense of the life of Silvia Diaz, this fierce-spirited yet gentle, caring mother and grandmother, in whose home I am so privileged to stay for these weeks. Last night I had some quiet moments to just think about her life and I tried to write down both what she and other family members have told me and what I imagine from having heard many stories here:

When you were a child, your father told you stories of "yanquis," of how they came and took over Nicaragua as if it were their own. He told you about a hero named Sandino who fought against the more powerful US Marines, until he was finally killed in 1934.

You are a woman of Nicaragua's Sandinista Revolution, age 48. You were born in a city of 30,000. You live in a house which is neatly kept. Your dirt floors are swept daily. Your house is beside the small river which runs through the town, convenient for washing clothes, a weekly chore that involves standing waste deep in the river and scrubbing on carefully placed rocks.

You can remember the days of 1978 and 1979 when Somoza's tanks moved past your home on your unpaved street and when Somoza's planes bombed the houses in the West barrio with families still inside them. You can remember when the center of Estelí was left barren by Somoza's bombing.

After a day of heavy fighting that included your husband and your father, you were told about how many had been killed and how Somoza's hated "Guardia" (National Guard) stacked bodies in the local schoolhouse. You went and found your husband's body there. He was shot full of holes from machine gun fire. His throat was also cut and his body was charred almost beyond recognition after having been set afire with gasoline.

But you also remember the "triumph" in July, 1979, when Somoza was finally driven out of the country, and when Estelí was renamed "Estelí Heroico" (Heroic Estelí) after the whole town joined together to defeat Somoza's Guardia in the final and decisive battle in the campaign to end one of the most brutal dictatorships in Latin American history. You saw new life unfold in your country. You were taught to read for the first time in your life along with other adults. Your seven children were inoculated against polio. You became a regular participant in your barrio's Sandinista Defense Committee. Your twenty-two-year-old daughter became part of a sewing cooperative, gaining not only a new sense of self-respect, but also a modest income for the household. Your older brother, who has worked as a campesino for most of his life for 32 centavos a day, visits you with stories of a new national minimum wage for farmworkers and the pride he feels in being a part for the first time of an organization to support the rights and work condition of campesinos.

But it was not long into the revolution, 1981, when it was clear that a counter-revolution was under way, once again, supported by the "yanquis," the USA. The strongest talk in the country turned to passion to defend the sovereignty and the gains of the revolution. Young men are drafted into the army to fight for their country. Posters appear all over the country showing young soldiers being embraced by mothers and wives. You agree with the need to defend and fight, but you also have mixed feelings since you have three sons who are of draft age. Two of them join the army. You give them your support, even though you really feel on the inside that you've had your share of war and death. after both your father and your husband were killed in the Revolution.

Six months after his enlistment, there is a knock at your door. It is a military officer who has come to tell you that your younger son was killed while fighting heroically in the mountains.

So you prepare for another funeral, more wakes, with gun salutes and a simple coffin hauled slowly to the graveyard in the back of a pickup truck. Dozens of friends walk with you and weep with you. They understand. Not a one among them has escaped losing someone close to them in the years of war.

You weep beside the grave as two women friends who have also lost husbands in the fighting, help you sit down on the ground. When your eyes clear you notice ten open graves beside the fresh grave of your son. You remember that so many young men from Estelí are being killed that there is a need to keep graves ready every day. You wonder if the fighting will ever end.

You walk home and get on with your life, making tortillas, beans, and rice for the family, clothes to sell to earn a little extra for the household.

The weekly class to teach adults how to read continues to meet in your living room.

You stand tall and strong with broad shoulders and a friendly smile. You have the tender heart of a grandmother but it is very clear that you are a "warrior matriarch" very much in charge of the household. Your 48 years in Nicaragua has known what you know as freedom for only the past 5 years, and that freedom has came at great cost and continues to be costly.

Silvia, you have become one of the important teachers of my life. I am grateful.

*2020 notes: We were fortunate to have among the NICA participants in 1984, Julia Lesage and Chuck Kleinhans, both professors of filmmaking at Northwestern University. Julia wanted to make a brief film on family life in Estelí and asked if she might interview Silvia and me as part of it. We honored to be chosen. I was especially grateful that Silvia was so willing to share her story as a part of the video. As of this writing it is still available for viewing online. Here is the link:* **https://mediaburn.org/video/home-life/**

## Sunday, July 29, 1984
*Human Beings or Ideology? What Comes First?*

Sometimes it seems like the NICA program here begins with ideology, the ideology of this Socialist Revolution, and then responds to people as individuals only through the lens of this ideology. I believe in trying to connect with people first and then move to how ideologies and systems may improve their lives.

I believe we all have conscious and unconscious assumptions that keep us from seeing each other fully as human beings. It seems that we all are in some way trying to protect the values and ideologies that we have internalized.

I am becoming more aware of how much I want to see this Revolution as a successful one for the people on the bottom. I have also grown up with all that democracy means in the myths and history of the U.S. How democratic is the Sandinista Revolution? I am far from able to fully evaluate this right now. What I do notice as I live with this family day by day is how much they talk about having opportunities and services that they did not have during the Somoza years. This includes food, health care, education (including adult literacy), and more. If democracy means that families such as Silvia's family have lots of control over their day to day lives right here in their barrio, I would have to say that the Revolution has been a great success for democracy.

But the passionate ideology of the Sandinistas must make it difficult for anyone who may disagree with them.

## Wednesday, August 1, 1984
*Digestive Adventure*

The difficulty gringos have with food and digestion in Latin America is well known. Someone explained to me that after a while it gets easier because our stomachs adapt by growing new bacteria in the gut. Whatever the cause, last night I had a magnificent case of "diarrhea plus regularity." The regularity came in that what happened took place at almost exactly two-hour intervals: midnight, 2 a.m. and 4 a.m. Running to the john is not an ordinary undertaking here, especially in the dark. It required three trips across the courtyard, which seemed at least 50 yards long, to get to the outdoor privy. I did have a flashlight and a few stars were shining, but still felt like I had to make a long trek over treacherous and unfamiliar terrain. I am not the only one going through this. Others in the group also have their stories of Montezuma's Revenge, as it has been called.

I survived. A friend and I have discovered a small diner that serves "leche con banano," milk with banana. It seems to go down well and cause no problems.

## Saturday, August 4, 1984
*Meeting the "Mothers of Heroes and Martyrs"*

After hearing Silvia's stories of both harsh losses and new hope, I have become keenly aware of the heavy loads that the mothers of Nicaragua carry, especially during the years of the war. Now it continues as young men continue to be killed or disappear in the fighting against the U.S.-supported Contras.

From the notes I took today, I will allow the Mothers to speak for themselves. The names here are the real first names of both mothers and fallen sons.

Gertrude - *'My son worked clandestinely before the Triumph (the overthrow). After July 1979 he continued as a fighter in the mountains. He died there in 1981 and three days later they brought his body to me."*

Virginia - *"My son also worked clandestinely. After the Triumph, he worked as a volunteer policeman. Later he went back to school, but died in an accident in May 1983. I am now serving in the militia myself"*

Rosario - *"In the September insurrection, Somoza's plane flew over and dropped bombs. A bomb hit the house where my daughter was and killed her. I still have two children. They do not have a father but they do have me."*

Sebastiana - *"I lost two sons in the fighting. Santiago was killed 1978. He volunteered for a mission that no one else wanted to take. Bombs fell at the place where the mission was to be completed and killed him. I was able to get to the place where his body laid, but I was afraid the Guardia would kill me. During his burial the planes were still flying over. Ernesto survived being tortured by the Guardia. Later he was released. I wanted him to go to Managua where it was safe but he felt that he had to continue fighting. I did not find out about his death until after the Triumph. He died in the same zone where Carlos Fonseca died.*

Marta Lucila – *"My son Mario Jose was a part of the April 1979 insurrection. He went to Leon to school for a while then came back to Estelí to help build barricades here. Eight planes were flying around the city dropping bombs. Many Guardia came from Managua, captured them, took them to a hospital, killed them. Then they put all the bodies in the back of a truck and took them away so I was never able to bury my son. For sixteen days no one was able to leave the city.*

Lucia – *"My son Mario was industrious, a shoe shine boy. He was one who awakened ideas in others. He wanted to destroy Somocismo (the regime of the dictator). When my eleven-year-old daughter was raped by the Guardia, my son said he felt this in his own body. At age 7 he became a messenger for the FSLN in Estelí. At about age 12 he fought in the mountains with his .22 rifle. He was 22 when he was killed. He had worked to share ideas at night and fought by day. Children here were persecuted for being young."*

## Saturday, August 4, 1984

*Eugenio Rodriguez del Socorro, one of my housemates here at Silvia's*

Anytime I think of him I see first a broad smile, a warm and enthusiastic greeting. I think of him gently picking up one of the small children in the house, being extra careful because he only has one hand.

Yesterday, Eugenio, 16, took me to see the simple grave of his father who was killed in the Revolution. It was very clear how proud he is of his father for being willing to give his life for a better life in Nicaragua.

Eugenio is 16. In the same month that the Sandinista Front finally drove Somoza out of Nicaragua, the streets of Estelí were filled with mortar fire, bombs dropped from airplanes, tanks and submachine guns. Women and children joined in the effort by stacking the loose bricks used for paving street to build barricades.

He was 11 when the fighting in Estelí surrounded his house. Mortar fire tore into his body and caused the loss of his right hand. His abdomen was torn open, but a long stay in the hospital helped him return to a normal life.

Eugenio is now a young man with much compassion and many possibilities. When the time is right, he will go to Cuba to acquire a prosthetic arm. For the moment his life is full of school, friends, and family. *(more on Eugenio below in 2/17/87 entry)*

*Cooperative farm outside Estelí*

## Sunday, August 5, 1984
*Work at the Agricultural Co-op*

Today about ten from our group walked to a local agricultural co-op to join in the work there. We shelled dry beans and did some sorting of potatoes and we learned how important such co-ops are in the future development plans of Nicaragua. I learned enough about co-ops to make me wonder why we do not see more of this business model across the world.

As our work there came to a close there were visitors to the co-op, officials from the National Sandinista government. Vice-president Sergio Ramirez was among them. Dressed in Levi jeans and a sport shirt, he radiated a lot of warmth as he greeted the members of the co-op. Ramirez is a writer and intellectual who changed the course of his life to join in the Sandinista Revolution. He was enjoying the life of a writer in Europe when he heard of the gains of the Sandinistas in the late 70s and returned to Nicaragua to join in the struggle.

## Monday, August 6, 1984
*Friends from El Salvador*

This afternoon for our seminar time we heard from a group of refugees from El Salvador who are now living in Nicaragua. It was a good experience of the close collaboration of the Sandinista government with the Faribundi Marti Liberation Front (FMLN) in El Salvador.

They spoke of theme that have now become familiar: lack of significant land reform that, if fair, would allow farmers to have the land they need to grow food and make a living, massive repression and violence by the government, Salvadoran refugees trying to flee and get to a safe place.

Just this past March, Napoleon Duarte was elected president, considered by many a puppet president of the United States while head of the military Roberto D'Aubisson continues to murder Salvadorans who show any evidence of supporting the FMLN.

Many Salvadorans do seem to be able to escape to other countries. There are now two United Nations-run refugee camps for Salvadorans in Honduras, many in the United States and apparently more throughout Central America. They offered some estimates of where Salvadoran refugees are at present: 500,000 in the U.S. 50,000 in Honduras, 60,000 in Mexico, and a few thousand in Costa Rica. They believed that about 50,000 have died in the fighting there.

They spoke highly of the hospitality they have received here in Nicaragua. While Salvadorans in other countries are not allowed to work, here they are. Apparently, some have arrived here as families and have been able to find work and send their children to school here. Some spoke of their solidarity with the Sandinista Revolution and their willingness to help defend it.

Sandinista passion is certainly being passed on to the poor majority in Nicaragua. The same seems to be true in El Salvador. But I feel like what I have absorbed here so far is simply the reality of human stories here. The stories matter so much more than whose politics are the best.

## Wednesday, August 8, 1984
*Friends from El Salvador*

This afternoon for our seminar time we heard from a group of refugees from El Salvador who are now living in Nicaragua. It was a good experience of the close collaboration of the Sandinista government with the Faribundi Marti Liberation Front (FMLN) in El Salvador.

They spoke of theme that have now become familiar: lack of significant land reform that, if fair, would allow farmers to have the land they need to grow food and make a living, massive repression and violence by the government, Salvadoran refugees trying to flee and get to a safe place.

Just this past March, Napoleon Duarte was elected president, considered by many a puppet president of the United States while head of the military Roberto D'Aubisson continues to murder Salvadorans who show any evidence of supporting the FMLN.

Many Salvadorans do seem to be able to escape to other countries. There are now two United Nations-run refugee camps for Salvadorans in Honduras, many in the United States and apparently more throughout Central America. They offered some estimates of where Salvadoran refugees are at present: 500,000 in the U.S. 50,000 in Honduras, 60,000 in Mexico, and a few thousand in Costa Rica. They believed that about 50,000 have died in the fighting there.

They spoke highly of the hospitality they have received here in Nicaragua. While Salvadorans in other countries are not allowed to work, here they are. Apparently, some have arrived here as families and have been able to find work and send their children to school here. Some spoke of their solidarity with the Sandinista Revolution and their willingness to help defend it.

Sandinista passion is certainly being passed on to the poor majority in Nicaragua. The same seems to be true in El Salvador. But I feel like what I have absorbed here so far is simply the reality of human stories here. The stories matter so much more than whose politics are the best.

## Wednesday, August 8, 1984
*Four deaths, one funeral service*

Today a group of us accompanied families where some in our group are living who have lost family members in the fighting in the past week. Four young men were buried in one funeral service. The grief of the mothers was overwhelming to watch. They were buried in four graves in a row, with eight more open graves already dug and waiting. Apparently, there are enough deaths of young men from Estelí that graves need to be dug and prepared in advance. I could not fully comprehend this. How could I understand the lives of people who have had to live with so much continuous war and violence?

To conclude the service, there was a uniformed soldier who fired a one-machine gun-salute to the fallen. He pointed the gun straight up in the air and keep it firing for about thirty seconds. It was terrifying to watch but the people are apparently accustomed to this. We have heard of complaints about this in the city because the bullets shot up into the air do eventually come down again. Some have fallen into local houses. It is obviously a dangerous practice. It is not clear whether this is an official government-sanctioned practice or simply an expression that is way out of order but simply tolerated. I suspect it is the latter.

### Thursday, August 9, 1984

*Today our speaker was Robert Fretz, Consul General from the U.S. Embassy in Managua*

NICA leaders have been clear that their mission is not to offer a "balanced" program, with points of view from both those for and against the Revolution. All the content has been heavy in favor of the Revolution. Apparently their sense is that we have received plenty of information about the point of view of the Reagan administration and the U.S. government. It was good today to hear from someone speaking on behalf of U.S. policy.

Here are some of the points he made along with some of my own comments:

*"In December 1981 the Reagan administration made the decision to support the Counterrevolutionaries ("Contras"). But since May 1984 U.S. assistance to the Contras has been discontinued."*

*2020 notes: It seemed obvious to us at the time and we would later learn that this was simply untrue. This was long before the secret Iran-Contra scandal became public in which the administration was secretly selling arms to Iran, an enemy of the U.S., and using the proceeds to support the Contras which almost became the worst scandal of the Reagan years.*

*"Some of the goals of U.S. policy in Nicaragua are:*

*1. To halt the export of this communist revolution to neighboring countries."*

*2020 notes: The Cold War had not yet ended in 1984 but the Vietnam War had. Vietnam might have been an important lesson about the futility of trying to stop communism anywhere but the lesson was not learned. Sometimes it seemed that President Ronald Reagan had a strange obsession with this very poor country of just 3 million people, and an absurd fear about the threat they posed to the United States. Still, the posture of the United States was to fight Communism in all of its forms, no matter the cost to our national dignity or to the waste of money and human lives.*

*2. Reduce the Nicaraguan armed forces to the size of neighboring armies. For example, Somoza's Guardia never had more than 14,000 troops, Honduras has 16,000, El Salvador 32,000 but the Sandinista Army has 55,000 and there are at least 8,000 Cubans in Nicaragua, many of them there as military advisers."*

*2020 notes: It certainly was true that the Sandinistas had a large army and at times it was unnerving to see soldiers walking in the streets carrying sub-machine guns. But I did not experience any sense of fear of the military, as I would later in Honduras, whose soldiers also carried sub-machine guns. It also became ludicrous to say that Nicaragua was more militarized than Honduras. The U.S. had built 11 airfields in Honduras, each of them with a runway large enough to accommodate large C-130 transport planes that could fly in tanks and motor vehicles whenever it might be deemed necessary. The U.S. had joint military exercises with the Honduran army and U.S. troops. Cuban and USSR military support for Nicaragua did not include troops, only advisers and armaments. The U.S. was the only outside nation there that had troops present and bases established. The hypocrisy of saying Nicaragua should be less-militarized was appalling.*

3. *"Promote internal democratization of Nicaragua"*

*2020 notes: This policy goal would have been an honorable one, including supervision of elections, if the U.S. had not violated a number of principles of democracy with its ongoing interventions in Central America. So much of U.S. policy and practice in both Honduras and Nicaragua was so antithetical to democracy that this goal sounded ludicrous then and still sounds ludicrous today.*

Other comments by Robert Fretz:

*"We do agree that more houses have been built in the past five years than in the last twenty years under Somoza."*

*"Social development is good under the Sandinistas but there is no economic development."*

*"The U.S. is still Nicaragua's number one trading partner."*

*"In Latin America, Cuba and Nicaragua are currently the only two countries with no opinion polls."*

*"The U.S. is the only country that thinks support for the Contras is a good idea."*

*"The U.S. Embassy here has 45 Americans on the staff and 250 Nicaraguans. We are the embassy that is seen as doing the most in Nicaragua."*

*"Nicaragua's government is not totalitarian but it is in the process of becoming one."*

*"As far as I'm concerned this government is rotten."*

*"We have no economic sanctions against Nicaragua. Of course the mining of Nicaraguan ports probably does not help much."*

*"We are the only country that thinks support for the contras is a good idea." But many have genuine doubts about the future of this government."*

*Should there be any relationship between people of Nicaragua & U.S. policy? Presently there is none.*

*"I cannot think of anything in international law which gives one country the right to intervene in another's sovereignty. But we do have a moral right to be doing this. There is something worse than fighting. It is living under a totalitarian government."*

## Friday, August 10, 1984

*Today's Speaker - Alfonse Ponce, church leader, a layman, in organizing "Base Communities" who works for the Guardian Agricultural Service, a private company.*

"Communidades de Base," or Base Communities, has become an important movement within the Catholic Church in Latin America. The movement grew out of the strong liberation theology movement which was based on the "preferential option for the poor" that many progressive bishops and priests in Latin America believe is the heart of the Christian message. Base Communities are groups of grass-roots people, usually poor, who come together to talk about how they can improve their lives in light of the Gospel, sometimes in opposition to oppressive structures and people in power. Alfonse Ponce shared with us from his experience with Communidades de Base here in Estelí.

Senor Ponce comes across as a calm, middle-class businessman here in Estelí. Some notes from his comments:

*"Communidades de Base take many different forms in different places. There is no one way to characterize the conversations that take place. People come together to talk about common concerns in light of the gospel. I know of about fifteen Communidades de Base here in Estelí. The groups do not talk about religion and politics as much as the situations of their lives.*

*"For example, one group here came together to talk about the shortage of soap. They started a soap factory in Estelí.*

*"People simply come together informally to talk about things that are important in their lives such as how to raise kids and the struggles and joys of that. Men abandoning families is a problem here, so both the Sandinistas and the church here are trying to get parents to reflect on what it means to be a parent. Often there will be a reading from the Bible at the end of the meeting.*

*"No one comes into these meetings with high expectations. It is not a movement to try to fix things. Sometimes women's and men's groups meet separately at the beginning then come together at the end. A lot of the organization happens through the women. And the groups may include non-Catholics as well as Catholics.*

*"Two priests in Estelí, Padre Luis and Padre Pedro, train leaders of Communidades de Base here.*

*"Jesus proclaimed the reign of God among the poor. The poor feel the presence of God more"*

He quoted from Mt 11:28-30: *"Come unto me all you who are weary and carrying heavy burdens, and I will give you rest....for my yoke is easy and my burden is light."*

*"I work for the Guardian Agricultural Service which is a 100% private company. It has been here for 27 years. It continues to do its work as it always has. Nothing has changed since the Sandinistas came to power.*

*"This Revolution has a mixed economy, private and public or socialist. The government supports the work we do here, which is providing chemicals for agricultural production.*

*"We have a trade organization called ENIA, the National Enterprise for Importation of Agricultural Products. We are currently importing products from U.S. companies Dow Chemical and Abbot Laboratories.*

*"We try to avoid the most toxic products, especially for food crops such as tomatoes, potatoes and beans. They are used only very early in the life of the crop. Minimum to zero toxicity are used in later stages."*

*Cotton is one of Nicaragua's primary exports. The billboard reads: 152,000 manzanas (1.7 acres = 1 manzana) of cotton is our goal"*

Regarding Pesticides that the Company Sells:

*"We do import a defoliant from the US and Germany called Drope which is a more toxic chemical for cotton crops.*

*"Our company is the second most important company in Nicaragua after a state-owned and run company. I have worked eight years with the company and have never been asked whether I am Catholic or Sandinista. About 65% of the production in this country is in the hands of private citizens. And workers are free to organize.*

*"There have been conflicts about the setting of prices by the government."*

## Sunday, August 12, 1984
*Fear of Living Out What I Say I Believe*

Oh, how I hold on. Oh, the time and energy that I expend convincing myself that I should not move more deeply into the roots of everything. Oh, how I fear my ideals and my passions. Oh, how I run to safety at the first thought of a friend who might not understand. Oh, how I cling to psychoanalysis when it is time for surrender. Oh, how I cringe at the thought of the ridicule that would be mine if I were to take a stand for the poor. Oh, how I run to the idolatry of career when the radical vision is all around me. Oh, how the spirits of Martin and Gandhi touch me and call me to a new place that I am afraid to go and see. Oh, how I run to rational processes when the peace of trusting moves within me. Oh, how I rationalize consumerism when the challenge of simplicity calls out to me.

Freedom is yet more than I can bear. I will return home. I will mean it. I will return to processes and paperwork at church that matter somehow. I will be careful not to offend other affluent Christians who are full of fear. I will impress people with how open I am with doubts about my lifestyle. I will tell tender stories about the history of my Nicaraguan family and touch people deeply.

I will do all of this and much more like it. In the process, my life will be full of "I." And in all of it something will be constantly incomplete.

*2020 notes: I feel some embarrassment by these overly earnest words by the 35-year-old me and was tempted to cut them out. I have left them here because they do honestly express an inner struggle that I felt much of the time then. My life was being influenced by mentors and other friends who were making some radical decisions on behalf of peace, justice and what it means to be a follower of Jesus. Questions that often haunted me then included: Why I am not getting arrested? Why am I not doing some time in prison? Where is the congruence of what I say I believe and the actions I take? I felt the anguish of still living inside the conventions of my "career" as a pastor, in which such expressions were appreciated in my denominational tribe but not widely practiced. I enjoyed "visiting" a community of people with more radical forms of witness, but was either unwilling or not called to "go and live there." I often felt that I enjoyed being seen as a radical (or maybe someone "sort of radical") but really did not want to pay the price of moving more deeply into the way of Jesus.*

## Tuesday, August 14, 1984
*The CIA*

*2020 note: This entry connects so directly with what we observed and heard at Corinto, Nicaragua on our first trip to Central America. See entry for March 10, 1984 above.*

This afternoon one of the speakers talked about how pervasive the presence of the CIA is in Central America and how long it has had such a large presence here. Again we heard that distinct pronunciation: "La CI-A " (la-SEE-yah). The way the word is spoken is its own evidence of how much the people here feel the presence of the CIA. I get the sense that it is not only people in the military and the government are aware of this presence. Two or three times in recent days I have heard mention of "La CI-A " by ordinary citizens. I get the sense that most everyone in Nicaragua has a strong sense of the presence here of the CIA, probably much more than any of us who live in the U.S. have.

I learned a lot about the CIA and how often it has intervened in Latin America when no significant U.S. security interests were at stake. Here are a few significant moments in the history of the CIA:

1947- CIA established by Congress with no congressional intent to authorize covert action.

1953- Major covert operations are going in 48 countries

1954- CIA overthrows the democratically-elected Jacobo Arbenz government in Guatemala.

Mid-1950s- Pan American Airlines arranges with the CIA to provide agency personnel access to baggage in planes transitioning the airport in Panama City, Panama, and to provide agents with mechanics overalls.

1961- CIA institutes a special program called "executive action" for the specific purpose of developing assassination capability.

1961- The New York Times conspired with the CIA to suppress the story of the Bay of Pigs invasion

1961- In Ecuador, the CIA recruits as secret agents the country's vice-president, members of the cabinet, head of police intelligence, and the nephew and personal doctor of the country's president.

1963- CIA authorizes a plot to kill Fidel Castro which involves the gift of a skin diving suit with a fungus that would cause a chronic skin disease.

Mid - 1960s – In Miami- CIA organizes an intelligence service among Cuban exiles.

1965- In the Dominican Republic, Rafael Trujillo is shot by dissidents who were in close touch with the CIA and State Department

1970-1973- In Chile - ITT and the CIA work closely on a variety of secret operations in the overthrow of democratically–elected president Salvador Allende.

*During the fighting in the cities in the '79 Revolution the people used paving stones in the streets to build barricades for protections. Children and youth were often used in the building. The barricade (barricada) became one of the important symbols of the Sandinistas and the name given to the official Sandinista newspaper. Bottom photo: Repaving the streets of Estelí after the fighting ended.*

1976- In Bolivia - Use of US missionaries in getting information on dissident groups is confirmed.

1976- In Chile -Report confirms use of Jesuit Roger Vekemans as a conduit for millions of dollars of political-action funds.

## Wednesday, August 15, 1984

One of this afternoon's speakers told us the following story:

It was an incident that shows both the brutality of Somoza's National Guard as well as how connected people on opposite side were to one another. Omar and his family lived beside the river in Estelí. After fighting with the guerrillas during the revolution against Somoza's people in the mountains, he and his brother would be careful to hide their military clothes when they came home, since house to house seizures and shootings had become common for "the Guardia." Such discretion was not always enough. Often the Guardia would enter homes and demand that the men remove their shirts so that scratches or other evidence of guerrilla involvement would be visible.

The Guardia entered the tidy house beside the river. Both Omar and his brother had recently returned from the front. The marks on their bodies were obvious. The entire family was marched out into the dirt street. It was the custom to shoot families out in the open in order that maximum fear could be instilled in the neighbors. There were five children and Omar's brother.

But as yet one more brutal massacre was about to happen, a voice came from among the Guardia called out, "Omar, Omar, hermano (brother)." One of the guard who had been adopted and raised by Omar's brother recognized him. He persuaded his fellow Guardia to call off the killing.

*2020 notes: Colonialism*

*In the years preceding and into the 2020s, many White people in the United States have been coming to terms with widespread and unconscious participation in racism, especially in its systemic forms which have plagued our nation since Europeans first began to arrive in the Western Hemisphere. I believe the same can be said for colonialism, in which the "settlers" in the "new world" felt that they had a right to any land or other resources that they came upon. President James Monroe made this more explicitly in the 1820s with what came to be known as the Monroe Doctrine in which he declared that there would be no further colonization in the Western Hemisphere by European countries, Great Britain being the one exception. In other times, U.S. leaders would refer to Latin American countries as "our back yard."*

*I do not remember any frequent use of the word colonialism during our time in Central America in the 1980s. But looking back now, its reality was present in a number of ways. It has been most disturbing to see clear evidence of its unconscious presence in me in the writings from this journal.*

*It seems that national policies and assumptions often take form in very personal behavior.*

*One aspect of it seems to be an unconscious sense that as the U.S. citizen I am the "Give ER" and Hondurans are the "Give-EEs." In working with people who had little access to education, many of them unable to even read, it was very easy for both sides in any interaction to slip in modes of colonialism. There were times when I felt I could see it in a certain submissiveness by some rural Honduras in my interactions with them. My being white, male and taller than average certainly added to the reality.*

*The primary area of experience and expertise that poor campesinos (rural people) had that I will never have is the capacity to simply survive and raise a family in a situation of severe poverty. Since we were there as part of an agency to assist them in dealing with poverty and improving their lives, it was easy to fall into a "helper" mentality. I knew the politically correct language of people in our wider network about standing beside the poor and learning from them. But it was much more difficult to really practice this.*

*I do remember one experience in 1987 when this reality did become utterly clear in a rare moment when I was left to be the "teacher for the day" with a group of campesino men. Our Honduran co-workers all had to be doing things in other places so I had been asked to serve as a "substitute teacher" for the day. I was with a group of about eight farmers. The Christian Commission for Development (CCD) had carefully prepared "charlas" or brief talks on various topics. They were neatly arranged on outer board, often with illustrations to make the words very clear and communicate with any who were unable to read. So as the substitute teacher for the day all I had to do was read the charla to the men. this seemed easy enough. I proceeded with a lot of confidence.*

*I don't remember exactly how it happened but early in my simple presentation there began to be a murmur with lots of smiling faces among the men. Here I was an urban gringo who had never raised a crop of corn serving as a teacher to men who had been raising corn for years. In this case we all somehow "got it" about how ridiculous this was. It was a rare moment when my own colonialism was fully exposed. We were able to talk about it and have a good laugh about it. Then I continued reading my "lesson for the day" about which I knew almost nothing from direct experience.*

*In the case of Honduras with parallel realities in many other Latin American countries, colonialism on an international scale was much more serious. The clearest example had to do with land. The most fertile land in the country was located in the north coast area. With a predominantly rural population constantly short of food, it obviously made sense that the country's best land would be used to grow food for Hondurans. But this has not been the reality since the late 1800s when Honduras became the original "Banana Republic" and the best land was taken over by U.S. companies to grow fruit as a cash crop for export to the U.S. and Europe.*

*The Monroe Doctrine evolved over the decades and centuries, especially as the United States became a world power with the military to enforce its declarations, whether they were just or not. It reached new level of imperialism in 1904 when President Theodore Roosevelt added the Roosevelt Corollary to the Monroe Doctrine which declared hat "in cases of flagrant and chronic wrongdoing by a Latin American country, the United States will intervene in the country's internal affairs." It was this extreme version of colonialism that was at issue in U.S. policies toward Central America in the 1980s.*

## Thursday, August 16, 1984

*Padre Miguel Guardado, Worker-Priest*

Today our speaker was a "worker-priest," Argentine priest Miguel Guardado. Here are some of the things he said about himself and about Nicaragua:

*"My political position is fundamentally based in my Christian beliefs."*

*"I'm not in Nicaragua of my own will or for political reasons. I'm a political exile.*

*In Argentina, I was a political extreme. I left there 8 years ago. The military regime would not tolerate positions such as those I held. My faith compelled me to have political convictions.*

*"I see the FSLN is more a vanguard of a people than a political party.*

*"I feel thrown forward by the Nicaraguan people. Siding with the poor is based on my Christian faith. Having a political position along with Christian faith may be offensive to some. But I am with the poor. I have chosen the option of liberation.*

*"I left Argentina in the mid 70s. I lived and studied in France, later lived in Mexico and served for 3 years here in Nicaragua as a parish priest. I am 61 years old.*

*"Currently I work as an electrician and superintendent of maintenance in an agricultural school here.*

*"I do not believe the Christian Base Communities are very strong here in Estelí. But the strength of Christian practice within a revolution is more important than any structure. It may be that for the first time in seventeen centuries it is time to reinterpret Christianity and really live it.*

*"The Nicaragua Revolution has given me so much more than I could ever give to the Revolution.*

*"An alliance was formed to overthrow Somoza that included the established Catholic Church here including Bishop Obando y Bravo. the majority of the bishops here sided with this alliance but also maintained its close ties to the bourgeoisie, more upper class people. Historically, the hierarchy of the Church has been aligned with the wealthy here.*

94

*"When Somoza was overthrown, the alliance ended. This was normal because its purpose had been satisfied."*

Regarding Violence in the Work of Christians to stand with the Poor:

*"I believe violence is immoral. But there is no such thing as an absolute bad. One cannot say that war is good or bad. One must ask what the fight is about.*

*"Use of violence by the powerful over the powerless is immoral. Use of violence by the oppressed is moral. It is an act of love.*

*"If a poor family is about to have taken what little it has, who can deny the right of the father of that family to take up a rifle. I saw children in Argentina, the breadbasket of the world, die of hunger. A child who dies of hunger- this is violence. This is the violence we are struggling against."*

*"During first 40 years of my life – no priest had spoken against violence. Anti-violence talk began in 1960s when Argentina priests began to speak against starvation.*

*"What violence are we talking about?*

*"The Catholic Bishops of Nicaragua put out a pastoral letter on forgiveness, and yes, forgiveness is fundamental. But the bishops have applied it badly. Jesus never talked about pardoning enemies without conditions. Catholic teaching says God forgives the sinner who transforms.*

*"How did Jesus practice forgiveness and love for enemies? He was constantly confronting them, the Pharisees, Caiaphas. The very presence of Jesus in his society produces a confrontation. When Jesus says "love enemies," it does not mean don't have enemies. It means an attitude of being in which every enemy could someday be my friend. I have to look for ways to transform my enemy not my friend.*

*"The apostles of Jesus were armed and not secretly so.*

*"Class struggle was not invented by Karl Marx. Marx says the history of humanity is a history of class struggle. Eternal struggle is between the rich and the poor – between those who produce (workers) and those who take advantage of those who produce. The structures will disappear. I'm not concerned with structures."*

# Friday, August 17, 1984

*Carlos Manuel, Governor of Estelí*

Our speaker today was Señor Carlos Manuel, the governor of the region of Estelí. He was among the earliest of those who joined the Sandinistas to go underground in the 1960s. He has been in office for eighteen months. He was appointed to his position. The country is in the process of writing a constitution. He emphasized that it took the United States fifteen years to adopt a constitution and that Nicaragua would have one in five years. He spoke with a lot of passion for the Sandinistas, acknowledged they have made some mistakes but says that most of them have been rectified.

In responses to many criticisms from the U.S. that elections in Nicaragua will not be fair, he acknowledged that supervisors at voting places were a majority Sandinista.

But he went on to say, *"A rule was set that each party would need 20,000 members to have representative at each place. Of 346 voting places in this region we have representatives from all the parties in only 14 of them. We believe this is because they simply do not have enough sympathizers. Even our enemies here have not been able to find anything wrong with our plans for election."*

*"Many things in the structure of the government are currently unclear. We inherited a government structure under Somoza that was very centralized in Managua. We are in the process of decentralizing. For example, before registration of vehicles was done in Managua. Now there are regional offices for this."*

One in our group had a comment and question: A retired U.S. colonel visiting Nicaragua accused the Sandinistas of choosing not to wipe out the Contras in order to use the war for propaganda purposes. Is there any truth to this?

The governor responded: *"We know how difficult it is to sustain an army in the mountains because we have been there. No one can do that without sufficient help from the outside. The Contras are surviving only because of help from the U.S. which has bases in Honduras within 20 miles of the border They get supplies dropped to them from planes and helicopters. There are about 1,000 Contras now fighting. We have good defenses to keep them from getting support by way of land. But the air support makes it possible for them to move easily in any direction for hundreds of kilometers.*

*"The only foreign country to have military bases in Central America is the U.S. There are military advisors here from Cuba and the USSR but no bases and no troops.*

*Just last week there were four spy flights over Estelí.*

*"We know that the United States is well-prepared to invade Nicaragua with its own troops. We think this would become more likely if we should defeat the Contras. In 1978, the U.S. was still supporting Somoza, even though your Congress had passed a law prohibiting it. In Honduras right now there are 70 war planes. We have only planes captured from Somoza, of the kind used in the Korean War. Every place in the country has a trench for defense. We have given over 200,000 guns to the people. We have no weapons factories in Nicaragua. Nor do we have people trained in sophisticated weapons.*

*2020 notes: We would later visit the major U.S. base in Honduras, Palmerola Air Base. It was massive, with long runways that could accommodate the large transport planes that could carry tanks and rough terrain vehicles if necessary. Joint military exercises by U.S. and Hondurans troops were carried out openly, probably to intimidate the Nicaraguan government. In a country the size of Tennessee the U.S. built 11 runways, all of them capable of accommodating the largest planes.*

*"We have to be as ready as we can be. But we have had enough war here. We want no more!"*

*"I graduated from a Catholic school run by Catholic brothers and later studied law. We are called communists because we work with the poor and try to help the poor. This is the bottom line for us — our commitment to the poor.*

*"Many of us have lived with the poor and shared their poverty. This is our alliance forever. This does not mean we will eliminate those who are not poor. We believe that we can all live in peace here. But we do not wish to have some with privileges and some without.*

*"Everyone tries to make us look Cuban or Russian. No one helps us to look like ourselves. The model we are proposing does not have*

*another one like it in the world. We want a mixed economy. Having enough of the basics is always a great challenge for a country like ours. We want to work with all countries in the world as long as they respect our sovereignty."*

> *2020 notes: This became an important theme for me, that not all governments based in part or mostly by Marxism were the same. Nicaragua enjoyed support from the Soviet Union and other communist governments but was very different from any of them, and they were all very different from each other. Christianity as practiced in the U.S. has never been willing to take a deep look at the many themes of Marxism that are congruent with Christianity. This continues to be a costly limitation and an ideological poverty aspect of democracy as practiced in the U.S.*

*"One key to our economic development is to improve the agro industry, especially basic grains of beans and rice. We would also like to move beyond dependency on coffee and cotton as export crops. Currently we export raw cotton to the U.S. and Japan and then it comes back to us ready to make into clothes. We would like to do it all here."*

*"We want peace. We want to live and work in peace."*

## End of the 1984 sojourn and return to life in Seattle

After these five weeks in Nicaragua, I returned to our life in Seattle and to my work as Minister of Outreach at University United Church of Christ. But the experiences of 1984 had set me on a course toward Central America. It was becoming clear that a chapter of my life was coming to a close and that I had my eyes set on more time in Central America.

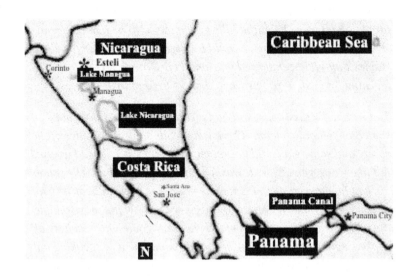

# CHAPTER 3
# COSTA RICA

*By early 1985 we had decided to move to Central America with promising possibilities from earlier conversations that we would be able to find some kind of meaningful work positions there where we could continue to learn and be of some service. We rented our house (and cat) in Seattle and moved to Costa Rica*

*The first step was an intensive course in Spanish.*

*We needed to learn Spanish well enough to function without a translator. From September until mid-December, 1985 we lived in Santa Ana, Costa Rica outside San Jose and attended the Spanish language school, Centro Linguistica Conversa. We were housed with a family there which was an important part of learning to speak Spanish all the time.*

*Every day for two months, Monday through Friday, we would ride a*

*large van up some beautiful hills to what used to be a horse farm.*
*We had small classes so we could learn faster. The horse farm had*
*stables that had been turned into small classrooms. We were*
*learning Spanish in rooms where horses used to live.*

*The "stable" classrooms still had dirt their original floors but*
*somehow felt quite clean. There were walls soon some sides of the*
*room, and some walls did not reach the ceiling. Air flowed freely. It*
*felt like we were outside. It was a pleasant space for us. The school*
*cooked lunch every day. I can remember that after an hour or two*
*in class the wonderful aroma of lunch cooking would move among*
*the open-air classrooms. The food was very good. Our teachers all*
*spoke English but kept to the school's commitment of speaking only*
*in Spanish throughout our days there, whether in class, over lunch*
*or playing volleyball.*

## Sunday, September 22, 1985
*Day 10 in Costa Rica*

I have studied Spanish three and one-half hours today. More to
go. Rain falls on a metal roof – peaceful. Rain muffles many sounds
that are very close – television, the groans of a handicapped woman
next door, the sounds of motorcycles on a street that is very close.

Our room is very close to the house next door. Our room in our
house is close to the room in that house where a severely handicapped
young woman apparently spends most of her time. She cannot speak,
we are told, but she can make sounds with her voice. From this room
one does not have to actively eavesdrop in order to hear her. I can
only guess as to the meaning of her sounds. Most of them seem to be
sounds of anguish. Some are sounds of contentment, I think. Perhaps
others are requests for assistance.

It does not seem time yet to go and meet her. Perhaps in time we
will.

In the meantime, it is not a bad spiritual discipline – to at least live
close enough to hear the cries of anguish, even if one is living in
comfort. A good symbol for these rather well-insulated opening days
in Central America.

Last night I read part of Love in a Fearful Land by Henri Nouwen. That final part tells of a priest who feels drawn to go and replace a martyred friend in a parish in Guatemala. Part of his struggle was discerning whether or not his urge to return was a result of some hidden death wish or martyr complex. Last night I dreamed of a house in which a bomb was to explode. Even though I was feeling sad I felt drawn to the house. There was some realization that this tension lives within me – between a vain urge and need for heroism, and a simple tender desire to love and suffer with others. I never seem to escape a mixture of motives.

I do have some fear of acting out of motives that will finally make the actions soul-less. But I have more fear of not acting at all for fear that motives may not be pure (which they never are).

**Tuesday, September 24, 1985**
*Day 12 in Costa Rica*

I like the process of learning a language within a context that has many parts and requirements, such as intense, even fanatic memorization, a family of Spanish-speaking people surrounding us, teachers who engage students in conversation and relaxation. There is a receptivity, intense attention, and a "dive-in the deep water" attitude toward the unknown here.

**Thursday, September 26, 1985**
*Day 14 in Costa Rica*

This morning I noticed myself feeling very uncomfortable and even defensive while a Canadian student in the program continued her relentless criticism of the United States. "How dare you talk about my country like that?!"

Later at lunch a U.S. businessman who works with a U.S. fruit company in Honduras expressed his view that mining a harbor was among the least evils required to fight communism, and that it was good that the U.S. chose to exercise restraint in its use of violence. At this, my inner tables turned, and I launched into a recitation of U.S. abuses in the history of Central America.

*2020 notes: Then as now I had strong feelings about United States policy and practice in poorer, dependent countries such as Honduras. The reference to the mining of harbors was about the CIA of the United States secretly bombing oil storage tanks in the Nicaraguan port of Corinto in 1983. Having visited Corinto in 1984 we saw the ruins of the oil tanks in the only port city in Nicaragua, as noted above in the journal from March 1984.*

Nationalism just won't go away. I seem to live in a tension between a longing to love my homeland and a conviction that its ugliness must be seen and changed. I feel a little hope that the two can exist together.

"Con mucho gusto." These are the words one often hears after a "muchas gracias" in Costa Rica. Con mucho gusto – with much pleasure when in English we might say "you are welcome." In other Latin American countries, the more likely response was "por nada" or "de nada" meaning "it was nothing." But in Costa Rica it was always "with mucho gusto."

### Sunday, September 29, 1985
*Day 17 in Costa Rica*

Had lunch today with Melita Wall, Central America Secretary, Latin America Council of Churches. She told us a story: She was in San Salvador with the 5-year-old daughter of a friend. A bomb went off far in the distance.

*"I am afraid,"* the little girl said.

*"But why are you afraid?"* The adult answered trying to comfort her. *"That bomb is very far away and it can't possibly hurt you."*

The little girl replied, *"Yes, but it will hurt someone and they will blame it on me and I'll have to go to jail and be hungry."*

### Tuesday, October 1, 1985
*Day 19 in Costa Rica*

Remembering a visit with Melita Wall on Sunday. She said she hoped she could last two more years in her job. She feels she is "on the list," to be detained or even killed in Guatemala, El Salvador, or Honduras. Making any public statements about repressions in those countries puts one at risk. Melita Wall's name had been public many times as part of her work with the Episcopal Church.

She also mentioned the situation in Costa Rica, sharing an incident in which an office of the Episcopal Church here was broken into. She seems to feel that members of the Costa Rican "Guardia Civil" (the National Guard in Costa Rica, the nearest entity the country has to an army) are a part of such break-ins.

I had moments with her when I wondered if she had a tendency to over dramatize situations. Then I remembered the number of people who have said similar things about the pervasive danger in Central America. It seems safest, for the sake of the truth, to lean toward trusting the word of such people. There is plenty of evidence to support them.

*2020 notes: Costa Rica had disbanded its military in 1948 under reformist president Jose Figueres. It was most definitely a safer country for anyone than any other Latin American country and liked to call itself "the Switzerland of Latin America." Its national guard apparently was at times repressive and operated outside its legal purpose. Costa Rica remains unique especially in this and in other ways among the countries of Latin America.*

## Thursday, October 3, 1985
*Day 21 5:30 p.m.*

Today the afternoon rain is falling much more generously than usual. The day is comfortable. Raindrops sound on the metal roof to silence all that would disturb the peace of this place. All is well in the one hundred or so square feet of space that Kathy and I call our own in this room.

The "senora" (the lady of the house and the one in charge) here, Ligia (pronounced LEE' he ah), loves to talk. She jokes constantly and serves food with a continuous spirit of joy and service. Lately she is inclined to put her hand on my shoulder as she makes a joke or makes fun of the usual duties of getting a meal served. I cherish those moments when Ligia moves close enough to touch me.

In the midst of all the questions and issues, regardless of the culture, I seem to live from love to love. "Vivo de amor a amor."

In between moments of touching, those moments when the universal sacrament of love is most real, I manage to work, learn, sleep, eat, pray, and relate. I also play and listen, talk and use the bathroom. But I think that in my honest moments I would have to say that I live for those sacramental moments when love really finds me.

## Sunday, October 6, 1985
*Day 24, Manuel Antonio National Park, Quepos, Costa Rica*

Ocean roars here. White surf sparkles. Yesterday was filled with blessings – good close times with Kathy, long and fine beach walking, sticky hike through the seaside jungle, and a closing dramatic encounter with white-face monkeys. Last night, I wrote two long letters and enjoyed writing in a way that I have not for many weeks.

This morning I may be all "written out." The waves and water here seem to be all there is to my morning reflections.

I am missing lately the intimate quality of prayer that I knew during the Ignatian experience. The Ignatian exercises includes entering into scripture with active imagination and imagery and seeking a sensuous experience of the presence of Jesus. I think that I only need to persist more in order to have more of what I want here. It is not at all like the deprived situation of Nicaragua last year when it was very difficult to write or pray. Here the amenities to support this are much more present. I am even learning to study reasonably well with noise in the background.

*2020 notes: Parque Nacional Manuel Antonio was a beautiful place. We took a short plane ride from San Jose to get there. We stayed a few nights in a very small "cabina" right on the beach. It had cement floors, and two hard cots for us to sleep on. It also included a small tropical jungle with walking trails. I can still remember the moment when we walked into the jungle and were met with the overwhelming and terrifying noise of wild animals. We soon looked up and could see the source of the noise — white-faced monkeys, sometimes called howling monkeys. Once we got over our initial terror at hearing them it was wonderful to see them as they moved so fast through the trees above us including out into the palm*

*trees on the beach. We also saw a sloth hanging down from a tree*
*limb. It was so motionless that it looked dead, but it was holding on*
*securely to the limb.*

## Sunday, October 20, 1985
*Day 38, 6:30 p.m.*

Remembering Nicaragua last weekend. Tears of a woman named Clellian because children can't get the medicine they need. Buses full, people literally hanging onto the sides and riding on top to get a ride. Prices – beans increased from 5 Nicaraguan Cordovas per pound to 50 Cordovas per pound within one year. Heat, "bearing down on you" heat in Managua. Money changing chaos - 700 Cordovas equals $1.00 U.S. at legal changing houses. Shortages – everything is short. Hotel room for three - $70.00 and must be paid in dollars. Friend Mark Benjamin's back and forth reactions to the situation: sympathetic then skeptical, then all over again.

## Wednesday, October 23, 1985
*Day 41, 6:00 p.m., back in Costa Rica*

A quiet hour in our room at Ligia's, in spite of televisions blaring from both directions – this house and the one next door. The music on cassette of the monks of Western Priority provide what quiet is possible.

It is not a tranquil week, compared to others. I feel distant from Kathy, always the most difficult distance to bear. I am also a bit unreceptive to bridging the distance, feeling a bit hurt probably, which results in a good bit of inward condemnation of her, including an attitude of "by God, I've done my part to bridge the distance between us – now it's her move." I pray that something in me will soften soon. I need her, and I need me to change back to a receptive person.

There are not many friends to embrace here – or who embrace me. The heart gets hungry for friends who hold and to hold. No marriage can provide all that is needed in the nourishment of tenderness. Perhaps this harder spell is a forerunner of more struggle to come – struggle that may be ours not because we are too pessimistic, but struggle that comes from trying to reach out and love in new ways in places strange to us.

The disciplines of running, sitting in silence, praying, and yoga are very fundamental for me. I'm sure that I will never arrange them into any predictable daily or even weekly pattern. But I do need to press on with them in order to allow good quality freedoms and joys to find me.

I am starved for silence – for alone time. I shall keep seeking it.

*2020 notes: Much in Costa Rica brought on challenges for us as a couple. We had very little privacy in the house where we were staying. We were without any close friends and had no real support system. As I look back I am amazed that we lived through all of our experiences with the grace that we were able to find in spite of the difficulties.*

## Saturday, October 26, 1985
*Day 44, Camp Roblealto, near Heredia, Costa Rica*

We asked around for a place where we might get away for a few days of quiet. Having usually depended on Roman Catholic friends and institutions for retreat space, we began to ask around among Catholic churches in San Jose. Noting that we were not Catholic they assumed we would want a non-Catholic place. I realized we were not in the progressive Catholic environment we had known in Seattle. We were told that a Seventh Day Adventist Camp called Roblealto (tall oak) would be a good place for us. So we hired a ride there and found ourselves in the midst of an Adventist youth retreat being led by one of their pastors. My primary memory of it looking back from 2019 is how cold we were when we slept there. They gave us sheets but no blankets. It was not a great retreat. I shivered too much to have any sense of humor about it.

Later that week I got into a heated conversation with another member of our Spanish class in San Jose. The school where we took Spanish usually served U.S. businessmen who needed Spanish to do business in Latin America. One man was there from Florida where he employed dozens of Spanish-speaking farmworkers and needed to learn Spanish to communicate better with them. He said: *"Now I believe, present company excepted,"* (meaning us) *"that when a bunch of do-gooders go into a combat zone, I don't think the U.S. government has any reason to protect them."* He was talking about the presence of U.S. church people along the San Juan River in Nicaragua who were finally captured by the U.S.-supported Contra rebels. Such people were precisely the kind of groups that we wanted to support. The "Contras," Nicaraguans paid by the U.S. to attack their own people, were terrorizing people in Southern Nicaragua near Costa Rica.

He continued: *"But what happens, to take a hypothetical situation,"* (although it really wasn't one) *"when a group of guerrillas are threatening and harming the lives of Costa Ricans near the border, and neither the U.S. nor Costa Rican government does anything to stop them? Who then has the responsibility to go and help those people.*

*"Well the government does, of course."*

*"But what if the government is not doing anything to help? What if the government is not acting? Who acts then?"*

*"I don't know, but before I go into some strange conflict, I'm going to be sure to check with my government first."*

The friendly argument went on for some time getting into the church's responsibility under Nazism, why Jesus was so threatening to Herod's government, and how the Bible was written.

He made his money off of pesticides and other agricultural chemicals. Though one of our fellow students in Spanish – he was a source of another form of education, the kind that leads one to see what kinds of consciousness, what perspectives U.S. citizens bring to Central America. It was good for me to meet someone who's life in Central America was all about making as much money as he could.

In an earlier talk with him I had confronted him when he criticized laws that protected agricultural workers in the U.S. I let slip a prejudgment that his work in agriculture had been to make big-money more so than to help the lives of farmworkers. He demanded an acknowledgement of my prejudgment, which I gave along with an apology. Later in the conversation he acknowledged that he had been in agriculture to make big money.

Reading today in Walter Brueggemann's *The Land* about its religious significance, I am reminded anew of what happens when land's religious significance is not acknowledged or celebrated. From where I am writing I can look out across a meadow and see a coffee field, patch, parcel whatever they call them here. The land is bountiful, and the land will be bountiful if its spirit is respected. On this matter we in the human race are still learning.

## Don German (pronounced "hayerman")

Don German (don is another word for mister but carries more respect and is often used for older men) is the man of the house. He is 75 or more, a slight man. He walks with a limp. His work on the "finca" (the small farm located on the property where we are staying) is the orchard. He keeps the fruit trees growing in what he calls a work of love.

He has a twinkle in his eye and a smile that constantly invites conversation – Don German is everybody's uncle. I remember the day I was introduced to him, he was building steps out of rock and concrete on one of the walkways. His first reply was "if there's any way I can serve you here, please let me know."

When he came to me one day and said he wish to "conversar" (have a conversation) with me, I was highly complimented, both because he is a warm and well-liked person, and because Don German is reasonably well-read. He is something of a campesino philosopher, and I usually feel a special quality of wisdom in his presence.

When the time came for our talk, he was careful to take me to a private spot. This surprised me a little, but I was also thinking that his wife had died of cancer only a few weeks before, and therefore that a more personal conversation might be helpful to him.

When we sat down, he explained to me that certain conversations needed to happen without women around.

This quickly captured my interest.

Then he began to tell me the famous story of one of his favorite ex-Costa Rican president. One story had to do with an event when the president was sitting at a corner seat at dinner, his own legs astride the table leg. The president was at a table full of women.

Purposely or otherwise, I missed the punch line, but it clearly had to do with a play on words related to the position of the president's legs at the corner of the table.

Later in the conversation, he leaned close to me and told me in warning tones about a Salvadoran teacher we both knew who felt El Salvador was a better country than Costa Rica. The depth of his nationalistic feelings was very apparent. The conversation moved on to Nicaragua, about which we clearly disagreed. I was saddened to note that his criticisms of Nicaragua were all based on inaccurate images, none of them based in facts or reality.

*2020 note: One Costa Rican friend told us that Costa Ricans are often "presumido" or proud, sometimes so proud of their country, feeling that it was superior to other Central American countries. I found some valid reasons for this. Costa Rica had disbanded its military in 1948 under reformist president Jose Figueres. Because of this they never seemed to get entangled in the wars that seemed so continuous in other Central American countries. During the Central American conflicts of the early 1980s President Oscar Arias of Costa Rica played in central role in bringing together opposing sides for conversation. For his work for peace there in the 1980's Arias was awarded the Nobel Peace Prize in 1987.*

When I talk with Don German now, I feel the same gentle, loving presence as I did the first day I saw him. I can see his face very clearly, and it is always smiling in my mind.

I also see a victim, a sensitive man who loves his country, but who somehow in the schemes of how national power translates into individual lives, was never given a chance to see his region of the world like it really is.

I think it is not so different for the rest of us, even when we try to stretch and look more closely at the world that is ours.

**Wednesday, October 30, 1985**
*Day 48, Santa Ana, Costa Rica*

At "home" in the house where we are living.

There's only a little more than a week to go here in the language school. We are anything but fluent. We are barely functional. I have trouble understanding the Spanish of the natives. Speaking is less of a problem for me.

The last few days have not been the most pleasant ones. My dreams reveal some inner strife that I do not know how to process outwardly. I would very much like to have three days of silence alone.

In recent days, I am missing being a pastor. I think of meetings in an office with coffee, lunch with a parishioner, phone calls that communicate caring, the monastic process of writing a sermon, the tender moments that go with serving communion, playing with children in the narthex, planning worship, or a special moment in worship, organizing a new program that has promise.

Today, as October comes to a close, all the good sensations that go with being a pastor are close to me – and far from me. I do feel the longing.

*2020 notes: Our decision to move to Central America was a radical departure from both of our career paths. It was very reasonable to ask if we had any business doing what we had decided to do. But we were both people with a lot of social concern and we had both been captured by the people and the difficult political realities of Central America at the time.*

The dreams of a better world are intoxicating for me. My hungers run deep – to see some genuine nuclear disarmament, to see Nicaragua be given a chance to grow as a nation. My imagination takes off in thousands of fantasies as to how I might be a part of it.

But when I come back to earth, it's clear that I'm just a person trying to do his job well, and trying to respond to the world like I found it. There have been a lot of "parsons" (one United Church of Christ word for a pastor which simply means person) like me before me, and there'll be a lot more like me after I'm gone.

The impact of one's life is always greatest when it grows out of being oneself, out of one's spiritual rootedness.

In this Central American sojourn, I am a pastor in exile, of sorts, away from settings where I would know more naturally what to do with myself. But it is an exile with purpose, an exile that will deepen the perspective out of which parish ministry needs to happen today.

## Friday, November 1, 1985
*Day 50, 6 a.m.*

I'm having stomach disturbances the last few days. Nothing serious and not unusual for U.S. folk living here, yet I suspect that it is also complicated by the pressures we are feeling. Our psyches certainly seem to be going through some deep transitions. I can feel it in my whole body.

Last night I remarked to Kathy that I was really missing Seattle, and that I felt I needed to have a good long cry. This kind of liberating grief does not come easily for me. Yet I feel that I may be using a lot of energy holding on to old feelings and old patterns.

Now I can only assume soberly that if some inward release does not occur for me consciously or unconsciously, then I may have even more psychic turmoil to go through as we bump into the next set of readjustments.

I feel I could use a good funny movie to go see.

## Saturday, November 2, 1985
*In the Church, Santa Ana, Costa Rica 11 a.m., some solitude*

Remembering a dream of 9-22-85 in which there were hints that I'm drawn to places of tragedy – the frightening possibility that much of what I thought was love may be but a martyr complex.

Maybe – but so what! Who says I'm the creature in the world who ought to have all the perfect motives?! Who says I should spend all my time pondering the motives circling my navel instead of getting on with what love and creativity are at my disposal.

My lot, it seems to me, is to try to look the dream straight in the face and allow it to speak to my life with healing and wisdom.

Today's call is to creativity. I have been swimming underwater for a good many days. Perhaps when the surfacing comes, I will find there's more Spanish in me than I realized. It is time to stop worrying. It is time to get on with things.

*11:30 a.m., same day, same church. A Conscious Examen*

*2020 note: A conscious examen is an exercise that has grown out of Ignatian Spirituality in which one simply sits quietly at the end of a day and recalls the moments when Grace/God had seemed especially present.*

Moments today when the Grace of God was especially present for me:

-When the thief came up behind me without my noticing and took things out of my backpack, a woman saw it and told me what had happened. I was able to recover what had been stolen.

-The wonderful moment when I saw that Mark Benjamin was in the travel agent's office as I walked in.

-The hilarity of Ligia in her Halloween mask.

-The pleasure of dreaming about a future in South Seattle when I woke up this morning.

-The wonderful energy of prayer time in the church.

-The intimacy and peace that has come with all the struggle lately.

-The joy of seeing a spot of sun this morning.

-The interest of ten-year-old Victor in me when I got up early to read this morning.

-The pleasure of feeling my body healing.

-Exciting ideas for the "actas," the skits in our class next Friday.

And so much more

Gracias!

## Monday, November 4, 1985
*Day 53, 9:30 p.m.*

Electricity drowns the good
sounds of a night that
would be silent
and gifted,

Were not anxieties charged
with current
and with fear of possibility.
Frontside gifts
find only our backs
turned,
while we front to electric
currents that spray
our souls full of non-possibility.
Facing up to silence
has its own shock,
the sweet screaming
step through the doorway
to peace.

The evening quiets as bedtime nears. Dreams blink lightly in the
fatigue of day's end. A book of readings looms worth more thinking.
They might be stories – snapshots of people, of struggles, of some
truth, or of some truth that did not quite make it.

Tonight, beneath all that has stressed us here, beneath all that has
distorted our energies and made us to see the world more scarce than
abundant – tonight a quiet glimpse of the something wonderful here
in Central America whispers through the brittle cracks in my heart.

I have touched parts of me that were deep and rich and good. I
have moved into some of the deeper regions. Perhaps I did not always
know what to do when I got there. Perhaps I knew less about what to
do when I got back.

There is yet hope that my fear will not always rule. Grace abides
gently to forgive and energize.

The day is the gift
The future is open.

*2020 notes: During the years in Central America I wanted so much
to become a competent and published writer. This theme recurs
throughout this journal. Looking back, I think I was overly obsessed
and ambitious about this. It would have taken more energy and
discipline that I could find in myself during those years. We did
publish fifteen issues of a newsletter, that we called Vista del Sur*

*which was a satisfying piece of work. It was mailed out to a few hundred friends and supporters in the Seattle area. But that was about all the writing I was really capable of at the time, except for this journal. I had also really underestimated how much time and energy it would require to do the work that was ours to do as part of the team we worked on as well as the energy required simply to learn to live in a new culture. This journal became the book I could write.*

## Saturday, November 9, 1985
*Day 58, 12:20 p.m. in the church, Santa Ana, Costa Rica*

Six pews in front of me Kathy sits and prays. Above her right shoulder, in the distance Mary stands stately, aloft, still, comforting one of her needy children. And hanging still from one of many very rustic pillars, her boy Jesus bleeds on his cross. And I sit breathing on a wooden pew padded only by the skin of my thin body.

Shadows of the pew on a stone wall that is three feet thick, somehow remind me that beyond the chains that I tend to tie myself with, there looms the promising glimmer of transcendence, easily more literal than my self-imposed chains.

There constantly abides the yearning for personal needs to be met. There is also the constant sense that these needs are the means by which I will break into liberation. I do not make light of personal needs – food, human touch, embraces, listening, sexual expression, status, and more – they are good parts of creation just like the rest of creation. They deserve time, organization, creativity, and intentionality. But they also find their place in creation more securely when they move within the subtle, literal shadows of transcendence. They are richest when the something larger has possessed us. They are gifts rather than oppressions when they exist "off-center" in our lives. They deserve to be part of the journey. They are not destinations.

## Saturday, November 9, 1985
*A note to Nancy Weber*

> *2020 notes: Nancy Weber was a good friend from Seattle who herself had made a courageous trip to Central America before we*

*went after she had been diagnosed with cancer. She was also active among "liberal Republicans" in Seattle, spoke Spanish and was a valuable guide and supporter. I must have written this after we knew that she was dying.*

Dear Nancy,

Your life, your laughter, your faith, your vision, and your great joy in being on the planet for a while has been a source of unspeakable hope for me. I have seen you laugh so often in the midst of suffering that was constant! I have seen you weep for love of a friend, for love of a child, for love of a nation, and for love of many nations. I want to be more like you. I want to carry laughter with me wherever suffering may take me. I want to be as comfortable embracing the weak as the strong. I want to keep laughing and giving the gifts that I have to give.

## Wednesday, November 13, 1985
*Day 62*

We have begun the active work of looking at position openings in Central America where we might be of service with the experience, skills and interest we bring. Our first visit was to the Commission for Development and Emergency (CODE), later renamed the Christian Commission for Development (CCD). We flew first to the capital city, Tegucigalpa before the long drive to "La Granja" (the farm) which was in need of a resident couple.

*In the cathedral, Tegucigalpa, Honduras*

> Upon seeing a woman, old, proud,
> cheerful, begging in the plaza:
> As you took from me
> all that was mine
> but which I never had
> I held my suffering heart proud.
> And even though poverty has
> wrenched me
> and kept my love in exile,
> You have been the poor one.

115

Tegucigalpa feels calm, relaxing and clean. My last time here was not particularly satisfying – rainy, overscheduled, and fraught with group conflicts. I am surprised and glad to be having good feelings in being here.

## Thursday, November 14, 1985
*San Pedro Sula, Honduras in the Cathedral*

> *2020 notes: San Pedro Sula is one of the two largest cities in Honduras, located in the northern part of the country close about an hour from the Atlantic coast. As the crow flies Tegucigalpa was much closer to La Granja ("the farm") but there are no passable roads that run directly between the two areas. This made it necessary to drive a triangle route, first north San Pedro Sula, about 4 hours, and then back to the south for another six hours to San Marcos, Ocotepeque and La Granja*

Simple people light candles to go with their prayers. Traffic roars.

Four candles burn near a side altar. Perhaps for friends who are sick – or for family members.

We go on to San Marcos today for more time with the staff of the Christian Commission for Development (CCD) and to look at the farm where we might live. I am very aware as I sit here that my thoughts are with the youth of Nicaragua. I pray today for more of an open hear to the situation at the farm, but presently I have real doubts as to whether it is an appropriate situation for us. Even in writing this my thoughts go to Nicaragua and to attempts at reconciliation. My head is full of ideas. I will need to work very hard in order to spend time listening and listening.

## Monday, November 18, 1985
*Day 67 in the hotel room, Tegucigalpa*

Back here after demanding and enriching days in San Marcos, Cololaca, "La Granja," the remote village of Coyolillo – and other places far beyond my usual reality. After the trip I find myself much more open to the possibility of living in San Marcos. However, I do not turn loose easily of Nicaragua and so much of me that wants to be there.

It is a little early to begin listing pros and cons. I am pleased to find myself in more of a state of openness to things here.

One thought occurred to me – that maybe I simply need to be strong enough to follow Kathy whatever choice she wishes to make. I really hope that we both will try to be quiet and listen for God. The possibility of new depths of spiritual surrender does seem to be with me. The fact that I am open to the farm life is one sign of this. The decision should take a few days – hopefully not many.

## Tuesday, November 19, 1985
*Day 68, 12:00 noon in the church, Santa Ana, Costa Rica*

We are back "home" in Costa Rica, and the inner struggle to decide begins. Kathy and I have not talked a lot to each other in terms of pros and cons between Nicaraguan Baptists and Honduran CCD programs.

*2020 notes: We made a second trip to Nicaragua to see if there might be a position there for us. There was. We were invited to work with youth in the Baptist Convention of Nicaragua. The position description was not all that clear but it would be a position among friends we had already made. I also felt a lot of loyalty to Nicaragua and to the achievements for the poor there after its 1979 revolution. We were told that if we were to work there we would need to have a four-wheel drive pickup and that it would be up to us to raise the money for the vehicle. This was very reasonable given the financial realities of our denomination, of the Baptists in Nicaragua and of our own independent means. We were not necessarily expecting to get a salary for whatever our work would become. But this was very different from the Honduras situation where the resources were somewhat better and where the work to be done was much clearer.*

I am full of emotion about the decision. The trip to San Marcos touched me and changed me some, but it did not nearly neutralize the feelings and sense of connection I have with Nicaragua.

I feel a little resentful that we had a more thorough experience in Honduras than in Nicaragua – perhaps a little like "my side did not get a fair chance."

Ideas still take off in many directions as I think of Nicaragua.

I have thoughts that there my mission, my calling is clearer, perhaps more "noble", because I would be closer to a revolution that had been successful in many ways on behalf of the poor.

I also feel the question in me that in Honduras, the depth of simplicity and the difficult lifestyle could affect a conversion in me that could be just what I need for future decades in my life.

In any case, I am now praying that we will break out of the "my choice vs. your choice" mentality. It may not be easy. God has many layers to work through. I pray that I may listen.

I do not wish to run from history. In Honduras (in San Marcos) I think I would feel rather insulated from history – from having to involve myself in the conflicts that really open up human life possibilities.

But then again, maybe an engagement with the very poor at a grass-roots level could be just what I need to deepen my roots in God's history-making.

Many of my needs call me to Nicaragua – needs for status, needs for success, needs for challenging work in more familiar areas, needs for more public attention. These needs are not bad needs. They may be the very ways in which God is trying to speak to me. I do not want to lapse into the wrong kind of self-denial here. I am a human Christian with human gifts and human needs.

I wonder how it is for Kathy. She is sitting six pews ahead writing in her own journal.

I think she is more likely to want to go to San Marcos. She does not have the passion, the feeling for Nicaragua that I have. At least if she does, I have not seen it.

She is a little more at home in agriculture than I. CODE's work in San Marcos is likely to be more fulfilling for Kathy. Her comments are all about CODE. I don't hear her sharing any visions, excitements, possibilities about Nicaragua.

I may be more adaptable than she in this environment. Certainly Central American culture is likely to be more hospitable to the gifts of a man than to the gifts of a woman.

I wonder if I could "go with her" to San Marcos without feeling the wrong kind of resentment. I know I could not do it without feeling regret and grief. This could be my one chance to deepen the friendships and possibilities I have come to cherish in Nicaragua. I won't be able to give this up without some pain.

Still this keeps us from moving into the "our" decision category. Is there a way within the prayer that God has given us that a clarity of "our" can emerge? I am enough of a realist to believe that decisions made well do not necessarily turn out to be "right." Yet I believe in the process. I believe in the discernment process that brings us to a readiness to move. If, after this readiness is established, free will and events turn life in a sour or fragmented direction. It is time to discern some more, whether to endure or change.

I am aware of some feeling that I might "let Tomas down." (Rev. Tomas Tellez is the head of the Nicaraguan Baptist Convention). I think he does have affection and a sense of connection to me. I do not want to let him down. Yet this is not a way to make a decision. God is with the Baptists in Nicaragua. And God will be with them whether I am or not. I need much more than "making Tomas feel good" etc. in order to be effective in Nicaragua. I believe that I have it.

In reading from another journal, I ran across a quote from Dag Hammerskjold in *Markings* – *"Never look down before taking your next step; only he who keeps eye fixed on the far horizon will find his right road."*

*2020 note: What I did not note in my journal at the time was that in Honduras there was clear work with women where Kathy's gifts and energy would be better used. This was not nearly as clear in the invitation to Nicaragua.*

## Wednesday, November 20, 1985
*Day 69 at noon in the church, Santa Ana, Costa Rica*

Why am I here? What callings brought me here? What expectations did I bring with me? What do I want to be able to say;

119

what do I want to be able to have done when the two years have ended?

## A look ahead in order to look back on paper

*2020 note: I decided to do a writing exercise as if I were in the future looking back, trying to imagine what it might be like after three years in Central America from both Honduras and Nicaragua, our two options. Below, the entry for September 14, 1987 reflects back on the time in Central America.*

January, 1988 – Managua (written in 1985)

In two weeks, we'll be going back to the United States. I am remembering back in the church in Santa Ana when we were trying to work out the decision as to where we would go. Here we are – it is all over. What happened to that time? Did we do what we came here to do?

We did reach some of the youth in Nicaragua – never as many as the Baptists here wanted us to reach, but we did plant some seeds. It took much longer than I expected at the beginning to get through the cultural differences and find some structures, some channels within which we could work. It took months just to be able to understand the Spanish the kids spoke. They were patient with us. I think they knew we wanted very much to care for them and help them grow.

I leave now ready to be a pastor again in the United States. We had a few big successes here – big hits – the drama night, the two convocations – and more – but I did not come close to establishing the "mighty" program that I came here to establish – and I do not think this was my role. God had different things in mind.

As I look back now, this time has been productive. I think the people feel satisfied with our work – and that we have made a real contribution. I hope so. But beyond this, this time has been the richest part of my life. It has been a time of reflection after acting, of having to look deep into myself for tools to work with, for gifts, that simply were not visible to me before I arrived. This has been the miracle. It has probably also been the quality that has touched others the most.

January 1988 – San Marcos

Our two years "in the campo" (countryside) have come to an end. They have been special days, although ordinary and full of difficulty. I do not know if all the lifestyle adjustments were worth whatever it was that we may have accomplished here.

The images do make us look good on paper. I am glad to have had the experience in a very deprived Third World environment. Much, much love has been given to us. I hope the place has affected in me a substantial part of the conversion for which God brought me here.

It may not be easy now to go back and work in the United States. I have less idea now about the meaning of career. I'm sure God had something in mind. Maybe we need to think about staying more years here in San Marcos. The UCC does not have many positions for those who have skills in raising rabbits.

But now I know I can bend to work with lives I could have never worked with before. The new breadth of my life is a good gift. I feel closer to earth, closer to life as it really is, more able to relate to people just where they are. *(end of the writing exercise)*

*And back to November 1985*

What do I want to have happened when the two years are finished?

-I want to have been profoundly educated, changed, converted – so that my being may enhance fresh, alternative visions for others.

-I want to have worked closely with people here, on issues that really matter to them. I want them to feel after two years that I have been present to them as servant in every possible way that I can that was appropriate.

-I want to work for peace. In whatever way possible, I want to use my gifts to influence peacemaking – to work with those who are seeking a new era of possibility between my country and Latin America in general, Central America in particular.

-I want to have deepened my spiritual life by living more simply, praying more regularly.

-I want to do some writing that will be helpful to others.

-I want to use the gifts that I have to give.

-I want to help people laugh and celebrate life.

## Thursday, November 21, 1985
*Day 70, 7 a.m., Ligia's house, Santa Ana, Costa Rica*

Yesterday, after quiet time and writing in the church, Kathy and I talked quietly on the church lawn for about an hour. The "central existential question" was just as I had expected – Kathy was leaning toward San Marcos – and I was leaning toward Nicaragua. She was having problems seeing a role for herself in Nicaragua, and I had some of the same for me in San Marcos (although the real issue for me is simply my deep attachment to Nicaragua). We talked without trying to convince each other of anything, but it was clear that we were in different places. We decided to go back into the church and pray out loud together. We did so, near the front, in a pew just a few feet from a very large crucifix – maybe seven or eight feet high.

We do not naturally or frequently do this kind of praying together – probably less than five times in five years. The few times within memory are rich memories for me – as was yesterday. We prayed quietly – sometimes with more feeling – we prayed for people in Honduras and Nicaragua. I prayed that if I needed to let go of Nicaragua, that I would be able to do so. I found some release and even some tears. Walking away from the church with Kathy I felt some peace. I also sensed that the letting go had begun – and that for me the day's nudging had been in the direction of Honduras.

The afternoon moved on with little activity but with a lot of fatigue. It is taking energy from both of us to live with indecision.

The afternoon also moved into an evening of anger for me – intense anger. In Exodus 16:8, Moses and Aaron were saying to the "murmuring" resentful Israelites, who were longing for the safety of Egypt, "your murmurings are not against us but against the Lord." Yesterday it may well have been that my murmurings against Kathy were really murmurings against the Lord.

Whatever were the murmurings, I was an angry man last night – still am to some extent. I felt like something central, a treasure in my life – had been taken from me.

Nicaragua – the place in the world where there is a hope that the passions of both socialism and capitalism might live together in hope, in the development of one struggling county – were it not for the sheer ignorance and immorality of the U.S. government. The place where the church is alive and creative, even though ripped apart by conflict and suffering. I wanted and I want so much to be an active part of this. What happens to those dreams and those passions now if we are being led to Honduras? Were they that bad? Were they not more, ever so much more, grounded in goodness and peace than in something less? I feel resistant, rebellious, and angry about having to let go, but if this is what God wills, then things will probably work, and broader richer possibilities will emerge all over the place.

I already have had a vision of an "adoption" program between the 18 villages of the San Marcos program and 18 local churches in the United States – all of this as part of a D. Min program on the local church and the Third World.

### *11 a.m. – Same Day – In the church – Santa Ana, Costa Rica*

The morning goes on. Now I am in one of those times when I feel saturated by an idea – I have the village adoption program on paper now. Ideas take off like crazy – an evening campfire once a week at La Granja for all the campesinos who can come, clearing an area that could be used for games – perhaps using the new games foundation model, delivering a new-born goat, learning to talk with the campesinos in their language.

Perhaps it is best if I have a role distinctly different from all the others – working some way that allows me to be who I need to be without threatening the turf of anyone else's work.

Development of video pieces to use to tell the story of the villages – or to use in setting up a study program. Exchange of videos between the villages and the U.S. churches.

Today, not much within me is quiet. I am ready to go to work. I am full of ideas. I am not full of anger or grief about Nicaragua. I want to get moving with the next chapter in my life. I think it's close enough to where Kathy is that we can work together just fine.

*2020 notes: I can remember how hard it was for me to let go of my hopes to live and work in Nicaragua. I was like a squealing pig. But Honduras was clearly the better option for us in many ways.*

## Friday, November 22, 1985
*Day 71, noon in the church, Santa Ana, Costa Rica*

*2020 note: Escuela Para Todas, translation "school for everyone"
was a publication we saw in a number of places in Central America.
It included "farmer's almnac" entries, stories and news, written in
language easily understood by those who have limited education.*

The peace with San Marcos seems to be continuing. There is still
a sense of hurt, of loss, of resentment and anger in the background.
But I am making my peace with life at La Granja. Ideas keep flowing
like crazy. So far I have a village adoption program, a weekly
campfire event, a work room in San Marcos, a curriculum on
Honduras using The Land by Walter Brueggemann as a guide, using
Escuela para Todas as a teaching tool, getting a video camera and
using Chuck & Julia to put together video pieces on Honduras, having
my parents visit the farm, being a kind of pastoral presence in
campesino homes as appropriate.

I seem to be letting go of Nicaragua. I can only take this
letting go and the strength of the ideas that are flowing as a sign that
God is now leading us to Honduras. If that Loving Spirit of Power
and Creativity is indeed our leader in these days of deciding, then the
rest can only be peace and fulfillment and creativity.

The scripture that found me today was from Psalm 57:2 - -
*"I cry to God most high who fulfills his purpose for me. He will send
from heaven and save me."*

## Saturday, November 23, 1985
*Day 72, noontime in the church, Santa Ana, Costa Rica*

The wind is strong here today. This stone building with walls 2 ft
thick is standing firm but the tin roof is sounding off.

Kathy and I are now moving ahead as if San Marcos is the place
we are going. It probably is. All will be well. Yesterday we talked
amid many tender feelings. I may be a little numb from all the energy
it has taken to decide.

Today I am not filled with passionate ideas about San Marcos. I
have more of a sense of the things we must get done – letters, packing,

transportation, newsletter. It's not that overwhelming, but it does seem to be the time to get moving.

I also feel a little numb from the loss of Nicaragua. I was hurt, angry when Kathy spoke of her pessimism about the success of the current Nicaraguan government as a reason against going there. We had a minor spat over this. If the U.S. destabilization and war process does succeed to the point of the collapse of the current government, this to me would be all the more reason to go and be there with the people.

But to play out the pessimism a bit, it is hard to imagine what would happen if the government were to collapse. The hills of Nicaragua would be full of "guerillas" who would not need CIA salaries to be committed to their cause. We (the U.S.) would have driven Nicaragua to the ugliest violence, possibly in all of its history.

Perhaps my calling now is to get away from Nicaragua passions for awhile, or at least to see them from the perspective of Honduras, especially the poor in Honduras.

### Sunday, December 1, 1985
*Day 80, in the village of Tortuguero, Atlantic Coast, Northern Costa Rica*

We took a seven-hour train ride from San Jose to Limón (lee-MONE) in preparation for catching the twice weekly government boat from Moín (mow-EEN) (near Limón) up the canal about 7-10 hours to Tortuguero, a national park on the Atlantic Coast of Costa Rica, famous as one of the places where the giant sea turtles in the Caribbean return each year to lay eggs after swimming hundreds of miles back to the place where all of them were hatched. Upon arriving in Moín we discovered that the government boat was broken down, and would not be fixed for perhaps weeks.

After weighing options with some twenty other hopeful tourists, we decided to take a chance and catch a ride on a private cargo boat, not knowing how soon a boat would be heading back to Moín.

The trip up was a many splendored nine-hour adventure. A rather homemade looking boat, about thirty feet long, run by a very homemade diesel V-8 engine which rumbled at 8 km/hr until we finally pulled into Tortuguero with great relief.

*The boat to Tortuguero took us through a dense jungle area where we saw colorful exotic birds in the wild.* Photo credit: "Honduras-0515 - Macaw" by Dennis Jarvis, CC license 2.0. See photo credits at end of book for full details.

Many moments on the trip up were very memorable:

-The cargo itself, large stacks of Coca-Cola and beer, sacks of cement, an unpackaged stereo, and the rest of us – some 40 passengers – 10 or so tourists and the rest natives, dependent to these boat rides to get to and from doctors and other services available only by way of this eight-hour boat ride.

-The babies – three local mothers on board had babies of breast-feeding age.

-One mother had two pre-school boys besides. Kathy and I ended up holding these two during the last leg of the trip.

-The good conversation sitting on the bow of the boat. At one point I was in a circle that included a German woman, a Costa Rican man, a young man from Israel, and myself. I heard about electric power systems in Costa Rica, kibbutz life in Israel, and the lives of palm trees in Costa Rica.

-The steering mechanism on the boat seemed to be in less than good shape a good part of the time. It consisted of a steering wheel, with chain and cable which went from the steering wheel in front of the boat, down each side of the boat to the rudder in the rear. As the benches for passengers were also along the side, one could feel the steering cable rub along one's bottom as the pilot made left or right turns. It gave one a "get to the bottom of it all" feeling of being very much a part of the steering of the boat.

We arrived in the village of Tortuguero on Thanksgiving Day. We got a very simple room, and then waited for half an hour to use the only phone in the village. We called Seattle and had a good phone visit with Kathy's family just after their Thanksgiving dinner.

We then luckily found one place still willing to serve us some dinner. We won't forget that Thanksgiving meal – rice, beans, fried bologna, and lemonade. We felt lucky to find any food at all at such a late hour in such a remote place.

*2020 notes: I used the trip as an opportunity to try out my Spanish as we talked to people many of whom seemed to speak two or three languages. During one meal with others I was trying hard to keep a conversation going in Spanish, but was humbled when a man, frustrated at not being able to understand my bad Spanish, said, "why don't we just talk in English." I still had a ways to go before my Spanish would be adequate for conversation!*

*November is not the time here when thousands of baby sea turtles hatch and make their run for the sea before they are eaten by ravenous sea birds and other predators, the time when most tourists visit. But the trip did include miles and miles on the canal through the Costa Rican coastal jungle where we saw numerous tropical birds in the wild, especially toucans and parrots. It was an unforgettable trip.*

## Tuesday, December 3, 1985
*Day 82 in the church, Santa Ana*

Psalm 103:6 – *"The Lord works vindication and justice for all who are oppressed."*

I hope to be in contact with this verse when life in Honduras has begun.

From this vantage point, I cannot see much that gives evidence of vindication and justice for the poor in Honduras.

## Saturday, December 7, 1985
*Day 86 in the church, Santa Ana*

The week has not been an easy one psychically. Seems that the fears, uncertainties of life in Cololaca have overruled the possibilities, the riches of life there. I am not having all that many saintly thoughts or feelings about going to work with the poor. Whatever romance there was in the venture seems to have faded fast.

I continue to feel some disappointment that we won't be in Nicaragua. I'm not having images that get at the essential beauty of the campesinos in the San Marcos area. I've worried some that they won't know how to express appreciation for our presence there (I've been used to a church where I felt well-loved, supported, admired, appreciated).

Read today in Walter Brueggemann's *The Land* when the people of Israel are air the Jordan River about to cross into the land promised:

*"The Jordan is entry not into safe space but into a context of covenant. The gift is for celebration. It is based on the risk that satiated people can stay in history and keep listening. It is a bold*

128

*question, as yet unresolved, whether only the hungry will listen, or whether satiated people can stay in history with the Lord of History."* What I feel in response to this is some sense of being deprived of my own normal satiations – close friends to talk to openly, the status of pastoral office, intellectual stimulation, lots of meals in restaurants, plenty of familiar foods at home.

The irony is that in response to Brueggemann here, I don't feel sure right now that his sense of "de-satiation" is necessarily making me any more present to history. I can only hope so.

Brueggemann also speaks of the nature of land in Israel's faith as "the land given, the land of restoration, land by graciousness" as contrasted with "a life of coercion, in which land is held by fearful, wearisome duty."

The spirit of the latter has unfortunately afflicted me lately. At this point I am not sure if I know how or even have the spiritual or emotional capacity to go to Honduras and experience the people, the time, the place (i.e. the land) as a gift.

I like Brueggemann's words. I so wanted them to fit nicely into all my preconceived thinking categories for living in Central America. It is not happening. My world is rather topsy-turvy now.

A certain undercurrent of trust and purpose does continue. I at least am struggling to believe in the promise talked about Brueggemann. I want to believe. I may be realizing that in the past I have lived much more off of the surface issues of status and program rather off the essence of the promise. If the present deprivation will bring me a little closer to the essence of the promise, then I may have less need to worry about the surface content, along with more energy to work creatively out of the promise and into tangible expressions.

## Monday, December 9, 1985
*Day 88 in the church, Santa Ana*

A hard depression has begun to come over me today. I do not really understand its source or its meaning.

Writing does not come easily. Knowing what I want and really need now does not some easily. It is a hard state.

It is hard to pray, hard to cry, almost impossible to laugh.

My body feels tight. I have very little hunger, and all I can seem to do is brood on paper – not what I most like to do with my writing.

## Tuesday, December 10, 1985
*Day 89 in the church, Santa Ana*

The depression subsides some, and I feel better.

There is anxiety – not really fear, - for there is no object – about going to Honduras. Our decision was well-made. In the earlier quiet moments of the decision-making, there was peace and energy. Now in the anxiety, there is good reason to keep my resolve that all will be well in the long run.

Have been reading more in Brueggemann's The Land. He deals with Israel in the wilderness as a "landless" people living with only a promise. Then they come the Jordan, the boundary, and all their fears come over them – the self-image of grasshoppers up against giants is the dominant theme. Deuteronomy is one big sermon by Moses at the boundary, to remind the people who they are as they go into the land of abundance.

In going to Honduras, I feel myself headed more to a wilderness than to a land of abundance. Even in the anxiety of thinking about living without electricity, running water, ice cream, bookstores, and hamburgers, I start to "murmur," like the distraught, untrustful Israelites in the wilderness. My energy seems low. I'm having trouble shaking a cold. I think about Nicaragua. I think about my carpeted study back at our house in Seattle, where there was always coffee at hand, good fruit, and cookies abundant. I want my friends, a good lunch at one of Seattle's nice quaint restaurants. I want to be doing work that I know how to do – work that helps me feel secure. I miss the Burke-Gilman Trail where I can so easily get my body into better working order. I want again the familiarity of people who speak my language, good affluent U.S. church people, the kind who want peace, and write thank you notes but who don't make outrageous changes in their lives because of strange, perhaps neurotic, attachments to some Galilean carpenter.

Even before I step into the wilderness, I want my stability back. I want familiarity. I want a life so filled with duties and meetings and friends that I don't have time for all of it. This psychological fuss that

I'm going through, trying to be somebody spiritual and know what I'm doing here in the Third World.

Only heroic images call me on – Only the call of "courageous stands," "suffering for Jesus in a tight spot," etc. etc. which could well mean that I do not have what it takes to live with such a crisis. The call of today: simple service, waiting, seems more of a trial than a gift for me. I don't want to get into the wrong kind of martyr psychology, but it may be the challenge of the day to day that will make me more whole.

We are in Advent. Emmanuel waits to arrive for captive Israel. As Emmanuel moves toward me, I feel myself sinking more deeply into the wilderness, and hopefully – into more hope.

*2020 notes: Doing God's Will - Following God's Call*

*A general definition of "doing God's will" or "following God's call to each person" usually means that one believes in some Divine leading of every individual's life and that this will of God can be discerned and known through understanding biblical teachings and listening to one's inner voice.*

*My years growing up in fundamentalist Christianity had an "either-or" sense about the meaning of doing God's will. I am sure that I remember this as being more rigid than it actually was in the minds of most people, but it felt like there was one road that was God's will and that all other roads taken were not God's will. There was some right road that I had to figure out and all other roads were wrong. This question was strong in me and caused me a good bit of torment well into my young adult years.*

*My Baptist deacon father gave me a hint once that his sense of doing God's will more human understanding in it than was usually taught when he told me a joke about the Baptist pastor who had been invited to serve in a larger church with a much higher salary. So, Daddy told me, the pastor said to his wife, "honey you go pack and I'll pray for guidance about God's will in this decision." I'm sure he had seen a number of times when there was a high correlation between God's will and being better off financially.*

*A mentor in my life had responded to a sense of call he felt early in his life to become a Jesuit priest. He later felt called to a marriage, thus to live out his call from then on from within his marriage. After about thirty years of marriage looking back on that decision, he once said to me, "I think I could have gone either way. I could have stayed in the priesthood or left, and on either path remained within God's will for his life.*

*Another source of guidance for me in understanding the meaning of God's will more compassionately comes from a well-known prayer written by Thomas Merton that includes the words, "...that fact that I think I am doing your will does not mean that I am actually doing so. But I believe the desire to please you, does in fact please you..."*

*I believe I had a genuine desire to do God's will in my decision to move to Central America. I am also aware that there were a variety of emotions and motivations at work in that decision— some ambition, some desire for adventure and to leave current comfort zones, and some sense that the human community had so many urgent needs that there was a universal call that went out to everyone that to question simply getting on with life as it has always been lived. I am also a bit uneasy whenever anyone seems to know the details of God's will beyond the shadow of any doubt.*

*Kathy and I had decided that we would give ourselves at least one year and maybe two for this sojourn. Then we would return to our lives in the U.S. I know that I wanted to "help" the people while we lived there without having nearly enough consciousness of what a red flag this wanting to help can be. I had learned the "correct" language of wanting to be in solidarity with the poor and accompany them. I knew how to use the correct language. I would have a lot to learn about moving into the receptive spirit that this sojourn would require.*

*My faith has evolved into a simple knowing and trust that "God adores us" as one teacher puts it, and I believe that God was with me every step of the way with all my blind spots as well as good intentions while in Central America, especially Honduras. I admire that young man who was me who was willing to make some out of the box choices about what directions my life would take.*

*Another factor in going was that we had enough financial resources that we could take a year or two on much-reduced income and still live as we needed to live. This was not the case for most of my colleagues in parish ministry. It is a profession in which a lot of good education and preparation does not result in income close to the amounts earned by many others in our economy with the same education and credentials. I was privileged in this way. I could afford to take strong stands on social justice issues in ways that were financial impossible for many colleagues and their families.*

*While acknowledging that "wanting to help" can lead to unfortunate outcomes, it is relevant to ask if our presence in Honduras was an asset to the people and programs that we were invited to be a part of. I can see many ways that my presence was a help to the work being done. Much of what I see takes very practical forms. For example, among the ten of us on the working team in San Marcos only four of us had driver's licenses. Getting people and necessary provisions to remote villages required a lot of driving. I was able to serve as a driver on many occasions. We served as resident managers at La Granja which was an important training center for people from eighteen surrounding villages. This included buying large amounts of food and hiring people who lived nearby as cooks and kitchen workers. We took care of the animals on the farm: goats, rabbits, chickens, and a donkey, all of whom had a role in improving the lives of the people we worked with. As U.S. citizens we felt that our presence in a sensitive area so close to the war in El Salvador provided some deterrence to abuses of local citizens by the Honduran military.*

*Along with the ways we felt we were helpful it also became significant to ask how long it takes for expatriates such as I to become sufficiently acclimated to life in Honduras so that we become more self-sufficient assets instead of learners who required a lot of emotional support and practical instruction. It was easy to see that in my final months in Honduras I had come to feel at home in ways that were not possible for me within the first year. It is not unusual for U.S. citizens to want to give a year or two abroad in order to be helpful in some situation of human need. At what point is one sufficiently acclimated to be able to give far more than one needs to receive from host staff? This is not an easy question to answer. My sense is that we often tend to assume that our presence will be helpful when in fact it takes a long time for most people to feel sufficiently at home in a new setting in ways that do not require extra energy on the part of the host agency. Sometimes it seemed that just as U.S. people were ready to wrap up their time and head home, they had finally become accustomed enough in the new situation to practice the self-sufficiency needed.*

*I have come to believe that there are a number of important hallmarks for knowing if one is "called" to some place or particular work. Among them are: (1) Call requires some careful attention to one's inward journey, whether the path is a fit and whether it put one on a path to becoming his or her most authentic self. (2) Call will give us some connection to people who have been made poor and marginalized by society. (3) Call will likely be costly in a number of ways yet be found worth the cost involved. (4) Call will "feel right" for the path of a particular life journey. It will lead to a sense of joy and meaning even if it is difficult at times. By these and other criteria, I look back at my time in Central America as very much on the course of my discovery of authentic selfhood. It was clumsy, imperfect and messy at so many points along the way. But it was crucial to my ongoing discovery of who I was and am and how I was called to live in the world.*

*Was I "doing God's will for my life" then during my time in Centra America? I don't finally know. I hope so, at least some of the time. Now I believe that we simply do the best we can to follow our call and that God takes it from there and makes something out of both our good and not so good choices and efforts.*

### Thursday, December 12, 1985
*Day 91 in the church, Santa Ana*

The last day in Costa Rica, at least for a while. We leave early in the morning for Tegucigalpa, and I am so happy.

I feel very good today. Seems that all my feelings are with me – at my disposal. Joy, love, anger, anticipation, ideas. My cold of many days standing has about ended. My energy is up.

Our friend Mark Benjamin is back from traveling, and we get to have one more visit with him – the highlight of this day. Today I heard myself uttering a silent prayer that our friendship with Mark would last a lifetime – then fantasized telling him of this wish, recognizing, of course, all the forces natural and not so natural in the ebb and flow of friendships. There is a beauty and a compassion about Mark that is surely one of God's finer gifts to my life.

I feel ready to give my best to life in Cololaca, with some coming together of zeal and determination that lets me feel it may be one of the great chapters of our lives. I so want it to work. And of course, my unfortunately significant ego needs remind me that I need it to work and that it would be rather painful if it did not.

Then, of course, we have not even begun There are many interesting and rough roads yet to be traveled, especially that 15 mile/one-hour jeep ride from San Marcos to Cololoca.

# CHAPTER 4
# LIFE AT LA GRANJA (THE FARM)
## DECEMBER 1985-JUNE 1987

*13 – Fri – arrived Tegucigalpa*

*14 – Sat – Tegucigalpa*

*15 – Sun – Tegucigalpa*

*16 – Mon – Tegucigalpa*

*17 – Tue – Tegucigalpa*

*18 – Wed – Tegucigalpa*

*19 – Thu – arrived San Marcos*

*20 – Fri – took things to La Granja – returned to San Marcos*

*21 – Sat – First night to sleep at La Granja*

*22 – Sun – at La Granja*

*23 – Mon – at La Granja*

*24 – Tues – at La Granja*

*25 – Wed – at La Granja*

*2020 note: This is an important time of transition, our move from Costa Rica to San Marcos and La Granja in southwestern Honduras. From December 1985 until June 1987 we lived at La Granja*

*To explain place names:*

**Tegucigalpa** *is the capital of Honduras and the location of the main office of the organization we will be working with the Christian Commission for Development (CCD), previously known as the Commission for Development and Emergency (CODE).*

**San Pedro Sula** *is the second large city in Honduras besides Tegucigalpa. It is located in the north coast area of the country not far from the nearest port city. To travel from Tegucigalpa to San Marcos almost everyone travels through San Pedro Sula because there are no good roads directly from Tegucigalpa to San Marcos.*

**San Marcos** *is a small city which at the time had only gravel streets and is the location of CCD's regional office near where we would be stationed. It is in the Southwest area of Honduras near the borders with both Guatemala and El Salvador.*

**La Granja**, *the farm where we lived for a year and a half, was another 15 miles from San Marcos, on a very rough road toward the El Salvador border. The 15-mile drive often took an hour because the road was so rough then. We have heard it is better now.*

**Cololaca** *was a village on the road between San Marcos and La Granja. It is about two miles from La Granja. Two members of our team lived in Cololaca, both of them local farmers or campesinos. Five more team members all lived in San Marcos.*

## Sunday, December 22, 1985
*La Granja, Cololaca, Honduras*

Last night, Saturday, December 21, was our first night to sleep here in La Granja. Arrived in Honduras 12 days ago – after we spent five days in Tegucigalpa. Now we are finally "home" at La Granja. The days here move slowly.

*2020 notes: An explanation of the mission of La Granja ("the farm") and of the work of the Christian Commission for Development (CCD):*

*Serving about twenty rural villages near San Marcos, CCD was a Christian organization whose mission was development for people living in rural areas, often in small villages that were accessible only on foot or horse back. Our CCD co-workers, seven Hondurans and sometimes the two of us, visited each of the villages about monthly in teams of two. The visit might include lessons in such areas as health care, nutrition, Biblical reflection, increasing crop yield, raising vegetables, and use of rabbits, fish and goats to supplement diets in an area where hunger and malnutrition was widespread. La Granja served as a model for raising vegetables, chickens, beans and corn and as a conference center for frequent five-day workshops when people from the villages would come together. We served as the resident managers of the farm which meant to provide some welcoming hospitality, take care of the goats, rabbits and chickens, and later a donkey there for breeding purposes. When week-long workshops were held, we would hire local women to serve as cooks for the week. La Granja's location between the civil war in El Salvador and the United Nations refugee camp for Salvadoran refugees in San Marcos meant that it was in a sensitive area. There was a sense that having two U.S. citizens in the area might serve as a deterrent to abuses of Hondurans and Salvadorans by the Honduran military.*

## Tuesday, December 24, 1985
*Christmas Eve, La Granja*

Sunday's entry got cut short – I don't remember why – perhaps the rabbits needed to be fed, perhaps a visitor arrived. The days move slowly. They also require an immense amount of energy – just to maintain ourselves. We seem to feel content in being home, but time will tell if we can endure and master the hard life.

This is a beautiful spot. A tile roof house on a hillside overlooking a bean field of about three acres. Breezes blowing.

Feeding the seven rabbits, the chickens, and the goat is fun. Cooking food and washing clothes – this is very difficult. Already I'm thinking of how we might hire someone to take care of these two areas for us. My mind is taking off with hopes of more time than I've ever had to write. I dream of a worthwhile published book coming out of this experience. It may be only a dream. If I could get to a point of more inner self-surrender along with commitment, I think the writing would come.

But today is Christmas Eve. A tender child born to campesino parents comes to us anew. "El Nino de Dios," the day is called in Spanish. We are lonely for family at Christmas, but how right it seems for us to be here – in the campo – as we celebrate the birth of this child.

Luke 1:46 ff  Mary's Magnificat
> *"My soul magnifies the Lord,*
> *And my spirit rejoices in God my Savior,*
> *For he has regarded the low estate of his handmaiden."*

Of the campesino women we have met so far, all seem generous. We've already been given oranges, tortillas, and home-made bread – items that could not have come easily for any of them. There is a part of me that wants to indulge in so-called reality today – a form of disbelief. I think I am tempted to say, 'I can't imagine these women rejoicing like Mary did.' And yet the simple gifts reveal a promise and a hope that the child did come – directly to the poor – to the poor first. There is promise that he grew out of land promise – out of roots deep in David's soul.

"He has scattered the proud, in the imagination of their hearts,"

He has put down the mighty from their thrones."

Has he? Honduras is run by the military which is very evident on every drive on Honduran highways. There are many checkpoints on roads where soldiers with sub-machine guns ask questions. A few of them are as young as 15 or 16. "Where did you come from? Where are you going?" And it's possible that there's one thing worse than Honduras' human rights record in recent years – and that is the way in which it is presented as a democracy.

One reason that we are being stationed here is that La Granja is located just a few miles from the El Salvador border where a civil war is happening and some of the most active fighting is just over the border from where we are. And back in San Marcos there is a United Nations Refugee Camp called Mesa Grande for Salvadorans who need to escape from the dangers of the war. La Granja is in between the border and the refugee camp. This means there is a lot of traffic of Salvadorans to the camp. Honduran soldiers often patrol the area, looking for "subversivos" (subversives or leftist rebels). Hondurans sometimes get caught in the middle and become vulnerable to abuses by Honduran soldiers.

In 1980 the U.S.-supported army of El Salvador launched an offensive against the Faribundo Marti Liberation Front (FMLN) the rebel group fighting against the Salvadoran army near the Honduran border. Innocent Salvadorans were caught in the middle and hundreds tried to escape across the Rio Sumpul into Honduras. But the Honduran army would not let them cross the border. Estimates of the number killed ranged from 300 to 600. Our CCD leaders believe that having U.S. citizens stationed here could serve as a deterrent to abuses by the Honduran soldiers.

Here the mighty have not been put down from their thrones. Still on this day – Mary's hope shouts at us, and shouts for us. The mighty have been put down from their thrones. The victory is won. There are leftovers yet to be cleared up, like Honduras, but Mary's vision, Mary's affirmation, is with us.

*"He has exalted those of low degree."*

Here in la Granja, we are in the hands of the campesinos. "How does this adobe stove work? What can the rabbits eat? How many times a day does the goat need to be moved?"

Neither my experience nor credentials count for much here. At this point we really haven't much to give to the campesinos. We are the receivers. There is a beauty to this – much like, I think, "the exaltation of those of low degree."

And so, Christmas Eve in the campo. It may hurt a little. But it won't be soon forgotten – and it may be the most truthful Christmas we've known.

## Wednesday, December 25, 1985
*Christmas Day, La Granja*

> *2020 note: We wrote the following to be sent to friends in the U.S. as a Christmas letter for 1985.*

Christmas Eve 1985

We arrived at La Granja, the farm, on December 21 in time for Christmas, but with no real plans. After a hearty and warm Christmas party, much like at home in the U.S. with our new co-workers in San Marcos, (15 miles and a one-hour drive from the farm), we decided to stay on or near the farm for Christmas.

The day began like any day on this farm. We got up. We fed the chickens, ducks, rabbits, and the pregnant goat (arrival due Dec. 29). After an hour-plus struggle, I finally coaxed pancakes out of a thus-far obstinate and smoky adobe wood stove.

We made a plan for afternoon and evening. We would visit some of our nearest new neighbors and then go to the church services in Colaloca, a fifteen-minute drive.

Our first stop was our nearest neighbors Noe and Pascuala and their 3 sons, 5, 2 and 10 months. She had not met us before, but opened the simple gate to her yard, slat by slat, to let us in. Noe was not home, but she invited us into her dirt-floor living room where the baby had slid off a straw mat onto the floor. He had a certain dirty but happy look about him. Pascuala took him into the corner of the room partitioned off for sleeping, and washed him a little. She put him back on the mat and then went to 2 other rooms to get 2 of their 3 homemade chairs. We sat down, feeling welcomed, although as usual, a little uncertain of our Spanish.

We chatted for a few minutes. But I still felt so far from fluent in Spanish, especially now that I was among campesinos many of whom have no teeth (there are no dentists here; the only treatment for dental problems is to pull teeth) and who speak in an informal Spanish dialect with many words we are hearing for the first time. But I did feel some confidence reading out loud from familiar writings. So I asked if she would like to hear a few verses from the Christmas story in Luke. "Me encanta!" she replied. "I would love it." As I began to read, she unselfconsciously gave her breast to her baby boy. She smiled, and I noted that she was as completely toothless as her baby.

And so with the rhythmic background music of contented sucking sounds, I read about a baby born in a stable. Pascuala was very still. Animals moved nearby in their yard. Verse by verse, I read – but paused once to look up and felt a keen and fleeting moment of wondering if Pascuala was Mary. She sure seemed to understand the story. I did also, better than I ever had before.

Then time for gifts. We had managed to get some peppermint candy and gave them to her and her well-loved but less than fully nourished sons. She too had gifts, the primary sign of Christmas sharing in the campo – "Tamales de Chancho," pork tamales, a tasty mixture of corn, mush, pork, vegetables, and spices in a wrapping of banana leaves. The tamales were definitely made to make the meat inside them go as far as possible. There was very little meat in each one compared to the other ingredients.

We left Pascuala and her boys. We were weighted down with their gifts to us.

After two or three more brief visits with neighbors within walking distance we boarded the jeep for the ride to Cololaca. Berna, another neighbor just up the barely-navigable gravel road, had requested a ride to the church service in Cololaca. When we stopped at her house, about ten people appeared, but only five got into the back seat – all children except Berna.

The children had a delightful case of the Christmas giggles which made the outlandishly bumpy ride a lot more bearable.

We arrived in Cololaca thinking that the service began at 6, but found that it was not until 8:30. We had time on our hands.

We went to the house of Lucio, our co-worker at La Granja and in our program, community leader, campesino, par-excellence, and coordinator of most of the projects at La Granja.

We went into his house lighted only by two large candles. Lucio's wife, Lidia, greeted us with an embrace, gave us a seat, and then returned to the constant movements of her Christmas Eve cooking, tamales, tortillas, and coffee.

We got a brief lesson in cooking both tamales and tortillas, enjoyed coffee and cake in the soft light of their burning oil lamps and generally enjoyed sharing the spirit of Christmas.

We left for church walking among God-awful sounds of firecrackers popping – one Central American Christmas custom I could do without. During the celebration of the Word service, outside, beside the church, under stars and a full moon on a warm night whose temperatures could not have been more perfect. The prayers and readings went on with firecrackers exploding all around. It really infuriated me, not only that the service was being so violently interrupted, but also that so few seemed willing to protest or stop the kids. I could not imagine that they were enjoying the firecrackers at this hour.

Later Lucio told us that the people were probably just too timid to call the hand of rude kids. I also had the thought that in a poor nation which has had to live most of its history as somebody's victim, it probably is not easy to help people claim even their most minimal rights to tranquility.

And as my ears rung during the service from the firecrackers, I also had the thought, "how appropriate," for in Central America, it so often seems that gunfire of some kind is never too far from even one's most tranquil moments. The firecrackers raged, but the Celebration of the Word went on.

After this service, we received what was for us the unsettling news that everyone in Cololaca, stays for the three-hour pageant from 9 p.m. until midnight. We wanted to go home and sleep, but we knew that our passengers would want to stay. We decided to "stick it out."

This took us back to Lucio's house where by now the tamales were almost done and more coffee was ready – coffee, direct from beans grown in small plots of coffee trees nearby. We would learn that many Honduran campesinos had a small coffee crop, and many had enough to sell at least one bag of coffee beans each year.

The village of Cololaca had electricity once through a large generator, but the people decided they could live better without it. There is no longer any electricity in the village. After dark the only lights are from kerosene lamps, kitchen fires and flashlights. The houses are all adobe, most with dirt floors, perhaps some with one or

144

two rooms with cement floors. It always seems that some room opens to the outside or to an inner courtyard. In the flickering shadows of the kerosene lamps, and with the rhythmic patting by Lidia on tortilla dough before putting them on the griddle on the open fire in the background, and in weather that was almost warm, it was an unforgettable Christmas Eve.

We talked about everything – local politics, plans for the family, the nature of life, here near the El Salvador border – many topics – but the topics didn't really matter. It was one of those conversations, in spite of our faulty Spanish, in which all the points seemed to find connections.

Then it was back to the church for hours of costumes, songs, skits, and simple dancing. It was a little more celebration than I had bargained for, but I was amazed at my patience. I was not sorry to finally hear the church bells peal at midnight.

We loaded everyone back into the car and added a passenger. Sleep would come easy on this night, and so would peace, and with a gentle depth that I could not have imagined, so would Christmas.

## Saturday, December 28, 1985
*La Granja*

Twice each day here, our routine is to feed the animals – the pregnant goat, the rabbits, the chickens and the ducks. For the first time in my life I find myself praying for very specific animals.

I have lived recent years in an environment very sensitive to the needs of animals. I am anything but a vegetarian, but I do have a deep admiration for friends who are sensitive to the pain that animals suffer, just to produce meat.

The hills in this part of Honduras are full of hungry children. Of the 18 villages served through CODE, over 80% of the children are considered malnourished.

I quickly deepen my appreciation for sensitivity to the suffering of animals. I understand why the Jewish Torah had such careful provisions to prevent pain when animals were to be slaughtered to become food. I remember the movie "The Gods Must Be Crazy" in which an African tribesman carefully explained to a goat that he was killing him only because he and his family needed food, and not because of any malice.

I also start to feel a little more of the place of animals in God's plan to heal a hungry planet. Our goats, rabbits and chickens have a role to play in the kingdom of God struggling to grow in Honduras.

For purposes of food, some of these animals will be killed. This won't be easy for me coming out of a pet culture that cares so fully for the rights and health of cats and dogs, but which sells meat by the ton in supermarkets with little thought that animals must be slaughtered to become the meat that we eat so unconsciously.

The animals here may be teaching me in important ways. While they live, they deserve every care and sensitivity. If they are to die, I see anew how their death is a part of the work of the kingdom. Death – sacrifice – can and does bring new life.

## Sunday, December 29, 1985
*8:45 a.m., La Granja*

*"Behold, this child is for the fall and rising of many in Israel."* *(Luke 2:34)*

What does the child's arrival mean for Honduras? Has Jesus never quite gotten here fully – what with the massive poverty and hunger of this place?

The wealthy military rule the country with minimal sensitivity to the needs of the poorest. U.S. power quietly reinforces all that is ugly and unjust in Honduras.

Is this child for the fall and rising of many in Honduras? What would this mean?

After one week here, we have not heard much of the people's hopes and dreams. We do not know how they feel about their government.

On Christmas Eve, when I offered to read the Christmas story from Luke to Pascuala across the road, her response was, "me encanta." "I would be enchanted" or "I'd love to hear it." Somehow it was a story that she knew. But how does it resonate in her soul. What feelings does she have as she spends her hours daily in a smoky kitchen to cook ever the same food for her hungry family. Does she get angry? Does she accept her lot and feel gratitude? Does she cry often? Is she glad she has those three children, ages 5, 3, 1? Is she sorry she has them? How many days each month, on the average, is she or one of the boys sick?

*2020 note: Looking back at these questions that come to me then, I am aware of how out of touch I was in most ways with the reality of just surviving for most Hondurans. The kinds of high-minded intellectual and lofty thoughts that I was and am prone to carry on, are just not a part of the life of the campesinos here, at least not in the ways I tended to articulate them.*

I visited her husband Noe (Spanish for Noah) briefly yesterday while he was cutting maisillo in his field. Maisillo – sorghum. For many here, maisillo is used for food only when the corn (maiz) has run out. Otherwise it is used to feed livestock. It is not a good sign when sorghum has to be used to make tortillas instead of corn.

I did not know what their corn supply was. He seemed very disappointed with his corn crop.

What would "the rise and fall of many in Israel (Honduras)," at its best, mean for Noel? Does he hope for better crops, for new ways to plant his corn and maisillo so it will produce better.

We are told that one of the problems here in development projects of any kind is getting the people motivated. It could well be that Noe really isn't interested in development programs, that he really does not see any reason to try to better the situation of the family.

If the coming of the child for the "rise and fall of many in Honduras" has any meaning, surely it must imply a hope of rising for Noe. What is it that will allow the child to live anew in Noe's life, or in my life as Noe's close neighbor?

The best of development work is bent toward helping people be self-sufficient, helping them to make use of the resources they have, meager though they may be. This too is kin to the coming of the child.

And if the child were to really touch me, the affluent U.S. citizen who wants to support good human development, and Noe, the campesino who has not been given many reasons to hope, if the child were to touch both of us – perhaps at the same time – I'll bet Noe's corn crop would begin to improve in almost no time.

## Monday, December 30, 1985
*7:00 a.m., La Granja*

Morning arrives gently, early with stars visible through the window from the bed. Wind blows cool. Skin tingles in cool air. Body warm under blankets of refreshing December morning, early in Honduras. Roosters announce the day. Body is rested. A day to look forward to – a party here for children, perhaps the birth of a goat, always the animals, and probably some surprise visitors. Yesterday Jose Enrique Espinoza, our Program Coordinator and Supervisor here, and his family, came for a delightful surprise visit. He is jovial, red-headed, very energetic, and has a warmth and friendliness about him that is quickly endearing. He is also a person of action who means business, whether it's planning a children's party, building a dam on the stream here, or repairing our Coleman lanterns, which he did so competently last night. He is certainly a gift in our lives.

## Monday, December 30, 1985
*8:00 p.m., The Day the Goats Were Born*

When we moved to the farm 9 days ago, we accepted the duties of caring for the animals, 7 rabbits, 3 ducks, about 25 chickens, and 1 pregnant goat. She has been such a content and gentle soul, willing to try out most any available grazing spots, although with spurts of stubbornness that left us having to pull hard at times on the rope around her neck.

In spite of living the first eight years of my life on the farm, I had never been present to witness the birth of any animal. When we were told that the goat entrusted to our charge was great with kid, we hoped for a daylight arrival, so we could be present.

Almost every hour on Dec. 29, we checked on "Salida," as we had been led to call her. We had been given few instructions, and no one with a lot of experience was nearby. We were fortified only with a Heifer Project International guidebook in Spanish, and our Spanish is not much stronger than our knowledge of goats.

But we read faithfully the chapter on birthing. We looked at the diagrams – what might happen if two are born, as is not unusual for goats.

We watched all the day long, finally going to bed after a bedtime check. No signs – no extra talking, no restlessness, no unusual affection, just the same steady stare in the face that we had come to know well in the twice-a-day feedings.

And then this morning – we arise again ready to check in every hour on the barn.

Long about mid-morning Kathy heard Salida begin to "speak" constantly, most unusual for her. By the time she made the thirty-yard trip down the hill and across the creek, there was healthy little five-pound creature wiggling on the ground, already showing the first signs of trying to stand on its feet.

We watched and waited, with our sleeves rolled up, our Heifer Project guidebook in one hand, and, as instructed, a soft towel in the other (I had always thought hot water was needed at time of birth. I was a little afraid the Heifer Project people had forgotten to mention this. I think I learned this from watching westerns on television as a child).

We stood by as Salida burst forth with a splendid array of the colorful and nourishing fluids of new life. She was doing so well that we could only assume that she must have read the Heifer Project book herself.

We had read that goat births come in twos almost as often as single births. And sure enough, as we looked more closely we saw that a second kid was trying to be born, but not nearly so easily as the first. Finally, a recognizable part appeared – a tiny head, and the, one front paw – only one – not a good sign because a smooth birth requires that both feet, either front or rear, come forth simultaneously.

I wiped the nose of the tiny protruding head, noted that it seemed to be breathing, and then we waited – we waited for what seemed like an eternity of some fifteen minutes, while Salida cried in agony and the tiny head and paw made no new progress toward the good earth.

We read some more. We hoped someone who knew more than we did would arrive soon. We waited. We wept. We wept because we were moved by the whole event, and also because of fear that either mama or baby number two might not survive.

The diagrams in the book were clear about how to assist with just such a problem birth as this. We hoped it would only be a matter of time and reminded ourselves that Salida knew a lot more about birthing goats than we did.

The struggle continued. No progress. We concluded that a gentle assist was in order. We needed to realign that missing front paw and right leg. Being blessed with long fingers, I reached in to do what I could to participate in the miracle. At first I could not feel a paw or a shoulder anywhere – Salida cried and pushed, cried and pushed. Only now in writing do I recall how intensely present I felt. My assistance seemed to be well received. I tried to reach farther.

Then there it was – a familiar joint, a little shoulder, a little goat foot under my index finger deep inside. I got my finger under it and gave it a gentle pull, exactly like the illustration in the Heifer Project book. Salida did the rest, in fact just about all of it as I now remember it. A second baby goat slid gently to the stable floor. All was well.

And the power of life had filled me in a manner unlike any I could remember. All the agony and the ecstasy of a fellow creature bringing some new life into the world. It was hard to believe God could have planned it any better.

Salida began to lick the kids clean as Kathy and I breathed a large sigh of relief. Within minutes the first of the arrivals was struggling onto his feet – and soon some twenty-five guests, arriving for a children's party, arrived to join our celebration and give what support was needed.

It would have been a moving enough event if it had been the birth of any goat – especially for people like us who had never witnessed a birth. But these births are part of other births trying to happen. You see, they were born into the family of Honduras' Christian Commission for Development on their model farm near San Marcos, Ocotepegue. The goats were born into an area in which the malnutrition rate among children aged 0-12 approaches 85%.

The new life involved was more than just the miracle of birth. It also was part of a larger vision – of the miracle of rebirth among the poor. As these baby goats grow, and as the campesinos in the surrounding communities visit them and learn from them, there is real possibility that more will own and raise goats, and that the goats will produce milk for children that presently just is not available.

Salida did not know all the wonderful implications of her birth process. She was just doing what God called her to do – being a goat. But oh the possibilities that spread out before us when any of us creatures manage to be something of what God put us here to be.

*2020 notes: Tim Wheeler and Heifer International*

*Any animal story from our time in Honduras will bring to mind Tim Wheeler, a remarkable U.S. Quaker who seemed to be pure Honduran sometimes. Tim was one of those people who can move to and live permanently in a country other than his birth and come to feel at home there. When we arrive to begin work at La Granja, Tim was the national coordinator for programs in agriculture and raising animals. He had history living and working in Guatemala and somewhere along the way met and married Gloria, a Honduran woman who was a native of San Marcos herself. They lived outside of Tegucigalpa in a house with property large enough for the two of them to raise their own goats and other animals and grow food in their own garden.*

*Tim was always in good communication with Heifer International and would later serve as Heifer's staff person in Honduras. Heifer was founded in the 1940s by an Ohio native named Dan West who had worked in relief during the Spanish Civil War in the 1930s. There he grew tired of handing out food and began a program to send animals to communities in need in countries around the world. The central practice of Heifer to this day is that when a Heifer animal bears offspring, it will be passed on to someone else in the community, and when any female offspring bears another, it too will be passed on, a multiplier effect in responding to hunger.*

*Under Tim's leadership the Christian Commission for Development served as the primary partner for Heifer in Honduras. Five-day workshops on raising goats were held at La Granja and on the final day a truck would show up with a load of pregnant goats. So each of twenty goats would go to a different village with the understanding that each one was intended to be the beginning of a herd of goats to serve everyone in the village. Our location at La Granja was ideal for this. We could do workshops, keep a number of goats ourselves, including male goats for breeding that would be lent out to villages as needed.*

*Tim was also experienced and wise in the ways of human rights and other political realities in Honduras. As a U.S. citizen with a Honduran soul he was a very valuable person and resource for the work of both CCD and Heifer International.*

*Tim and Gloria had three beautiful daughters who must be almost 40 years old as I write this in 2020.*

*Salida, our mama goat, a few days after giving birth.*

## Wednesday, January 1, 1986
*10:45 a.m., La Granja*

> *2020 notes: CCD's office in San Marcos had two vehicles, both of them four-wheel-drive Toyotas. One is a pickup, which is much-needed when we have to go and pick up supplies. The other is a Toyota Land-Cruiser. It has the look of the rough terrain vehicles one associates with the back country of Africa. Both are equipped with four-wheel drive which is needed occasionally to travel through mud in the road or climb hills. Of our Honduras team of 8, only 2 of them had driver's license. We were privileged to be able*

*to drive and it also helped to have more drivers on the team. Being able to drive and having access to any vehicle is very unusual for the majority of Hondurans as well as for organizations such as CCD.*

Driving home last night over the 15 miles of rough roads that require an hour from San Marcos, we found ourselves being followed closely in Cololaca, the village just 2 miles from us. The road is so rough in places that the red pickup won't go much faster than a person can walk. Some 8 or 10 boys, probably in the 10-14 years old age bracket began to run alongside us. We recognized them as the same group which had visited us at La Granja just the day before yesterday. They were in a good New Year's Eve celebrative spirit and it was easy to talk to them as we drove very slowly through the village of Cololaca. They asked us for a ride to "the bridge" (la Puente), and of course we were happy to oblige.

We drove on, and they gave us the familiar tap on the cab when they were ready to get off. We stopped, they all jumped out, thanked us. We said good night, Happy New Year, and that was that – or so we thought.

When we finally pulled our pickup in the drive at La Granja with the supplies we'd been waiting for days to get, we noticed one of our bags was missing. We didn't realize it at the time, but it had our expensive camera in it. But the real contents of value were this journal and another which represented many hours of work and reflections recorded over many years.

We decided to get back in the pickup and drive to Cololaca, not expecting much success but hoping to find help from some friends. On the way we met the large blue cattle truck owned by our co-worker Sebastian Melgar. In it were his two brothers Dorado and Margarito. We told them of the problem, and Margarito was especially responsive. He remembered the bag from having ridden with us in the pickup the day before. He promised to investigate.

We drove on to Cololaca to seek the advice and help of more friends, Alvaro and his wife, Luz, and Lucio and his wife Lidia. Only Lidia was at home. She was so supportive and promised to do what she could the next day.

We have done all we could do for the night and decided to head home.

We stopped where we had let the boys out earlier, noticing a light and music coming from a nearby house. But when I got there, I found only Dorado once again, and met a very nice family in a neat and congenial house. I explained our problem again, apologized for intruding, and said good night.

But just up the road a ways, we saw again Sebastian's cattle truck coming toward us. We noticed he was pulling off and stopping on the left. Margarito came running to our window with encouraging words. Soon the brown bag appeared, and we felt overwhelmed with gratitude.

He asked us about our camera, and it was only then that we realized the camera had been in the bag. Soon it appeared too, with a strap missing, but in generally good working order.

New Year's Eve ended with a note of relief instead of disappointment.

Kathy and I found a lot to talk about during and after all of this. We went through the feelings, "how could they steal our bag and especially our camera!? We had only yesterday welcomed them into our house!" "We trusted them and now this!" etc., etc.

We also took note of how our two trunks full of many things must look to poor young boys whose lives are very unlikely to make contact with all the consumer goods that have characterized our lives. We must be a temptation to both intrusive curiosity and petty thievery.

We talked about trust. Our trust has been damaged a little, but we were able to affirm that even if we had not been fortunate enough to recover the bag, it should not have been a devastating experience for us. It was a context within which we were able to affirm with new focus the unfolding purposes of our being here. We did not want our camera to be stolen. But it was something that was replaceable.

Like so many people of U.S. culture, we identify our personhood closely with things and property. It is easy to feel violated personally when property is violated. And we are able to carry in our two trunks more "stuff" than these friends will ever own.

It will be different here. We are no longer just one more house on the block filled with food and goods and with two cars out front. We now live in the nicest house for miles, and our two trunks of goodies represent a wealth not enjoyed by anyone within miles in any direction.

Our relationship to our things will be made new here.

*2020 note: Looking back, I am aware of how romantic and inflated this "made new" prediction was. When we returned to the consumer-intense realities of U.S. culture in 1988, we did not really make any fundamental changes in our patterns of consumptions. The deeper levels of conversion do not come easily.*

*The San Marcos Team for the Christian Commission for Development in January 1986: back row: Kathy Williams and Elmer Reyes with chicken, Enrique Espinoza, Ana Ventura with duck, Alvaro Melgar, with another goat. Front: Randall Mullins, baby goat, Teresa Gonzalez, rabbit, Lucio Guardado with another rabbit, Sebastian Melgar with another goat.*

## Thursday, January 2, 1986
*8:30 a.m., La Granja*

Just had forty-five minutes of some quiet time, a bit of scripture reading, and what I hope was authentic efforts to pray. As I think back now on this time, I note that most of it was spent dreaming, fantasizing, with real passion and energy. This is good. But there is an edge to it that is too bent on "being a success," "making a hit" with the work here. This won't go far, either spiritually or practically, in the long run.

This is not to apologize for the dreaming. It just seems good to keep a gentle self-critical edge to some of the longings and needs involved. It may be that the wholeness out of which I can best live and serve here will be more related to reflecting on what has happened rather than getting too passionate too soon about what might happen.

I need to think on this some.

## Saturday, January 4, 1986
*8:30 a.m., La Granja*

Yesterday was our first real official meeting with the CCD team. It was delightful. There was involvement, enthusiasm, ideas, openness, sensitivity. There was also the sense that a more authentic reality had begun. There were moments of honest struggle acknowledging a personality conflict between a team member and a campesino worker. There was talk of members of a community who have been unwilling to pay debts owed for fertilizer and other agricultural supplies. I don't like problems particularly. But there was a sense yesterday of, "now we are really here – now we are getting into what we came here to be a part of."

I don't think Kathy or I will have many answers to the kind of problems found here. We have much to learn in a new culture. But maybe we can be present in a supportive manner to the ongoing engagement with problems.

I woke up early this morning with a certain restlessness. Some moments later, I realized that I had a hunch as to what it was all about. Yesterday put me more in touch with the real issues we'll be facing here. I usually feel most fulfilled when I am involved, when I get myself "out there." Yesterday was a significant step in this – in seeing how I might begin to share my gifts.

And yet with my energetic style and at times "bravado" approach, I will need to be very careful. I so need to keep the posture of a listener, a learner. If I start to push too much, too soon, I could cause some real unnecessary pain.

It may be that the weaknesses of my Spanish will be a check against too much of my need to be so overly active here.

*2020 notes -- Enrique Espinoza*

*During our time at La Granja working with the San Marcos team we were fortunate to have Enrique Espinoza as a friend and our Regional Coordinator and our supervisor.*

*A man in his 30s like me, Enrique and his wife Maria were both native of the region. He grew up in a family that prospered more than most due to his father's life growing and marketing coffee, one of the major cash crops of the country and one that even poor farmers had some access to. Enrique had attended the university in the capital and graduated with a degree in agriculture, making him an agronomist.*

*It was clear from the moment we met him that this was a man of grace, with a warm heart as well as one well-seasoned in the life of people in the countryside. He could have easily found an easier and more prosperous life in San Pedro Sula or Tegucigalpa, the large cities, but he had chosen to live his life close to his roots. He remarked to us a number of times that he liked to live close to "la gente,"(la-HEN-tay) the people, by which he meant the country people who lived their lives in the face of so many challenges in hundreds of rural villages in the nearby area of Ocotepeque and Lempira.*

*He obviously enjoyed both the respect and the affection of others on our team. Everyone respected his knowledge and his understanding of village life. He knew how to help local farmers improve crop production on land where this was not easy. He had an active interest and skill in the Christian Commission for Development's newer programs in human relations, in which village people were taught new ways to communicate more clearly and at deeper levels of need and emotion.*

*When our San Marcos team obviously had some conflicts among us that were not being easily resolved, Enrique called off all other work for a day so we could have unrushed time to work through some of the differences that were preventing us to work with maximum effectiveness. I respected him for making that day possible and for much else. I was grateful for that good day of work to increase our understandings of one another, especially when differences of culture gender roles were so great.*

*Thinking back now I know there must have been times when he had to exercise a lot of patience with the two gringos who were well-educated and may have looked competent in some ways, but knew so very little about life in Honduras, especially in the nuances of local culture that take a long time for expatriates to understand.*

*Enrique spoke often of a strong role model and mentor in life, an uncle, also named Enrique, who was an artist and director of a choir in San Marcos. We were able to attend one choir concert in San Marcos directed by his uncle and witness the esteem and affection others in the community had for him.*

*Enrique was also drawn to art as his uncle was and wanted to study painting when he went off to the university. But his father insisted that he study something that would enable him to make a good income. In Honduras, this often meant agriculture, especially if one has access to a sufficient amount of good land. Income from his family came from his modest salary working for CCD, from Maria's work as a teacher in the local school and especially from the coffee he was able to grow on family land with hired labor and sell at the market.*

*When we returned to San Marcos for a visit in 1991, Enrique, unsurprisingly, had become the national director of agricultural programs for CCD, serving all six regional offices across the country. It was unsurprising that his many gifts were now being used more widely. It was also unsurprising that Enrique had worked out a way that he could carry on this wider work from his home town base in San Marcos.*

*We were blessed to get to know and to learn from this good man, so at home in the countryside among "la gente."*

## Wednesday, January 8, 1986
*3:15 p.m., La Granja*

The days are tiring. It is taking time to master getting "leña" (firewood), keeping the stove hot, getting water to boil, milking the goat, being gracious to visitors who come (with whom it is still difficult to communicate well and who often stay for two hours even if the communication is non-existent), hauling water, walking thirty feet to get flush water every time we use the toilet, and coming to terms with the reality that privacy will not come easily here, since most every CCD person considers La Granja part theirs, and since privacy simply means less in this culture than in others.

*2020 notes: Outdoor toilets were still more the exception than the rule in the rural area of Honduras where we were in the 1980s. The farmhouse where we lived included a remarkable exception. We had no plumbing or running water, but we did have a toilet that would flush and which emptied into a septic tank. Our water came from the creek (or quebrada pronounced kay-BRA-da) which was about twenty yards down the hill from the house. But a hose that ran from the creek farther upstream did keep a fifty-five-gallon drum full of water most of the time. The drum was just a few yards from the house. We had to keep a five-gallon container of water beside the indoor commode at all times to flush it. We were very glad we had this advanced form of toilet instead of having to use an outhouse or worse, "campo libre" (open land), the option that most people still had to use.*

*Firewood was a challenge but a small challenge for us compared to the people living around us. CCD paid a young man to bring us what we needed. But others have to walk further and further to find it, as all the trees finally get cut down. The smoke from cooking on a wood fire is also a difficult issue for eyesight of Honduras in the countryside.* Photo credit: *"Hombre cargando leña y su sombrero - Man carrying firewood and his hat; near Sonaguera, Honduras" by Lon&Queta, CC license 2.0. See photo credits at end of book for full details.*

The life here is wearing on us, perhaps more on Kathy since so much of the work is sheer physical labor – a little easier for my stronger body.

The setting here is beautiful and "tranquilo." The life is not all that tranquil. It is very difficult to find time for quiet, for prayer, even for rest. Now I have real doubts as to how much serious writing I will be able to do here. I think it will take some real determination, advance planning, and blocking out of time in order to do this well.

For now, I will try to keep writing with some consistency here, in this journal. Perhaps this is all the writing I am being called to do anyway – but I doubt it.

There may be within me a lack of emotional acceptance of the reality here. I think I keep wanting it to feel good, or to have more romantic sensations than it is having. I may be wanting something that just is not possible.

It is not romantic here. It is hard. Relationships are not all that easy. There is not a friend within miles with whom we can really talk openly. It is a hard life here, and I have not yet found its rhythm. Long before we came to Central America I had thoughts that I want to be "in community with the poor." This was mostly unrealistic. It is very lonely and difficult for me to be outside the familiarities of my own culture and customs.

Yet there is another level upon which my determination to "make it" is intact, and in which meanings continue to flow. The struggle has barely begun.

Here, there is time. There is no hurry. Nothing here has to move, or is likely to move as fast as I would like for it to move.

### Sunday, January 12, 1986
*4:00 a.m., La Granja*

Matilde is 7. She looks younger. She lives with her mother and brother in a house just down the road. She has many of the mannerisms and moments of excitement that I associate with a 5-year-old in the U.S. She comes to the farmhouse where we live almost daily, usually with a very dirty face, and always barefoot. She is at home in most of the houses nearby. Sharing is both a basic spirit and a means of survival in this part of the Honduras campo that we are coming to know.

One day when she came, she took note of our magazines with pictures that we had on hand. (We have not seen one book or magazine in any of the seven or eight houses nearest us.) Her appetite for pictures and books was hearty indeed. On a later visit we dug out the few colored marking pencils that we managed to pack, and put blank paper on our front porch table. Matilde marked away. Lots of color, very childlike drawings, but not a sign of a letter or a word.

This led us to begin asking the many children who have visited us at La Granja since we arrived, "do you go to school." The only answer we have received is "no." "Would you like to?" The only answer we have received is "yes."

After inquiring with friends nearby, we discovered the nearest school is an hour and a half walk (a demanding hike, even for a seven-year-old without hunger; well over half of the children in this sector are as malnourished in their stomachs as in their minds).

There was an effort in the past to petition the Ministry of Education for a school. It failed. The Honduras education budget is very low. One national leader told us that in one military exercise with the U.S. military, the Hondurans spent an amount for fuel that was more than the entire educational budget for the country.

Even fewer of these children's parents had a chance to go to school, so there is not much literate adult leadership to organize another effort to get a school. Most of the male children run loose until they are old enough to work in the fields, when work is available. The girls learn the ways of tending tiny adobe houses with no electricity and often with water a good distance from the house.

Presently, there are not many signs that Matilde will have a chance to learn even the basics of reading and writing. She may learn some counting – perhaps enough to count to 3 lempiras ($1.50), the maximum a woman can earn here for washing clothes, this too, only in those rare times when work can be found.

On Christmas Day, we were driving on the poorly paved highway that runs from Santa Rosa in the Department of Copan to the Guatemala and El Salvador borders. Winding down the highway with spectacular mountain scenery in the background were a host of

"Christmas gifts" for Hondurans – twenty-three – we counted. They were olive but shiny, new troop carrier trucks being driven to some unknown place in the trafficless tranquility of Christmas Day.

This is the U.S. investment in Matilde's future – army trucks. Yes, I have seen the U.S. embassy's figures about how much more goes for development assistance in Honduras than for "security assistance" which means weapons. Will Matilde even understand what the word assistance means? The problem with this is that driving through Honduras, one sees a lot of evidence of the security assistance, like military checkpoints on all the highways. "Where did you come from?" "Where are you going?" "You have space for two in your car – can these soldiers ride with you?"

Twenty-three army trucks. Assuming that the U.S. pays at least $40,000 for one of these giant machines, each truck would represent enough to buy the land, construct a simple building, and pay a teacher for at least three years in a school that make an immense difference in Matilde's life.

Sorry, Matilde. For Christmas this year, you and all the Honduran children only get "army toys." This is all that the boy children of your country will get to play with. There'll be lots more in the future, because we in the U.S. want so much for you to be "secure" in your life.

The Honduran tragedy goes on behind a façade of democracy, impressively and sometimes brutally maintained and dominated by U.S. interests.

One simple, one-room school house in the country? Sorry, not now. Not in decades of U.S. domination, and no signs of it in the near future.

The Honduran tragedy continues.

## Sunday, January 12, 1986
*9:15 a.m., La Granja*

At 4 this morning I woke with something to write in my mind. I got up, and I wrote it – then I went back to bed.

I am trying to commit to myself that in the night – if things come to me to be written, I will get up and write them. I was glad that I did this morning.

I am struggling with a little sense of "ought" in my praying. Maybe they're really "ought nots." But today during an hour of silence I had such an urge to write long letters to people – yet I felt I could not "leave God' to go and write a letter. I need to think on this. It may not be easy to discern. I know something of my capacity for compulsions – writing and other things. Yet at the same time it seems not quite right not to give these urges some expression.

Today I had the thought that if something is given me to write, I will try to write it.

O, how I need a dependable typewriter.

## Sunday, January 19, 1986
*11:30 a.m., La Granja*

The silence here is so often filled with love. Today, the wind blows softly. It is a day to rest some and reflect some after a week of meetings and traveling.

It is also the day one of our baby goats died. It all started with a simple sprained front leg – or so we thought. We left for meetings on Monday, noting the limp but no shortage of energy.

When we got back, her eyes were closed with congestion and she could not stand up, nor could she make her usual hearty squawks. Kathy managed to feed some milk into her a few times, but during the last feeding the little goat died in Kathy's arms.

It was the same little female who had a little trouble being born and who I helped to arrive here on the planet.

Kathy cried and we were both hurt by the death. She had been such a delightful little creature.

What remains now is to investigate a little in order to prevent similar deaths in the future.

*Rainbow at La Granja*

## Monday, January 20, 1986
*10:30 p.m., A Conscious Examen*

When was the grace of God at work in my life today:
- The good warm soup at Alvaro's house (Alvaro is one of our co-worker who lives in Cololaca).
- His family standing together in the door
- The warm sense of sharing with him as we drove, especially of Dr. King.
- Tears as I thought of Dr. King.

165

- The baby goat, running to me like a puppy.
- Good moments with Lucio, planting onions.
- The struggle with Kathy over Vista del Sur (newsletter), not feeling brittle, still a strong engagement and we got our decisions made.
- And so much more.

## Friday, January 24, 1986
*3:20 p.m.*

The days go so quickly. Time does slip away. Nothing here really has much of a set schedule. Meeting times seldom mean much to people. For example, today, we had set 10:30 as a time to sit and talk about things in La Granja with Lucio. He came at noon with his rifle in his hand for some target practice. The group of them, Lucio, Sebastian, and two friends, went and shot awhile. "Be right back" had been the word. Then, his two daughters arrived to say that his son was missing – perhaps run away from home. We had a hurried stand-up conversation, then they left, saying he might be back later. It was clear, however, that he would not be back later.

This is hard on my U.S. efficiency mindset, but it is a part of the life here. We will need to adapt.

While I write, Kathy is out on the "portal" (porch) with 14-year-old Andreas sanding blocks of wood to later be used for toys. I have felt quite free to keep myself in this room. This is good. It is time now to start claiming more reading writing time. I think there will always be a little guilt that goes with claiming this time for me. (Even though it is really more than for me – it is meant to broaden the love within me.)

## Sunday, January 26, 1986
*Thinking of friends in the U.S. in the sanctuary movement and of the price they are paying for justice.*

O tender Mother of Justice and Father of Hope, take into your arms this day, all those who labor in the Sanctuary Movement, but especially for Jamie and Donovan. (two clergy colleagues in Seattle whose church had become one of the first sanctuary churches in the country to house and protect Central American refugees). Thank you for the price they are paying with their lives. Thank you for your presence in their hearts which constantly recharges the hearts of others. Grant them tender words when tender words are needed. Grant them boldness even when the forces of darkness close in. Remind them ever that the tender power of Your love can never be overcome by the fearful forces of death.

And as we give You thanks for these and all who lead us in the way of peace, grant to all of us the sweet joy of Your victory. Nourish us with gladness, with love for friend and enemy, and with the fresh vision toward which you call us to work.

## Saturday, Feb 1, 1986

*9:30 p.m., La Granja*

After a week of frustrating meetings, diarrhea, and crowded quarters, we are back home in La Granja.

Our outdoor bath has been such a great sensuous gift.

We built an outdoor "dip and pour" bath in the utter privacy that is ours here after dark. Usually we leave water in the dark five-gallon jug all day so that by night the sun has it pretty warm, much better than all those cold hotel showers we have found in Honduras.

Tonight, we treated ourselves to water even hotter, heated on the adobe stove. The night was cool but not cold. The moon was absent but the stars were very bright.

O, how connected was everything in the universe during my bath. My body which is two-thirds water and which began in a warm water sack completely secure. Then this planet, three fourths water, brilliantly reflected with trillions of neighboring stars.

Water – warm water – a gift, running over my naked body in air cool, but not cold. Trees silhouette the darkness. Coleman lantern burns away inside the adobe house that is our home.

What complete joy! Not expensive. Something that most any campesino here can experience. Do they? Should we teach them?

Thank the good Lord for the gift of water.

*View of La Granja from the hills above looking into El Salvador*

*2020 notes: On one of the most memorable nights in our outdoor bath I had an unexpected visitor. For privacy we waited until after dark to take our baths. On one particular night there was a full moon. Stars were shining. It was warm but not hot and the warm water that had been heating in the sun all day felt wonderful. I wrapped a towel around myself and began walking the forty or fifty feet from the bath back to the house using a flashlight to show the way. About halfway back the light shone on a tarantula about six inches in diameter. I felt chills of fear run through me even though there really was no danger. Apparently we had more creatures living near of us than we were ever aware of, including these giant spiders and scorpions. Fortunately they were never a problem for us but the awareness that they were nearby did keep us alert!*

**Saturday, Feb 22, 1986**
*9:30 p.m., La Granja*

It has been twenty-two turbulent days since I have written in the journal. I am not surprised. These days have been full of fatigue physically, psychic struggles and personal conflict. There were many moments when the whole experience here seemed nothing but superficial and tiring. There is such an urge to write beautiful and positive things. They are present. But I am also feeling the difficulties of life here in a way that I have not felt difficulty for quite some time. Some tensions between Kathy and me, but with all we are living with how can we be surprised at this? Both of us have had little illnesses, and almost as many days with diarrhea as without it. She had a cracked rib and both of us people who have a great need to put forth an image that is pleasant, dynamic, and energetic.

Still the blessings do come through. Frank Bronkema is experienced in the work of Third World Development. He is an ecumenical leader from the U.S. whose initiatives had most to do with the formation of the Christian Commission for Development. It was a good gift a few days ago to have him come for a visit here.

There have been the many CCD people who have extended themselves to me in interest and in love, and over a language weakness of mine that continues to be immense. There were the devotionals when I could make comment and feel that I was being heard. There come again moments like this are when the pen flows across the page easily, there is peace in expressing myself in writing, and I hear birds singing and Kathy making conversation with Lucio, our campesino co-worker.

Still, there is the need to write about what hurts - what is missing. It is hard to feel silence, to sit and write, to pray, to cry. There really is no friend, especially male friend, with whom I can talk openly. This is very lonely for me. I am wanting enough centered energy and quiet to try to do some writing for publication. Unless grace comes to find me in some new ways, this continues to seem unlikely. I will continue to hope. My body gets tired very fast, both because the work we do is physically demanding, and because food is short and low-energy from frequent gastro-intestinal difficulties. I long to be able to relate to people with an inner spirit of tenderness and reaching out, but too much of the time what I feel is a sense of disappointment, deprivation, and anger which really means hurt.

I am now on page 100 in this handwritten journal describing a little of what began as an exciting adventure, but which presently feels like a very great struggle. It is tempting to think that maybe all this means we have no business here in the first place, that we should face facts, and get back to the United States where we belong. Yet there is an undercurrent of determination, maybe even peace and purpose, that tells me struggle and even a sense of hardship are not signs that one should retreat.

Even in the hardships, especially in the hardships, I am not here under my own power. Only the presence of grace can keep me here in the midst of so much that is new, difficult, and strange.

I can only hope I somehow am growing in human understanding. It will not be of my doing. I would also like to be growing in compassion for individuals. I am not sure this is happening at present.

The journey is very difficult right now. And yet the journey continues.

## Sunday, Feb 23, 1986
*8:00 a.m.*

Inner difficulty continues. Hard to write. Depression. Low energy. Grim feelings. Probably self-pity. Feelings not violent - just god-awful pessimistic.

*2020 notes: I notice that we are about 5 months into our time in Central America, less than 2 months into our time at La Granja. All that was romance and adventure has worn off by now. This probably means that it took at least this long just to begin to do some learning from being there. I know I did not expect it to be so hard. No matter how easy my life had been before, I had thought of myself as someone who was adventurous, adaptable and who had the physical stamina to hold my own in places of much-increased deprivation. One awakening was that almost none of this was true about me. I began to crave opportunities for what I called a "gringo fix," time for some comforts more like back in Seattle, such as a good meal in a restaurant, or a pizza or getting to go see a movie. I was not built well for life in the campo, but we were both managing to hang in there.*

## Monday, Feb 24, 1986
*7:00 a.m.*

*"And Jesus, full of the Holy Spirit, returned from the Jordan, and was led by the Spirit for forty days in the wilderness, tempted by the Devil." --Luke 4:1*

Lent has begun with our hardly having noticed.

Jesus in the wilderness- today I sense a little more of the depth meaning of this story. It needs more contact, I think - more of what Jesus had been filled with by parents, relatives, teachers in the temple. "You're going to be one of the great ones- I just know you are." Or "Jesus is such a nice lad, he's just not like all the rest," says cousin Elizabeth as Jesus stands there embarrassed with anger churning in his heart and sexual feelings dominating his adolescent identity.

He was tempted, but I don't think the temptations ended in the wilderness. Those forty days may have been something of a supreme test of his spiritual focus of whether or not he would choose that which he was being called to be. Did he ever make any wrong choices? Did he ever feel like I felt yesterday?

## Saturday, March 1, 1986
*Noon, La Granja*

This week has been serene. Last weekend, I had reached a depth of depression, the worst I have known since arriving in Central America. Kathy's initiative in getting us to pray together was a key element. We went and sat by the creek near the dam. We read Luke 3, and we prayed. We also read Psalm 88.

*2020 notes: The "dam" was an attempt by our co-worker Lucio to build a small dam in the creek to create a pool in which we might begin to raise fish (tilapia). It didn't work out. The water just came on too forcefully during the rainy season and we learned how difficult it is to build a dam strong enough to stop the water. We needed some beavers!*

The week has been for me a stretch of acceptance of the limitations here - limitations of physical energy, limitations imposed by duties on the farm, the difficulty of having energy and finding time to do serious reading and writing. I have not let go of my hopes of the "glorious" things that might have been "accomplished" but some kind of emotional breakthrough did happen. I have more peace now. I am more at home just being here at La Granja. I made a small step in coming to terms with the reality that I'm not likely to accomplish all that much while we are here. I am still seeking an inner quiet and contemplation that will allow more study to happen. I think this is possible. It does not come easily.

With all the hard work I do here, I do not feel my physical condition is improving all that much. I feel physically tired a good bit of the time. I feel the need for more work on the heart muscle. This is not easy here. Perhaps it is possible only in the early morning.

Gail Crouch's letters and tapes sure came at a good time. This was the other gift of this week.

## Saturday, March 22, 1986
*8:00 a.m., La Granja*

It has been so many days since I have written. Why? Lack of discipline, I think, except I do not want to be too hard on myself.

Here two years will pass so quickly. So rapidly will pass this opportunity to see and hear and experience from this perspective. I want to feel it more - without wearing down completely. I want some images to become clearer. I want some focus to emerge for creativity. All in all, I'm sure I want too much.

*Faithful farm dog Paloma*

Yesterday, I wept openly (and alone) for the first time in a while. It was in response to Dick Kroll's illness. It had been so long. Since I had wept so freely. I was relieved. Some, and healed some. I guess it didn't help Dick and Linda much. But maybe it did, because out of feeling my feelings, I was able to write and pray to and for them. If it transports a little love and healing to them, I will be grateful. But whether it does or not, some grieving on my part did bring some healing to me.

This makes me wonder why I am not (cannot?) feel more of the suffering of the people who are all around me here. There is hunger, poverty, lack of education, lack of vision, lack of freedom. There is a certain numbness to the life here. I have not seen any tears.

*2020 notes: I try to recall this numbness. I could never feel anything close to what it is like to live out of many generations of poverty and hunger. For me to try to experience the life in the campo, the countryside, and translate it into the psychological/emotional language of our lives in North America was very far from anything that is possible for any American. There were and still are a precious few U.S. citizens who have been able to move into the Honduras countryside and live much as the campesinos live. During our time there we heard stories of a Father Earl Gallagher, who was affectionately known as "Padre Beto," who had lived there for decades and had so completely won the hearts and the trust of poor rural Hondurans. We never met him. But the spiritual presence of such people is still felt by so many.*

Can the people have visions and hope if they cannot weep? I wonder. Is the pain of Honduras so deep that any grieving would just be too much to bear instead of a step toward healing? If the pain of a people is so deep that even grieving endangers emotional survival, then can hope be engendered when Jesus helps us to grieve on their behalf? If Jesus were to, so help me, would I be willing, able, to receive the help - to suffer with the people in the way that Jesus does?

I don't know. I seem rather set on working on my goals here, my priorities, my program ideas, instead of serving the people here on their terms, and trusting that all of my status and program needs will come out as they should.

So what if I should come out of this time without any articles published, or without a D. Min degree? So what?

*2020 notes: A number of my clergy colleagues who were around my age were completing Doctor of Ministry degrees, a professional degree that did not require the lengthy academic requirements of a PhD yet still made it possible for these ministers to carry the title of Dr. and Rev. Dr. I was aware that this sojourn in Central America was my version of a D.Min. It might have been possible for me to connect what I was doing in Honduras to some D.Min. program but I decided that just being there was enough. I was learning things there that few ministers in the U.S. would learn, but in truth time living in Central America was not usually an attractive point on a resume for churches who were looking for pastors.*

What are the essentials that will make these years the most worthwhile?

I believe the essential is to be here - to open myself to presence here with all of my being - to choose priorities and focus yes, but also to be faithfully sensitive to responding to what is placed in front of me. To give myself. To move toward the people, struggling, in my awkward human way, to love them, and leaving other important works to those who are better situated and better-equipped, to do them.

There is variety here. There are letters to write, woodwork projects to do, animals to feed, pastors to befriend, people to welcome, simple things to teach. They will work together best if I can manage to search within me for the love that God sent me here to give.

## Monday, March 24, 1986
*Monday in Holy Week*

Western Honduras has turned cold on us. We are in turtlenecks and flannel shirts. Thank goodness we have them. We notice that the people here in the countryside have few extra clothes to keep them warm in such an emergency. Perhaps we should be giving some of our clothes away instead of wrapping ourselves up in them.

Yesterday Kathy and I read the passage for Palm Sunday from Luke 19. We took note of a number of things: - the apparent "possessed" state of the followers "if they should keep quiet, even the stones would cry out." - Jesus weeping ever the city Jerusalem - "would that you knew the things that make for peace." - and the fact that the cleansing of the temple episode follows the triumphed entry in three of the four gospels.

It seems to me that "the things that make for peace" are addressed to cities and to nations. Kathy felt the words bearing down on our country. But the words are to be felt also on individuals. And this is my search. I do not think I have yet found "the little things that make for peace" in my own life. I am searching. I have been the route of peace organization and education. I have touched one low-risk moment of civil disobedience. I have made the decision to live for a time in Central America. Perhaps all of it together takes some significant shape toward joining in God's concern and energy for peace. But there is still that sense that the search is incomplete.

The words in Luke come during the week of creative sacrifice. It is not just any sacrifice that makes for peace. Nor is it immediate results that let us know our sacrifice has moved us toward peace.

I would like to know more of what this sacrifice is for me. I would also like to be able to do it.

I think of this sacrifice in relation to the sacrifice that allows for creativity.

I am yearning to love here in Honduras. I am also yearning for creativity.

## Tuesday, March 25, 1986
*Tuesday in Holy Week*

*From Luke 20:17 - The Parable of the Tenants in the Vineyard: "The stone which the builders rejected as worthless turned out to be the most important of all."*

I remember W. Brueggemann's lecture on history in Seattle - noting that the history that never got written turned out to be the most important of all.

It is with the people who make "non-history," that God is most present.

Honduras, where the people must endure poverty and constant domination from the United States - this is where God wants to be present with us. The verse helps me understand why I am here.

## Wednesday, March 26, 1986
*Wednesday in Holy Week, 7:15 a.m., La Granja*

The week is a quieter one. No team members, as all are on vacation. There are fewer visitors. The wind is blowing now for the sixth day, making the weather uncommonly cool for this time of year. Holy Week here seems to be a culture-wide time of observance.

Our young friend Andreas came by today as I was cleaning one of the rabbit cages. He was uneasy with my working telling me that this is "Semana Santa," Holy Week, and that I should not be doing any work.

I continue to struggle with many inner demons, the most difficult being those of presence and tenderness - being here, being present to people and place in this community - trusting that - - and struggling against the urges within that can be so filled with anger at times. I need to be involved in peace and justice work much because of my own inner struggle against violence.

This struggle is not being lost, I don't think, even though it seems far from being won. But there are moments when I feel pushed to tenderness even when tenderness is not necessarily my urge at the moment.

The violence in me at times is more than normal human irritations. It is a violence that I have managed not to use against people in a physical manner. Verbally, it is more difficult to distinguish between appropriate expression of anger, an expression that seeks intimacy, and an expression that comes from a less-whole source. This source for me still seems to be some old wound that I do not know, a wound that does not seem close to being healed. It is, I believe, out of this that comes my proneness to violence, and for which I pray a slow or a rapid healing.

Psalm 58 would seem to be from a person who knows what I struggle with. "Oh God break the teeth in their mouth!" (verse 6)

Holy Week is a time of reverence here unlike anything I have ever experienced. It seems like nothing is going on. Today our ten-year-old friend Andres came to visit while I was cleaning out one of the rabbit cages. He was troubled by this. *"Esto is Semana Santa"* he said. *"No debe trabajar durante la Semana Santa."* This is Holy Week. You should not be working during Holy Week. I was moved by his devotion and impressed that he felt free enough to reprimand me.

### Thursday, March 27, 1986
*Maundy Thursday, 8:45 a.m in La Granja*

*From Luke 20:27ff – The Question About Rising from Death.*
*Luke 20:39 - "He is the God of the living, not of the dead, for to him all are alive."*

This verse speaks so helpfully to me today just as it is that it needs no commentary.

What If We Began to Kneel Again?

I just can't help myself. I knew well that when the stadium packed and the color guard of soldiers march onto the field for the national anthem (why do people with guns always have to carry the flag), and the referees put their caps on their hearts, that we may well be reinforcing a myth that is ever doing deepening injury to our national soul. But what can I do? I love the passion, the abandon, the uncertainty, the talent, the physical expression, and the creativity that goes into football, indeed into all of U. S. sport.

As captain of my small-college football team and a high school coach for two years, I experienced both the positives and the negatives that sports can introduce into the lives of young people. I saw the discipline, the camaraderie, the self-respect emerge. I also saw the abuse of rhetoric, the in-school "class system" that developed, and young people lost in the superficial identity of athlete thoroughly unmotivated to develop other, and often more significant, gifts.

This is perhaps one of the more honest glimpses of our USA - that moment when the drum major raises his baton, when well-padded young men stand piously with helmet in hand, and other young expressionless men shoulder weapons near the flag, as if we can somehow protect the best of our national values from abuse by being ready to shoot their adversaries.

And what do the tens of thousands of spectators do in this moment. They stand reverently, dutifully, and I'm afraid in this moment, with fear of performing any gesture that would point toward a more promising national vision. Perhaps they also stand with no thought that in this significant moment as a citizen there could be a better way to love one's country.

It is always a moment of anguish for me. I usually give in to overwhelming social pressure and stand with the multitudes, expressing what can only be support for a mentality which says "death to any creature who would dare say we are not righteous." I am aware that this is not the meaning for everyone. But it does seem to be a religious ritual and that I am asked to affirm a religion that is not mine at all.

It is in this moment that I most long to say a word of love for my country, which is at once respectful, heartfelt, and pointed toward a vision that both acknowledges our flaws and calls us to the best that is within us. I do not wish to remain seated which would be seen as a disrespectful and less than hopeful non-action.

One day in Seattle it came to me with the stands packed and the field full of all the colors of the unyielding symbols. There was just room in front of the stadium seat for even my oversize body to kneel. As in churches with kneelers, my feet would fit neatly under the seat behind me. I could express, respect for nation while reaching for something not readily seen in this fundamental national ritual. With family and friends embarrassed and strangers staring, it would certainly be awkward, but it might just lead to the kind of dialogue that changes some hearts, mine and theirs.

Then the fantasy took off with me. What if at the playing of the national anthem at every U.S. sports event, we were to see hundreds, thousands kneeling, all seeking a common vision and purpose.

No, I didn't have the courage, nerve, or audacity (or some redemptive blend of all three) to go ahead and do it. I am also reminded of Tillich's words, that symbol participates in the reality which it symbolizes. Thus, I must recognize that the kneeling would fail to be an authentic symbol if within the kneelers there were not an honest longing for a nation more bent toward the best of its values.

Do such people show up in the stands at football games? Do any of them agonize with that moment of the national anthem like I do? Would I be more willing to kneel if a companion soul were kneeling beside me, holding my hand?

I don't know, and the kneeling might not change the national vision a lot, or even a little. But it might go a long way toward helping all the kneelers love their country in the ways that it really needs to be loved.

*2020 notes: I find this interesting in 2020 after Colin Kaepernick and other NFL football players in recent years decided to kneel during the national anthem in 2016 in response to racism in our country. I also have knelt a number of times during the national anthem before games since 1986.*

*The house from the bean field below.*

### Friday, March 28, 1986

*Good Friday, 9:00 a.m., La Granja*

My body is itching today in various places, and my mind is wandering. There is not much focus. Last night we went to the Last Supper service at the Church in Cololaca. I was glad that I went for the community contact, but the service was a tiring drain - nearly two hours. Too much reading and not very well thought-out worship. Fidel has such compassion but really not much ability in knowing what makes worship move.

Alvaro's reading of the Exodus story was strong.

In his reflections on the Exodus story Fidel spoke of Honduras 1821 independence from Spain as a parallel. I wondered how many people in the room felt as I did that the liberation of Hondurans had never really been given a chance to begin, and that this nation, as much as any in Latin America, is still awaiting its Exodus.

### Saturday, April 5, 1986

*La Granja*

God, I never want to see another fire! I'm sitting here smutty and sweaty after the third episode this week of brush fires when we had to stop whatever we were doing, haul cans of water uphill, and chase fire everywhere. This year in Honduras has brought a new set of phenomena - all of March and April without one drop of rain, and heavy winds for over a week. This combined with land clearing by burning and some not-so-accidental fire starts have left us tired of fires. The first night we were up all night. Fearing that the fire might reach the house we moved everything out of the house. We were relieved when we realized that fire would not be very large and could be stopped at the top of the hill around 5 a.m.

Easter came and left so quickly. We went to church in Cololaca. Word had come that a Honduran priest would be present to say Mass. He never showed and Fidel had the hard task as Delegate of the Word of leading a service in which all present had expected a Mass. He did the best he could in his wonderful loving spirit, but we could sense some letdown in the room. We sat through it all and found it meaningful.

*2020 notes: Fidel was a "Delegate of the Word" (Delegado de la Palabra) a Roman Catholic movement in Honduras and other Latin American countries where there is a severe shortage of priests, especially in remote places like Cololaca. Delegates of the Word are trained lay leaders who lead worship when no priest is present but are not allowed to preside at Communion. They also serve as leaders in other ways in the church and community.*

## Sunday, April 6, 1986
*10:00 a.m., La Granja*

The fires this week were very difficult for us. Neither of us is anxious to see a fire again soon. But the struggle did seem to bring us closer together somehow.

We are both very tired today, mostly, I think, from a week of fighting fires. Yet there is also acceptance of the life here, a kind of deepening that is happening for me. I would seem to be settling in to life here with some new depth, and perhaps new quality of seeking.

I seem to be getting here with more and more of myself. I still think of Nicaragua with real longing, but my thoughts and hopes and plans for now are here - in Honduras.

We are into the fourth month now of life at La Granja. We have shown ourselves that we can manage the life here even if it will continue to be difficult.

I am thinking of an article for the Christian Ministry on "the local church witnesses in the global family" urging local congregations to get directly connected to some place in the Third World.

*2020 note: We began a program that we called Amistad (friendship) in which congregations in the U.S. could become a partner with one of the twenty villages we worked with. The program resulted in visits by group from three congregations. Our goal in this was to educate US citizens about the realities of poverty in Honduras but do so in such a way that they would know the names of specific people in known villages impacted by this reality. We also included some teaching about how U.S. policies at the time minimized development for the people while using Honduras for its political and military objectives.*

## Tuesday, April 8, 1986
*La Granja*

Yesterday was spent, almost entirely, working with Lucio and Andreas to build a rabbit cage. It was a most satisfying day. There was lots of focus, a feeling of creativity and accomplishment and good fellowship with Lucio.

We also have our letters ready to mail for the Amistad program, 14 of them, I think. I feel a little overwhelmed by the task in front of me and us on this but genuinely looking forward to the possibilities.

Today begins gently with a good morning of yoga and meditation. I would really like to have the whole day to read and write, but need to work with Lucio today more on getting the adobe stove begun for the new kitchen.

*2020 notes: Throughout our time at La Granja a lot of buildings were added: a new dormitory with bunk beds that would sleep about thirty, showers, a large conference room and a kitchen separate from the house that was large enough to cook for the groups that came.*

## Thursday, April 10, 1986

*7:20 a.m., La Granja*

Yesterday, I got up, did some yoga, fed the animals, had breakfast and went to Corrazalitos, one of the villages, with Teresa and Alvaro. I so enjoy the conversations on those one-hour trail walks.

I came home, looked at the mail, worked on the lanterns a bit, feed the animals, took a bath, had dinner, wrote a letter and went to bed.

I am feeling physically tired these days, or this week, and having some continuous pain in my upper back/neck/right shoulder blade. The water carrying and daypack carrying seem to irritate it. It is not unbearable, but I wish it would go away.

## Saturday, April 12, 1986

*9:00 p.m., La Granja*

Days of real physical fatigue. I just do not have the young body that I used to have. This life is hard physically, and it is hard for me to sit myself at a desk to study.

Tomorrow I have invited people to come for games & stories. We'll see how it goes. I am tired but would like for this to go well.

A slow Saturday. Up at 7 or so. Some yoga and 7 minutes of rope-skipping (still trying to get the heart stronger). Had an hour or so of quiet then cooked breakfast, cleaned the porch and rested until noon. Helped water the garden, then rested some more. Got some things ready for tomorrow's games, then rested more. Then cooked banana bread with some third-class bananas we'd been given. Cooked dinner, ate it, cleaned up. Cooked more banana bread. Went to bed.

## Monday, April 14, 1986

*7:30 a.m., La Granja*

Yesterday we tried a session of "Games and Stories" just to see who would show up. About 6 boys did. We played, laughed, had some boring moments, and then in my nervous broken Spanish I tried to read stories. It was a good day. I want to try again. Then Felipe arrived. He had just finished a four-day workshop, a human relations lab, and was obviously full of the experience.

I have the urge to sit here quietly and tell you more about Felipe. But I have "duties." I must go and cook breakfast.

*2020 notes: Felipe was a leader in our group in the village of Junigual which is just two miles from us further out the main road. One of CCD's programs that had a strong and positive impact on the people were human relations labs in which trained facilitators led the people toward communicating at deeper emotional levels which were very unusual for Hondurans in general and perhaps even mores for campesinos. Felipe had obviously touched something inside of him and was full of joy about it. He could not stop talking about it. It was a joy to witness this, but his enthusiasm would not last.*

In the hard and glorious challenges that call one to creativity, I think one must finally hold a piece of work, or even a vision of a piece of work, in one's arms, and protect it from all intruders - from "duty," from fatigue, from loved ones - any intruder who would make you feel that you are not doing what you "ought" to do if you engage in the creative act. There is, I think, always some guilt that goes with creativity. Was it Rank who talked about this?

I am not a fancy person. I am a regular person. I do seem to have a way of being, or needing to be, a rather public regular person. Perhaps it is time to work with this more. Perhaps this is part of the mission in Honduras.

## Wednesday, April 16, 1986
*2:45 a.m.*

Sleep escapes me. A restlessness brings me to the desk, candle and journal. I am either up even earlier that the extremely early-rising campesinos or I am staying up ever so much later than they would ever dream of. The campo (countryside) is vibrating with the overwhelming silence of this hour. The wind is blowing. It is a silence that is somehow not quite still for me.

I know now and need to acknowledge that I am writing this journal hoping the words will be read and be helpful to someone. I'm sure this makes the writing a lot more self-conscious - I hope that it won't be too far removed from authenticity.

Good friend Felipe Melgar was back with us yesterday as the CCD group from Junigual met here at La Granja. On Sunday, he dropped in and shared, much from a human relations workshop of four days, apparently a very important and helpful experience for him. He is also becoming more and more a person that I think of as a friend. Felipe is in his early 20s, married, with three children. He is outgoing, friendly. Laughter comes easily for him.

The Spanish language has this fragile and beautiful difference between formal and familiar in its verbs and pronouns, the familiar being the forms used with family, intimate friends and children. Wanting to avoid being presumptuous we had decided that we would not move into the familiar forms until it had been initiated by others here. Being dignified and respectful they likewise always used the formal with us.

In Spanish, the formal word for you is "Usted," the familiar word is "tu."

It had all the innocence and beauty of a child bringing, that first color crayon drawing to daddy - that moment Sunday when I felt Felipe gently slip the pronoun "tu" into one of our conversations for the first time. For him it may have been a part of celebrating, out of his workshop experience, a new freedom to explore the personal, to enjoy the riches of human feeling and relationship. For me it was a moment rich with love. I have someone here who thinks of himself as my friend! This gives me joy.

I am able to find meaning in moments with children nearby, with people who just want to be friendly, and with people who are seeking help. But for a gringo in the fancy and big house, I know it is not easy for the people here to approach us simply in friendship. La Granja may be radically rustic for us, but living in a house with cement floors and a large bed, with water nearby and plenty of food, is far more than anyone has among the people we have met so far. I also know that for me the "service" aspects of being here can reach a point when it does do not do much for me. I need friends.

Felipe also represents some parts of my experience that were not altogether pleasant. He is a very enthusiastic member of the small but growing group of Honduran evangelicals. His Bible has that "always there" feeling of many evangelicals, that sense that "I must push this book at you," whether you want to be pushed or not. This part of evangelicalism seems to me rather distant from the Jesus who so often met people where they were, on their terms rather than his. I'm sure it also touches some of my own history with fundamentalism in which God was so cruel, cold, and overwhelming for me.

But with Felipe, one can also feel other parts wanting to come through. He is working hard as a leader in his village of Junigual, trying to push for development on all kinds of fronts. He is poor, like most everyone here. His house is not much larger than any one room of any house I have ever lived in. Yet he is also constantly at work on his half-acre of land, planting fruit trees (on our last visit he climbed his papaya tree to harvest one precious papaya to share with us), vegetables, making plans for goats and rabbits, and even building a new house, starting from the ground level literally, cutting the pine trees and then cutting the trees into lumber, and making his own adobe.

Felipe arrives at La Granja with a heart ready to share and a wanting to help. He will be one of the important people of life here in La Granja.

## Monday, April 21, 1986
*6:00 a.m., La Granja*

We just had a couple of days in San Marcos to rest a little and to attend an exhibition of paintings by an uncle of Enrique Espinoza, our Regional Director and Supervisor. Such a different perspective to go from the country to the "city" (San Marcos has no paved streets, a population of 5,000 at most). This is so unlike the days when we longed to "get out of town" for a spell from Seattle.

We got back last night in time to drink a little of the rum we bought and sleep in the big bed here in La Granja.

Being up so early, I'm wanting to write inspiring things but I feel a little rambly. I'm still having a little pain in the lower back. Nothing serious, but I wish it would go away. I think it must be from all the subtle lifting (some not so subtle) here at La Granja, but I also wonder if there's some unconscious stress to encourage it on a bit. I'm just trying to watch what and how I lift things.

I'm sitting on a stump behind the house about thirty feet uphill. Birds chirping and chickens squawking fill the air on all sides. Across the road some 75 yards away, conversations carry to where I am sitting. I can almost make out what they are saying.

Paloma, our skinny and now motherly, farm dog, runs enthusiastically up the hill to say good morning. She has seven puppies. Her ribs are all showing, not because we don't feed her (she probably eats better than many of the children nearby), but because her utter is immense at this point. It can't be true, but she often looks like she has a gallon of milk to carry.

Paloma is the first dog in my life since early high school, maybe even before. Since then, I have been busy, I guess, living the kind of constant moving from here to there life that does not allow for the attention that a dog needs. Oh, we could have had one at our house in Seattle, but I'm sure we both felt that life was just too busy for a dog.

Now we have eight. Paloma had seven pups about a month ago, and we feel their presence thoroughly when they begin to scream in the middle of the night. We enjoy them but we may not be altogether sad when they are all finally given away.

We are still waiting on the rain to come - "winter", - the rainy season - it's called here, the May-October season when the corn grows. There is no moisture yet, but it is a cloudy day, and we hope that rain can't be too far away.

*2020 notes: The rainy season, was called el invierno (winter) by most which was confusing since it had been cold but dry back in January during the "dry season." The rainy season also felt like Spring because it was the time when the fields would be plowed and planted and all the plants would turn green. Weather had its own unique patterns in Western Honduras. It was simpler to consider each year as having only two seasons, wet and dry. When the rainy season finally did set in completely, it was so predictable. Every day at about 5 p.m. the sky to the south of us over El Salvador would turn black. The rain would come and continue for up to an hour and then stop. It seemed so consistent to me during our time there. I doubt if it was always that consistent.*

*I do remember days when we would have a group on our large front porch, the "portal," while it was raining and cool. We would make coffee for everyone, coffee grown on someone's land nearby. We would drink our coffee together, enjoy one another, watch and enjoy the peacefulness of the rain.*

*Now in 2020 as climate change progresses, the land in Western Honduras, rocky hills that were mostly dry in the 1980s, has become so dry now that growing the basic crops of corn and beans has become impossible. This is one of the main reasons that so many Hondurans have come to see their only way of survival as migrating north to the United States.*

*Some of our regular visitors at La Granja.*

## Wednesday, April 23, 1986
*7:00 a.m., Front Porch, La Granja*

We spent most of yesterday helping Lucio build the new clay wood stove for the new kitchen that's being built. The work involves a lot of squeezing and kneading clay to mix it with sand. One part of it was walking on the mixture barefoot, using body weight to mash it all together. It was hard work but earthy work. We continue today needing to have two weeks of drying time before a May 5 workshop which will be the first chance for the new kitchen to be used. I'm afraid we won't make it, so Kathy and I are preparing ourselves for three meals a day being cooked here in the kitchen where we live as in previous workshops. It won't be easy for us, but then it looks like we won't have to cook that week. We can just join in the meals being prepared for those who will be here for the workshop.

*2020 note: The numbers of workshops and the numbers of people attending them increased steadily during our eighteen months at La Granja. There could be as many as 30 people present for workshops in all of the areas of CCD's program of "integrated development." It might be a week on workshops for health and nutrition, especially for nursing mothers, on how to increase the yield of the crucial corn and bean crops, Biblical reflection, building sheet metal grain storage bins, and raising rabbits and raising goats. These Monday -Friday workshops were a treasured time for people to get away from home and to be fed three full meals each day, which few were able to do in their own homes.*

We can hear the bombing in El Salvador today, like we do more days than we don't it seems. This is still something of a mystery to me - that is, how a government can expect to regain the loyalty of its own people by dropping bombs on them, by firing at them from helicopters. I know guerrilla warfare is a complicated thing. But I keep looking for evidence that the Salvadoran government, especially its military, has any genuine concern for their own people. And, of course, at least a large part of the roots of the violence there has to be my own country. One can easily guess where the bombs were made, where the helicopters were made.

We have a portable radio here. The only reception we can get well happens in the evening on a classical music station from El Salvador. It has not been unusual for us to hear gunfire and bombing from El Salvador with the music of Bach playing on our porch.

One of the villages with whom we work is Olosingo, a good 12 km from the nearest car passable road. Last week a characteristic incident happened there.

The people of Olosingo trade freely, and share life, with people on the El Salvador side. The river, where both peoples bathe and wash their clothes, is a symbol of the common life that they share.

On the El Salvador side, which is the province of Chalatenango, the Salvadoran guerrillas control much of the territory. Last week, as apparently happens often, a helicopter flew over and fired at what it apparently thought was a group of guerrillas or guerrilla-sympathizers. One Honduran man from Olosingo was with the group, returning from having driven cattle on the El Salvador side of the border. As the group ran for cover he was the only one hit - a Honduran having nothing to do with the conflict, just driving his cattle, doing the kinds of things that campesinos do as they live there from day to day.

We both have visited most of the other villages except for El Rodeo and Olosingo, both of them on the Rio Sumpul. It has been decided that Kathy and I should not visit there, because it is just too dangerous.

*2020 comments: The Rio Sumpul was the site of a horrible massacre of Salvadoran farmers and their families in May 1980, just over 5 years before we arrived. They were apparently trying to escape into Honduras to get away from the Civil War in El Salvador. As they waded the rivers the government's army helicopter flew over and began shooting. El Salvador authorities admitted 135 people had been killed but other counts placed the number at 600. And it happened in such a secluded area that few people might have ever heard of it had it not been for Father Earl Gallagher, a U.S. Capuchin priest from Brooklyn who worked in this part of Honduras, made sure that news of this tragedy made it into Honduran and international news. But the world still knows too little about it, the Rio Sumpul Massacre.*

As I write now I'm watching our farm-dog Paloma nurse her seven pups. She lays so serenely on the concrete porch, while the pups suck and fizz, and spin their feet on the floor, making what sound like desperate noises to get fed. They crawl and climb all over each other, they lose their grip on Paloma's tits, and go plummeting to the floor, only to get up instantly and start the climbing, crawling desperation all over again to get themselves fed. It is quite a study in contrast - Paloma with her calm demeanor, and seemingly limitless supply of nourishment, and the pups in their desperation grinding away as if this were the last possible chance that they will be fed.

I think this must be a parallel to how the divine - human relationship sometimes moves - God at the center of the universe effortlessly providing all the nourishment humans could need, and the little human creatures all crawling all over each other to get what they can, convinced that if they (we) don't get it now, we will certainly perish before too long.

I wonder what would happen if we could all patiently wait our turn at one of God's mammary glands, trusting that no one in front of the line would take more than their share, that there would be plenty left when we got there. And because of this the waiting time in the line would be a time of joyful fellowship and creativity.

It's a nice thought. But when I think of our neighbors, the campesinos here near La Granja - the image falls flat on its face. They've been waiting in line for many generations. I'm not sure but that some of them are unaware that the people at the front of the line are clinging to the nourishment far beyond their appointed time. I'm not sure all of them believe God has something better in store for them if the chubby puppies up front will just get out of the way, or at least stop eating long enough to do a little real celebrating, with the other people in the line.

The heartening stories of campesinos from other parts of Latin America, who at least are capturing a vision for themselves, and feeling their energies moving toward liberation, are absent here. What I sense most days is a complacent "this is the way it has been, this is the way it is, and this is the way it will be" attitude.

Perhaps God's liberation is tugging at their hearts in ways that I cannot see. I hope so. Meanwhile I think I would like to see some of our neighbors get angry about how the structures here have oppressed them and continue to oppress them.

*2020 notes: Here I seem to be judging Honduras and Hondurans according the best stories I have heard about liberation movements by the poor in other Latin American countries. Hondurans and people from all other countries deserve to be judged on the basis of their own realities. Honduras is not like any other country. Many leaders in human rights and resisting oppression have paid a heavy price for the stands they have taken, including death for a number of them. No one from the outside has any right to speculate on what courage should look like for the people of Honduras.*

## Thursday, April 24, 1986
*6:00 a.m., La Granja: Alvaro Melgar*

He is one of those people in my life who makes my heart sing every time he shows up.

He is campesino through and through, from his campo sombrero, to the corn which he still smokes in his attic, to his anxiety to get back to his house in the campo every time he has to leave for a few days.

But this is no ordinary campesino. I think I knew this first when I watched the way he looked into the face of his son Leonel, and cuddled him in the back of a pickup as we drove fast on a paved road on a cold and rainy day.

He and Luz are the parents of six children by birth. I have watched them so many times interact with affection, interest, and joy with their children. A seventh child is adopted. Orphaned at age 10, Alvaro and Luz took her in.

Alvaro only has a sixth-grade education - formally. I say only, but in fact getting through the sixth grade in this part of Honduras is unusual. Apparently, a scholarship was awarded him to continue into the seventh grade and beyond through channels of one of the political parties, but was later denied when it was discovered that his father was a member of another party.

In Alvaro's case, one can almost be relieved that institutions were not given a chance to interrupt what has proven to be a steady and solid stretching of both his head and his heart. He is a very intelligent and resourceful man - in everything from sharing in Biblical reflections, to consulting with villages on how to get a water project to work, to his most-valued and most-used area of expertise, agriculture. Combining the natural experience of a campesino who has labored in the hilly and very poor soil of this region, with technical knowledge he has learned by getting himself to the workshops and people who do know of ways that farming in

Honduras can improve, Alvaro has become a treasured talent. He is at home in the campo. He looks and lives like a campesino. The people in the campo think of him as one of them. Yet he also has vision and energy which is always reaching for the better - in how to love one's children as well as in how to produce more corn.

*Co-workers Ana, Alvaro and Elmer on a trail to one of the villages.*

As a pious Catholic, he is an interesting product of the post Vatican II era in which the laity's place in the church was heightened significantly. As a young man, he became a Delegate of the Word, lay leaders trained to carry on the work of the church where there is a shortage of priests. He shared with me the hard conflicts he had with his own mother who just could not see why, for example, parents should have to attend orientation sessions in order for their children to be baptized, no matter how much Vatican II said that people need to understand the sacraments more in order to increase their efficacy.

Although no longer a Delegate of the Word, Alvaro remains one of the compassionate, and steady pillars of the parish in Cololaca. He is also secretary of Cololaca's chapter of the Parent's Society, a parallel to what U. S. citizens would know as the PTA. And at age 40, he has recently become a good enough driver to get his license. With the CODE pickup often available to him, and living in an area where there are less than ten privately owned cars within an hour in any direction from his home, he now finds himself with a crucial new means of service. In just a few weeks as a licensed driver, he has delivered a casket for a funeral in which the family had no other means to get one. He helped a woman who had gone for weeks with no medical attention to the hospital for an operation that may well have saved her life. And he has given countless rides to weary campesinos on the hot and dusty road between San Marcos and Guarita. I worry now that he may get too busy with the truck and such. Enrique Espinoza our Regional Coordinator and Supervisor has expressed concern that Alvaro is spending too much time driving the pickup.

## Saturday, April 26, 1986
*10:00 p.m., San Marcos*

We have been in San Marcos for a few days of rest, writing and change of scenery. We have eaten in little low-priced diners here. It is good to be free from cooking for a few days. Tonight we went to the local picture show. We have more money than can easily be spent here. I just haven't thought much about La Granja.

Tomorrow we take the bus for the two-hour, 15-mile trek back to La Granja. I look forward to the tranquility and the pleasure of having a place that feels like our home. But I must also acknowledge a certain dread about going back. I think it has most to do with just how physically hard life at La Granja is for me. The walking, the carrying water, the smoky, stubborn wood stove, and the resulting backaches are a challenge. It is not really disillusionment, I don't think. The sense of purpose in living is growing. It is just hard for me after I have lived a life so full of conveniences and comforts.

Yet even at La Granja, we have better food, access to town, money, and numerous other conveniences to make our lives ever so

194

much easier than our campesino neighbors. For example, they have to deal with hauling firewood daily, carrying the water they need from the creek to their homes daily, working in bad soil that does not produce food, and generally living a life that is as physically overbearing as it is inaccessible to income and education. And usually there are many children to raise in the midst of all the above.

In spite of all these demands, indeed, in part, because of them, we are here to say to the people, "you need development." From the way life often feels to me at La Granja, I wonder why we do not have more campesinos who look at us with exhausted faces and say, "how can we develop? We use up more energy than we have just surviving." And yet the slow march toward the fragile vision of a better life for them does go on. Many are interested in learning whatever they can.

Earlier this week we were stopped by a very friendly U.S. citizen, a physicist here to check the possibilities for geothermal power in Honduras. He told the story of how he had given a "very nice, expensive actually," he said, shirt to a Honduran youth only to be dismayed the following day when the boy was playing in the dirt with the shirt. "He just had not respect for the gift. He just did not realize how nice he could look if he would just try."

I felt some anger, was turned off by this attitude - that if the people of poor nations would just develop themselves on our terms, if they would just try to look like we'd like them to look, they would be so much better off. And yet I find much of this same attitude in me as I interact daily with our campesino neighbors. "Why don't you do the things for yourselves that to me would be so obviously good for you?" It's development on my terms. It may even be worthy projects based in appropriate technology. But if it's on my terms and if it grows out of my needs rather than out of the integrity of the campesinos own vision, it means nothing. It even denies the mysterious and wonderful ways that the Holy Spirit works in the lives of the poor.

I don't know how often I will be able to work on their terms instead of my terms. It has not been easy for me to genuinely stand beside our campesino friends and really see with them their visions that fuels their hope. And the few times when I thought I have for a moment, even then the vision seemed rather blurry to me.

I think development has a lot to do with just waiting - watching - blowing on smoldering coals that may go out if you blow too hard or choose not to blow at all. But the waiting, like good praying, tries the souls of those of us who strain so hard to have life under control.

In Honduras, no one can pretend to have life under control, not even the wealthy or the military. They may enjoy comfort, but in the long run, not much control. And the campesinos certainly do not. They are the victims of forces so vastly beyond their control.

And yet there is one sense in which the poor in the countryside may be the freest of all. I sense among many of them what may be a mixture of resignation and acceptance. The urge to strain and strive which I seem to need in my life is not much of an option for people for whom survival can be a regular struggle.

One day I asked our neighbor Noe (Spanish for Noah) what some of his hopes were for his three young sons. The question seemed to bother him some. I believe Noel loves his sons very much. But his response was, "I'm not even sure if God plans for my sons to live very long." In a country where up to fifty per cent of the children die before age twelve, one does not spend much energy on the future when survival is a daily issue for many families. I realized how out of touch with reality my question had been.

## Monday, May 5, 1986
*7:00 a.m., La Granja*

It is early but late. I want more time to just sit here and write now. I feel like I can't. A workshop for Delegates of the Word starts today. People are arriving. There is work to be done.

## Saturday, May 10, 1986

The rains continue in our part of Honduras. Today, the rain was so hard and the wind blowing so strongly that we all had to cozy into a corner of the front porch to cozy up to our coffee and stay mostly dry. The brown hills that we have known in our early months are all turning green. Everything is plush with new life. Oxen effortlessly pull a homemade plow to get land loosened up for the planting. Campesinos huddle in to themselves as they ride their mules home from the fields. One hand holds on to the reins while the other pinches a sheet of thin plastic wrapped around his shoulder, his only protection from the rain. Raindrops drip from his straw hat. They call this season winter here because of the rain but the energy is certainly that of Spring. People are more alive, on the move. It is the time of year with many things to do, many of them things that if they are not done now, cannot be done later. The soil is now at its richest, as rich as the soil can get in these rocky hills of western Honduras. The people resonate with the earth thrown open to give them all it has to give.

### Wednesday, May 14, 1986
*8:30 a.m., La Granja*

The first time of silence in many days. In that one line between the May 5 and May 14 entry are crowded many days of struggle, disorientation, anger and depression. It is always hardest for me to write when life's struggles are heavier.

I'm not really sure just what it is that I want so often that I don't seem to get. So much is here with me, available for the taking - meaningful work, neighbors to visit, time for silence, good food, good things to read, a new language to learn, animals to care for, letters to write, a nice big bed in which to rest, children who love to visit us here in La Granja, Kathy's energy and creativity. When serenity finds me, when I allow serenity to find me, these items seem so much more available. That is, I can see them. But when I run off in my anger and self-pity, I feel so deprived. I feel like I just must have more food, more to drink, must have some free days to read and write. I am really unable to see all that is here and present for the taking.

### Thursday, May 15, 1986
*7:15 a.m., La Granja*

We now have a donkey here at La Granja. He lives at Lucio's house in Cololaca much of the time, but he'll probably end up living here permanently.

The donkey's job description is very clear. For a nominal fee, he is to mate with any willing mare who seeks his companionship in order to increase the mule population here in the countryside. He seems to enjoy his work. CCD charges a modest fee for his "services" but the greater purpose is to increase the mule population in the area.

He does not have to do any of the heavy hauling that we see being done every day by the dozens of other mules and horses in the community. A few days ago when I was carrying a fifty-pound sack of chicken feed on my back the one hundred yards or so from the car to the house, I looked down and saw our playboy burro mating with his guest for the day. I felt a lot of resentment!! Central America is so full of injustices!! He enjoys the pleasures of the flesh while I carry heavy sacks of feed that would be easy for him.

*2020 comment: We named the donkey Solomon after King Solomon in the Bible who had many females in his life as our Solomon does. He is a large donkey. He was flown here from Kentucky by Heifer International. With the privileged life he lived in Honduras we joked that he must have flown first class. He looked so strong. I never fully believed it was true that carrying large loads might do damage to his important reproductive capacities. It would have sure been nice to have him haul the fifty pound bags of animal feed the one hundred yards from the car to the house, which we had to do about every two months.*

*It is still exceptional for campesinos families here to own a horse or mule. But for those who do, it is very clear what a help they are. They provide transportation for long walks to the fields and haul bags of beans and corn from the fields back home, which sometimes are miles away.*

*One day when we were walking on a trail to one of the more remote villages we serve we met a man on his way out with his mule. The mule was carrying two cases of empty Coca-Cola bottles. Later that afternoon on our way out, we met him again, this time with the mule carrying two cases of full Coca-Colas. Of course Coca-Cola does not provide the nutrition that we wanted for the people there. But it was a lesson about how well U.S. corporate culture and products had penetrated to even the most remote parts of poor countries.*

## Wednesday, May 21, 1986
*10:00 a.m., La Granja*

Today's workshop on raising rabbits was for women only. Kathy has been promoting this event for a long time and it is overdue. In our village groups one person, usually a woman, is appointed to be the leader for health and nutrition. She takes the lead in learning local remedies for minor injuries and illnesses and improvements in nutrition. We have about twenty leaders from our villages here today.

We decided to slaughter one large adult rabbit and four young ones for lunch today. The idea is to encourage villages to raise rabbits as a source of protein, especially for children.

*Getting the rabbits ready for cooking.*

There was this moment after lunch when I went and stared into the empty cage where the four rabbits we ate had lived and where I had helped feed them for four months. I did not feel sentimentality. I did take note, with a rather full stomach, that the rabbits I had fed for months were now inside me. I had not since childhood eaten an animal that had been killed the same day. I don't think I had ever taken note of the intimate relationship between my needs for food and animals in the world. It was a simple but good moment of realizing that in order for me to eat meat, some animal has to die.

*Kathy conducting a class.*

I am not a vegetarian. I am appreciative of those who are. There is a great need for more meat in the diets, especially for children. I do wish that the sense of being a kindred being with animals we eat could be acknowledged more.

A letter came yesterday from Seattle, from Frank Kelsey a retired regional minister and now a member there, asking if I would consider becoming a candidate to become pastor Pilgrim Congregational United Church of Christ in Seattle. As weary as I get here at times, I don't feel interested, but I will want to think about it with some seriousness, especially since it was Frank who wrote the letter. (Frank has been a good friend and mentor in my life).

Life is not easy here. Life is often hard here. But I so feel that I want to stay with it a little longer, even a lot longer,

I am still a pastor at heart. I still look forward to all the tasks that go with being a people's pastor. I still think about all that a lot.

Pilgrim in some ways could speak to my own ego needs as a pastor. In the inner city. It has some history of affirming things that are difficult to affirm - singles, gay people, street people, the unemployed.

Not many thoughts are coming here. I think I should write to Frank.

## Saturday, June 7, 1986
*10:00 a.m., La Granja*

A rare day alone here in La Granja. Kathy has gone to San Pedro Sula for a day or two.

We have had almost no extended time away from each other since arriving here. It feels like a good thing for me. I hope it is for us.

Life moves along well here, although I live with many hungers - hunger for relaxed time with friends, for a creative expression that seems hard to come by here, for a self-discipline that is freer, more loving, more creative, to see my family and love them.

Mark Benjamin was with us for four days - a wonderful respite of compassion and delight. Mark is truly a person who tastes of life in all of its fullness. I really appreciate his friendship immensely, and I value the things that seem to come out of me when he is around.

The day is quiet. I slept in until 7 today. It now takes nearly two hours to tend the animals.

I have a writing project begging for my attention today. I pray for enough stillness to produce something worthwhile.

## Monday, June 23, 1986
*10:00 a.m., La Granja*

*2020 notes: The "galera" is a simple outdoor shelter that seats about five under a thatched roof of straw. It was built as a place for outdoor classes and meetings and as a place to just sit and relax.*

Sitting in the galera trying to pray - maybe I did a little, that is if a few good private tears can mean anything. Tears do not come easily for me in Honduras - not even those light subtle ones that I have always depended on for a little help in my prayer life.

Why is it hard to cry here? Here where suffering is so much a part of everything? Where here is the friend in whose presence I can feel free?

Does God hear us when we pray for tears?

## Monday, June 30, 1986

*Rosalina's Journey*

The small village of Ana Sanchez is just a half mile up the road from us. The people there had not organized as an "official" CCD community even though we had regular contact with many there since we were so close. A few weeks ago the first CCD meeting was held at Ana Sanchez so now it is one of the official villages that are among the twenty or so that CCD serves in the area.

One symptom of the massive malnutrition among the children in rural Honduras is patches of white hair growing on their heads. When hair does not get the food it needs, it begins to turn white among people that have almost totally dark-colored hair. The children must wear this sign of their lack of food as a kind of badge of deprivation. One of our new initiatives recently has been to appoint a woman in each of the villages to serve as the nutrition leader for the village.

Rosalina is 18, an age when many women here are married and have children, but she still lives at home with her parents in Ana Sanchez. In Honduran rural culture, being 18 at home seems to mean that a daughter is still very much under the supervision of her father.

Rosalina was able to go to school long enough to learn to read and write. She is also a warm and friendly person, and quickly became one looked to for some leadership of the CCD group in Ana Sanchez. She seemed honored and delighted to be chosen as the Nutrition Leader for the village. Having gotten to know her and having watched her work and spirit at La Granja gatherings, we were also glad to hear this news.

But it was not a done deal until her father, Don Juan de la Cruz Guardado, gave his approval, especially because the program was to begin with a week-long workshop for leaders from all the villages 15 miles away in San Marcos. He decided that she would not be allowed to go. Since Rosalina seemed to be the only woman in the village available for this role, it would mean Ana Sanchez would not have a representative in the program.

Kathy has been nurturing the process with care and made the wise decision to ask our co-worker Alvaro Melgar to have a talk with Juan to see if he could persuade him to change his mind. He was glad to give it a try. We have no idea of what he said nor how he said it. But after a visit of about a half hour Alvaro came to tell us that don Juan had changed his mind and that Rosalina would be making the journey to San Marcos. We were overjoyed.

As a man who has enjoyed a number of places where my authority and power were respected, I imagined that for don Juan, used to being powerless in so many ways where he has been forced to live, needed to protect the few places of power that were still his, especially that of being a father. I also imagined that Alvaro who has lived through similar experiences of powerlessness to some new places of respect and influence, was able to relate to Juan in ways that none of the rest of us could.

Yesterday was the day of departure for the week-long workshop and I was the driver of the Land Rover to take about 8 of the women from nearby villages into San Marcos. As we were arriving at Ana Sanchez I saw don Juan standing beside the turnoff drive waving for me to stop. I worried that he had changed his mind and wanted to tell me that Rosalina would not be going after all. But as he walked up to the car window there was a certain smile on his face. I'm almost sure it was a smile of pride. He asked me *"will Dona Olivia be going to the workshop?"* Dona Olivia is a respected matriarch from Cololaca known by many. When I assured him that she would be going, he was pleased and waved us up the drive further into the village. About 50 yards more about 30 people from the village had gathered to see Rosalina off. Everyone available had turned out to celebrate the occasion, a high moment when a little girl in the village took a great step closer to full womanhood in the wider community.

Rosalina's 16-year-old sister Regina came out first as the lady-in-waiting carrying Rosalina's bag. Then Rosalina came out, dressed in her finest dress, smiling widely and walking with confidence and pride. She waved at the people of the village, took her bag from Regina, and climbed into the land rover as if she had been doing it for years.

It was simply one among dozens of routine workshops that CCD had held in the area for a number of purposes. But for Rosalina and her father Don Juan it seemed to be a large step forward on the sacred journey of a human life.

## Tuesday, July 1, 1986

*La Granja: Noemi Madrid de Espinoza, Executive President, Christian Commission for Development*

Sometimes it seems the great majority of the growth in the villages has to do with growth in the lives of women. We are fortunate to have a remarkable woman as head of CCD. In fact we would not exist without her.

Noemi Madrid de Espinoza was born into a farming family that was poor in terms of material resources but wealthy in matters of dignity and faith. Against extremely difficult odds her parents pushed Noemi and her brothers and sisters to study and work hard to fulfill their potentials. In a country where about 1% of the population is able to attend college, Noemi graduated from both college and law school and went into private practice. But after Honduras was devastated by hurricane Fifi in 1974, Noemi began to put her faith and abilities to work on behalf of the poor in Honduras. She has been involved in the formation and leadership of a number of people-serving programs in Honduras.

Noemi grew up in the village of Pinelejo near San Pedro Sula. She became a part of the life of the Evangelical and Reformed Church of Honduras and was baptized by U.S. missionary Gus Kuether.

Before she founded the Christian Commission for Development (CCD) in 1982, she was the Director of a UN related programs which served thousands of Salvadoran and Guatemalan refugees living in Honduras. The CCD (earlier called the Commission for Development and Emergency or CODE) came into being after a strange takeover of the board of the refugee program by very conservative Christians. When she saw the narrow and religiously exclusive way in which she would have to carry out her work, she resigned and with help from church leaders she knew in the U.S. and a number of European countries, she founded the Christian Commission for Development. Noemi has a strong and gracious presence, one who commands attention any time she walks in a room. She enjoys the support of everyone in CCD. With five regional offices across the country he only visits La Granja occasionally, but she obviously knows a lot about what is going on here and in all of CCD's regions. I consider it a privilege to work under her leadership.

204

Any program that serves the poor in Honduras becomes suspect as soon as it begins to show some growth. Noemi has apparently been "in good trouble" a number of times because of her work and her unwillingness to conform to repressive government policies. The word we get is that sometimes she has been able to avoid worse reprisals because of the influence of her husband Felipe Espinoza, a math professor at the local university. Over the years his students have included a number of men who are now officers in the military. We were told that he has been able to call on those relationships to assist Noemi in times of misunderstanding and trouble.

## Thursday, July 3, 1986
*9:00 a.m., La Granja*

Psalm 131 is an odd one:

*"O Lord, my heart is not lifted up, my eyes are not raised too high; I do not occupy myself with things too great and too marvelous for me. But I have calmed and quieted my soul."* Then it gets rational at the end: *"O Israel, hope in the Lord from this time forth and forevermore."*

Yesterday some maps I had ordered arrived which illustrate U.S. military presence in Central America and the Caribbean. As Kathy and I began to look at them, we found ourselves talking matter-of-factly about the reality that these maps could be risky things to have around. At first it felt like just any practical conversation that husbands and wives have around the house.

Then I realized what was happening - we were really having to think about, in our own home the risks of having certain literature present.

This is not to be melodramatized. We are not likely to be searched or threatened. And even if we were, our status here as citizens of Honduras' parent world-power would go a long way toward keeping us from having to endure a lot of trouble. Worst case scenario might be something like a lot of bureaucratic hassles. Yet we do have to think about the risk for CODE, already thought of as leaning toward subversive by some. We should not be the ones to cause extra suspicions for them.

The situation also brings to mind the risks that probably most of the Honduran citizens have to undergo if they want to seriously question their government or challenge its injustices. Another irony is that as I write this I can hear once again the bombing a few miles away in El Salvador.

*2020 note: Later on in the journal you will see that in fact these very maps had to be burned by our co-workers very fast before soldiers came to La Granja in 1987 while we were away.*

*Children in doorway.*

## Friday, July 4, 1986
*6:30 a.m., La Granja*

In our covered classroom space I lay face down on a mattress, looking out to the side in a quiet moment. A frog has gotten caught inside the little building. He is hopping around the perimeter of the wall trying to find an exit. Without some help there won't be one. I arose from my quiet and showed him to the door. He sat still in the outdoor sunlight.

There are moments when I too feel caught, feel sequestered inside a building with no exit. There are times when in my heart I don't think I can get out without some help from someone else. I am caught in a negative anger, and I have no psychic access to a larger perspective.

I feel caught in a loneliness that I may not know how to acknowledge. Only a sensitive friend can open for me anew the door of relationship. Or in rare moments, only the Spirit can reach to me in subtle and gentle ways, and hand me the liberation that I have been seeking.

The morning quiet and still - our dog Paloma, even more vigilant than we prefer - tells us with frantic barking that the first visitor of the day has arrived. The day is now coming to take us. But just before it does, a little more time to be here where the spirit of Words read themselves back to me and send me into the day a little more ready to greet all its strains and promises.

It is July 4, and today the nation will gather to celebrate the renewal of our lady of liberty - that welcoming statue, welcoming the tired and the poor longing to breathe free.

And I sit in Honduras, where most all the people I see every day are tired and poor, and not only this, they also live surrounded by poverty, violence and war ever ready to consume them.

*2020 note: At the time of this writing I had read in the paper about a major renovation of the Statue of Liberty in New York.*

Our lady of liberty needs a new chapter in her life as well as a renovation. She needs more than plastic surgery - more than a facelift. Maybe the engineers who did the renovation should have added some tears streaming down her cheeks for the next era of her service. For now, many, many of the tired and the poor are tired and poor because she couldn't quite see over the hazy horizon. She got scared, and she began to do damage to people she thought would threaten her liberty. In the process she lost her way. In the process, she began to get weak. And look a bit frazzled, joints creaky, frazzled in the morning, tired in the afternoon, and always inclined to shout at folks when the pressure was on. It is not that she is old, for in fact she is very young. She did look tired. Maybe she never had that quiet and reflective time that all need in some way to keep the heart fresh.

So now she has a facelift, and people will admire her outer beauty all over again. The surgeons will be praised, and people will weep at the glory of her restoration.

But this time is not like the time when she first arrived on the island. If she really still cares about the tired and the poor she may have to leave that island, and step off into some deep water. She may have to realize that while she stood gloriously at one gate to the refuge, fearful leaders were locking a thousand other gates. She may need to get on one of those ships, the kind that brought so many to her feet, and travel to the places where her followers have helped close a million more gates, such as right here in Central America, which, had they stayed open, might have helped the tired and the poor to breathe free on the land where their feet first touched earth.

## Thursday, July 10, 1986
*Noon, La Granja*

Today I seem full of old wounds, old conflicts that never healed, people that I thought maybe I should talk to but never did.

I remember asking a therapist in Seattle that I respected about whether or not I should initiate talk with two people at University Congregational Church with whom I had some conflicts. He asked, "Do you need to?" At the time I didn't think so. Now I do, and it has become a very awkward time to do very much about it. I still carry the scar, probably also much of the unhealed wound. Hurts and conflicts need to be talked about face to face. We may not always move to a point of reconciliation. But at least we will have the peace of knowing that we did what we could.

I think I was probably better five or six years ago at sharing my feelings, at being the kind of vulnerable person necessary for reconciliation to happen.

## Saturday, July 19, 1986
*Abadia de Jesucristo Crucificado (Abbey of the Crucified Christ), Esquipulas, Guatemala*

*2020 notes: The Benedictine Abbey of the Crucified Christ was just over the border in Guatemala, an easy bus ride for us. It is an incredibly beautiful place. There is a colonial era basilica there with the shrine of the Black Christ. It is probably the most significant pilgrimage site for Roman Catholics anywhere in Central America. Built right up against the basilica was a beautiful Benedictine monastery. It was modern architecture but was built to be very compatible with the basilica. The abbot was an authority on tropical plants so there were beautiful flowers everywhere.*

*The whole town of Esquipulas seemed to have a "pilgrimage-based" economy. There were numerous shops where one could go to buy candles, devotional statues, books and much more.*

*American Benedictines from Louisiana seemed to be the ones mostly in charge. The Benedictine Rule includes the words "greet Christ in every guest." They are known for hospitality. I felt like we enjoyed the best of both Benedictine and Southern hospitality.*

*The Benedictine brother who played the organ in the liturgies was also the chef for the community and made delicious meals. I especially remember how flavorful his black bean soup was. The grounds had orchards and lots of irrigation. It was obviously a place where the church had decided to invest a lot of money. There was a good library and even a television! After so much time in a dry and dusty setting, a retreat in the Abbey of the Crucified Christ was a most welcome respite for us.*

*The abbey had also been the meeting place of peace talks among all the Central American presidents a few years before out visit. President Oscar Arias, President of Costa Rica received the Nobel Peace Prize for his leadership during those efforts for peace.*

It is quiet here. Away for a week of some rest and for me work on the Amistad curriculum. This is such a tranquil place. It is in the shadow of the Basilica of the Black Christ, an immense and beautiful building with hundreds of visitors daily. Yet we are "behind the wall" with the always hospitable Benedictines and it feels so good.

The place is also plush - bath in every room, a color TV in a common lounge, an orange orchard for walking. Sleek modern architecture - probably the plushest place we've been in since we left the U.S., yet the rule here is silence except in certain areas. Maybe it is plush, but it is clearly the faith and discipline of the Benedictines that make this already begin to feel like a uniquely good place for the renewal of the soul.

I have a cold. But I feel ready to go to work. I should probably start rather slowly, and build up.

**Monday, July 21, 1986**
*7:00 a.m., Abadia de Jesucristo Crucificado, Esquipulas, Guatemala*

Kathy made it up in time for the 6 a.m. morning prayers today - a miracle in itself. It is brief so it leaves a good hour for solitude between this prayer and breakfast at 7:30.

We are both feeling so blessed here - not that close to each other really - this is not the purpose of the week. But indulgently wonderful gifts like private rooms, quiet lawns and orchards for walking, the always hospitable faces of the monks, and much more, are keeping us most uplifted.

Today I need to be at work on the study series. I pray for a gentle and receptive discipline, a quiet steadiness that will allow the session outlines to take shape in helpful ways. At this point, I am also praying that they will be used by someone!

**Tuesday, July 22, 1986**
*8:15 a.m., Abadia de Jesucristo Crucificado, Esquipulas, Guatemala*

The silence continues to do good work in my life. There are a few people I would like to write letters to from here - Gail, Frank, George, Barb, Judith. Maybe I will.

A touch of diarrhea has me slowed down a little, but I can't think of a better place to have diarrhea.

The work goes on - writing a study series for our Amistad program. It is not falling into place like magic but I think it is working.

Matthew Fox's *Original Blessing* is nourishing me in between all other doings here.

It is time now to not write, not work, not pray, not talk, not seek God, not think, not do and so to rest in the good darkness.

**Wednesday, July 23, 1986**
*8:30 a.m., Abbey, Esquipulas*

O, these good hours of the morning when the soul is most rested and ready. These are hours for me best used for rest, for quiet work (writing and reading) for dreaming, praying, enjoying and stretching the body, creative, letting pain be pain, listening to the darkness and the creative power of nothingness.

**Thursday, July 24, 1986**
*6:30 a.m., Abbey, Esquipulas*

I am realizing now in moments of quiet that in my life, which is any spiritual life, I have nothing to protect. I have no duty to cling to anything in my past or present. Nor do I have any duty to reject any part. The past is all there, as gift, waiting in the wings, vast, too many parts to use in any one day or any one year. I need not hide behind any part of it, and yet I am free to go and walk beside some part of the past for a short time, or a larger time.

I think now of parts of my past as friends, both seen and unseen, both strong and weak, both right and wrong, who are cheering me on.

It also occurs to me that each day that passes, I am being given a little more of a past to cheer for me and guide me into new days.

*Conscious Examen, how Grace has been present today:*

How has Jesus been good to me this week?
- Gerardo and his robust friendliness.
- Hugs by Kathy

- The energetic silence that has so helped me with my work.
- Songs of the monks
- Good, good food
- Large green fields
- The loving face of that kid, I don't know his name.
- Peasants kneeling holding candles in the basilica
- Readings from Matthew Fox

## Sunday, July 27, 1986
*In the park, San Marcos*

Jesus teaching on prayer.

v. 5ff. (About going to a friend's house and asking for bread at midnight and if he says no, knock again, and ask again). At first reading seem to be saying "keep badgering" and you'll get what you want.

It is hard to focus on this right now at great length, but the passage closes with "how much more then, will the Father in heaven give the Holy Spirit to those who ask him."

It seems to me that this is the end of all our longing, to "know" the "Holy Spirit" - to be connected to the Spirit that gives spirit to all created things.

Maybe we can finally only struggle and persist in this, to be "given" the Holy Spirit.

## Wednesday, July 30, 1986
*La Granja*

What Happened on Tuesday?

Up early - had an hour to pray.

Alvaro arrived, as usual, earlier than we expected him.

Had corn flakes - a rather hurried breakfast.

Off in the pickup with 3 women and various children headed for the health center in Cololaca. When we got there the health center was closed. We drove the women back to Ana Sanchez.

Then off with Alvaro to La Florida - a long hot walk. My energy was good but as usual, I arrived feeling sleepy after walking in the sun.

On the way in we talked about the situation with Elmer, the day he drove the car into the ditch, and how the news spread.

In the meeting in La Florida. we did the prepared lesson on parental responsibility with only 5 present - 1 man, 4 women. It was a good discussion.

On the way back we talked of fears of "gente extraña" (the guerillas) and of homosexuality in Honduras and in the U.S.

Alvaro walked over the bridge. I chose to go over the rocks in the river. That bridge is so shaky I am afraid to walk on it. Not Alvaro.

Back at La Granja I read the paper, sorted beans and had a very brief chat with Jose Angel Ramirez, a local evangelical Christian and tooth puller. He was on his way to pull a tooth.

*2020 notes: In rural Honduras there are no dentists. Occasionally a group of dentists from the U.S. will come for a week or so and see patients. Alvaro, who has had all his teeth pulled, was able to afford and travel to get dentures. But this required a lot of his money and a bus ride of about four hours one way. So the tooth puller in the countryside perform an important service and relieve a lot of pain.*

I cooked dinner with reasonable inner peace, washed dishes and went to bed. While I was bathing in our outdoor bath, the new white male goat came to say hello.

## TODAY, TODAY, TODAY

Reading some in Matthew Fox of late. He speaks well to me of depth, of creativity, of a vision of the world that I want to live by.

I feel thankful for pens and pieces of paper. With these simple instruments, I have kept my life in touch with good things that otherwise I would have missed.

God of Peace,

Give me peace. All that I cannot settle by talking or effort, by management or by trying, by words or by actions - all within me that lies unhealed and uncreated - I pray thee to give me peace with these things. Give me peace and give me creativity. And give to the silence that I can touch all that I otherwise find. Amen.

## Wednesday, July 30, 1986
*7:15 a.m., La Granja: A Conscious Examen*

Where was Jesus good to me yesterday?
- A sense of peace while feeding the animals.
- Good time of work planning with Gregorio, the carpenter doing most of the building here lately.
- The cup of coffee when the rain started to fall.
- Typed pages completed on the Amistad study program.
- A sense of trust when the typewriter would not work.

## Friday, August 1, 1986
*11:15 a.m., La Granja*

Today my heart is full of the question - What does it mean when the charge of "guilt-motivated" is directed at those of us who are critical of the United States.

What is guilt?

What is unjustified guilt?

What is justified guilt?

Is there such a thing as realizing that, yes, as a nation, we have done some rather wrong things, and to try to work to correct them? If this is guilt, then is it not appropriate guilt? And if the guilt is appropriate, is it not better to work with those inner emotions in a creative manner that seeks to right the wrongs done rather than to wallow in cheap self-criticisms and self-putdowns.

To deny that there is a reason for national guilt - is this not worse for the national soul? Do not all nations commit wrongs? Indeed, do not all entities of great power find that the power inevitably leads to wrongdoing? Power does not ride naturally with justice. Is this not a reality? And while this unnaturalness continues, what are the rest of us to do? We won't soon change the basic nature of how power tends to behave in large group collectives. But maybe we can, at least occasionally, make ourselves vulnerable when we find ourselves insulated, a part of, such power collectives. If we can't change the larger systems that inevitably misuse the power given to them, is it not, at the very least, worthwhile to work to keep those power systems from changing us?

I think that very few of us can claim to be totally apart from the power systems that use and hurt people. In some way or ways most all of us are collaborators. And as I say this, I do not feel myself laying a guilt trip on myself or anyone. It seems to me that one can have the maturity to acknowledge this reality and then go on to live as a forgiven, creative, reconciling person.

Is there unjustified guilt at work in the national soul? I must say that I do not see much. I have seen a lot of unjustified guilt in personal lines. It is a crippling and fragmenting tragedy to see people who feel they have been cut off from their rightful connection to the universe.

As a nation we lack a means of catharsis for unexpressed wounds and guilt than we live with too much unjustified guilt. We are not crippled by unjustified guilt, at present. Rather we seem to be "marching on," not inclined to give a look over either shoulder to see what people we may have trampled upon. I don't know if it is realistic to hope for ways in which a nation might turn and see, and then return to itself, be who it is called to be, and then go back and pick up those trampled people, giving to them the option of being restored to independence and dignity.

*2020 notes: In recent years in the U.S. we have seen numerous cities across the country acknowledge the racist policies of their histories and apologize to African Americans for the lack of care that resulted in so much terrorism and death. As I write we are still in the middle of a strong world-wide Black Lives Matter Movement that has included a lot of unprecedented acknowledgement of racism by cities, newspapers, universities and individuals. There is a long way to travel, but we at least and at last we have taken these small steps.*

Andres came today to bring firewood (leña in Spanish, pronounced LAYN-ya). He walks up the walkway leading his white horse, an old white horse, always with a friendly and welcoming face.

After he unloaded the leña, we sat and drank coffee. I was complimented that he accepted a second cup, unusual for a campesino.

I asked him, or tried to ask him - "what are your dreams, your plans for your life?" Andres is fifteen. He can barely write his name, but cannot read. He works in the fields and sells firewood. There is little likelihood that he will own a lot of land in his life, or that he will improve his reading ability.

Yet he seemed to understand my question. His reaction was not the polite kind of "life is as it is and always will be" response that I usually get when I try to engage a campesino at something more than a surface level.

He did not have specifics to share with me, but when I threw out possible visions such as family, animals, land - he responded with an animated laughter and a response - "yes, I want everything."

But, then, then he asked me what my dreams were. He asked if we wanted to have a family. I said that we had talked about having children but that we just were not sure about it.

He asked me about my dreams. The nature of our friendship took an important turn. I felt a touch, just a touch, of allowing myself to be a receiver of friendship in a way that I had not before with other campesino friends and acquaintances. It was a very good moment.

*2020 notes: Looking back this seems like a conversation I tried to have on North American terms with a person who does not live with any of the same assumptions and possibilities that I live with. More of my unconscious colonial consciousness showing. Now I look back at myself with compassion. I was doing the best I could with the consciousness I had then. Still working on this.*

## Sunday, August 3, 1986
*1:00 p.m., La Granja*

*2020 notes: I lived on a family farm in Mississippi until I was 8 on land that had been in our family since the 1840s, first farmed by my great-great grandfather. Returning to farming life for this time in Honduras brought up memories and reflections of my grandfather whom we all knew as "Grandaddy." Life at La Granja made me want to write letters to Grandaddy who had passed away in 1974. It was very interesting to compare the farming life I saw in Honduras to the farming life of my grandfather from 1910 to 1974. Most of the letters to Grandaddy from Honduras were written in August 1986.*

216

*I was in college in Memphis in 1968 when Dr. Martin Luther King, Jr. was assassinated just a few miles from our campus. My life as a Southerner went through a major transformation after that. Having been raised in an environment that practiced every possible form of racism, I became a strong advocate for racial integration.*

*Then and now I wanted to be a radically different kind of White Southerner, yet still a Southerner. One thing I could love about my Southern identity was my roots among humble farming people and a sense of connection to land and place. My grandparents bought a small farm for $300 from my great-grandfather in 1916 and lived there until my grandmother's death in 1983. They seemed to live from the land as well as on it. They belonged to the land as much as the land belonged to them. I continue to love this about my Southern roots.*

*I thought of my farming ancestors as humble country people, sometimes referred to as "country hicks." Many had little or no education. My grandfather could barely read. They were nowhere close to the plantation class of Southerners. It never occurred to me until recent years that our people were beneficiaries of "White Privilege." Even if I knew I tended to romanticize my farmer ancestors, I held on to the beauty and integrity of farming people as my people.*

*A main point of my 1986 "Letters to Grandaddy" from the farming community of Western Honduras was to notice the vast difference between a "small" Mississippi farm (100 acres) compared to a Honduran subsistence farmer who had to feed his family on 10 acres or less of infertile land. That comparison was striking.*

*What I began to sense from a 2020 perspective as I reread my Letters to Grandaddy from Honduras were the many layers of White Privilege in the United States which also extends across national boundaries.*

*One layer was the removal of the Chickasaw nation from what we now call Mississippi so White settlers such as my great-great grandfather could take over their land at little or no cost.*

*Another layer was that of enslaved Africans and their descendants who were forced into hard labor on the land but were never given any significant access to access to owning land.*

*And still another layer is the takeover of much of the most productive land in Honduras by U.S. fruit corporations leaving the worst land to poor subsistence farmers.*

*At age 72 I feel like I am only beginning to become aware of how much I still don't know about how systemic racism has benefitted my life as a descendant of White farmers and lower middle class working people. The evolution of land ownership throughout the Americas is much more central aspect of the larger picture of White Privilege than I had realized. Farmers such as my grandfather might seem humble and powerless compared to many in our country. But with the access to land that he inherited he was nowhere near the lowest class of farmers when viewed from an international perspective. This was true alongside the racism instilled into me by him as well as by just about all of those who influenced my upbringing.*

*Alexandr Solzhenitsyn said that "the line between good and evil run through every human heart." I find this to be especially true in the ways White people such as my grandfather and I have unconsciously taken systemic racism into our DNA. It has taken me a long to even begin to acknowledge this.*

*I still love and honor all that was good in my grandfather's life as a farmer. But his humanity and my own are dishonored if we cannot acknowledge the racism and privilege that has been a part of both of our lives.*

*Grandaddy, Hugh Ray Mullins (1890-1974) on his Mississippi Farm in the early 1970s. Photo Credit: Cynthia Jo Wilbanks.*

#1

Dear Grandaddy,

I ran off to the city when Daddy and Mother decided to move there, and you seemed to understand. I didn't think I was sorry to leave. At the time, I probably wasn't. You see, I loved you, Grandaddy, but it didn't work very well for you to be Daddy and Grandaddy both for me. What I mean is, when Daddy left every Sunday to go to Memphis and work, and stay in the boarding house, I always cried hard. Or so they tell me. I don't remember too much. Maybe something kind within us keeps us from remembering things that really hurt until we are ready.

So after we left the farm I was more or less happy in our little house south of town on Manson Road. Most of the folks in the neighborhood seemed to be a lot like us, country folks who had moved to Memphis because that's where the jobs were. Some of them planted big gardens in big back yards. We always had more tomatoes and butterbeans than we could eat. Sometimes we even had more than we could give away.

Don't get me wrong, but at the time I didn't care much for working in that garden. I was always picking the butterbeans before they were ready, and that usually upset Daddy. I'm afraid that as happens when kids move to the city, other things start to be more important than growing things - like baseball, or buying ice cream, or going to the public pool in August, or playing golf with rented clubs over beside the river.

So, I think I began to forget what it felt like to live close to the land. I mean things like walking barefoot on newly plowed ground that was cool and moist in springtime. Or putting on lots of clothes in August to protect us from chiggers when Grandmother would take me with her to pick blackberries. There were the cool October mornings when we rode to the field on top of a half-load of cotton, in order to fill the truck with more.

Those first eight years of mine, Grandaddy, I think I was kind of close to the land, able to know a kind of unconscious cherishing of if it all.

I can't really say I feel it was all bad that we left. Farming was hard, and when we finally moved to Memphis, Daddy came home every day instead of every Friday. That was sure better for me. But, the truth is, Grandaddy, I did leave the land. And I think it took me a lot of years to begin to feel a little of what I had lost in leaving.

I shouldn't romanticize. I never would have been able to hack it as a farmer. It was right for me to wander off to many places and seek what might rightly be called my fortune. But the fortune kept showing up in my dreams as your farm, Grandaddy. No, I know it wasn't a fancy or the sort of farm fit for making one money-rich. But in the most stunning of the dreams Grandaddy, the farm, (your farm, our farm, the farm), appeared as a fine plantation, with beautiful fences, and exquisite buildings. Everything was perfectly manicured. And the boundless hospitality of you and Grandmother were in the dream.

Yes, I know it's not a fancy farm, not at all. And now the fences are kind of rusty with a good many rotten posts that need replacing.

But I think the dream was true. I think the farm does have a perfection about it, I mean a good earthy, loose-soiled at-homeness kind of perfection - a place where all you need is really there if one can just manage to come home fully enough.

My coming home is still going. It has taken me, to all kind of places that you wouldn't know much about. I think maybe my coming home got started during those summer vacations from school in Memphis when I would go back to the farm to spend a week or two with you and Grandmother.

But as my coming home kept going, I found that the urge grew ever stronger to keep coming back to your house, and sit up close to you in one of those timeless cane-bottomed chairs so you could tell me more stories. Lots of relatives told me how good it was that I went to college and was doing interesting things, and that was nice. But, you Grandaddy, weren't too impressed with all that achievement stuff, or at least you didn't appear to be. You just stayed close to the land, watched the road for company coming, and somehow let us know you enjoyed us when we finally got there.

Still my coming home kept going, and I found some of home in places like Berkeley, Pennsylvania, Seattle, and now Honduras.

This is about as far away as the homecoming has taken me, and yet I think I feel closer to you here than I have any other place.

We live on a farm. In Spanish, we just call it La Granja or the farm. It's about 4 acres, a lot more than most of the farmers near here own. No, we don't do all the work here, not even most of it. I'm finding out all over again that I couldn't hack it as a farmer. But this place is helping me come home a little. Some days I almost think that any minute I'll be sitting in one of the old green rocking chairs on your front porch and listening to you tell me another story.

Even the house we live in is made of earth. Folks in Honduras call it adobe. Some say that adobe houses, if they're built well, can last as long as a hundred years. Ours looks nice. About half of it is front porch, which is also where we eat and where we just sit. You'd like it.

We have walls and a clay-tile roof, but no ceiling. That lets the air circulate because it gets real hot here. In fact, it stays hot most days except for a few nights in January or in the days of the rainy season. But even the rain is sort of a warm rain.

Not having a ceiling means we usually have a few more bugs than we need while we're sleeping. But it also means that the fireflies can get in. And on many nights, I go to sleep with fireflies dancing in the air above me. And as far as I know, none of them have ever bit me. I think they live just to make country nights beautiful, but I don't think they know that's why they live.

I remember the fireflies in Mississippi and in Memphis. In springtime they did their dancing all across the pasture, and you could see them for what seemed like miles. There must have been millions, but they never seemed to stay very long. Here there aren't so many, but the ones that are do seem to stay longer.

I'll tell you more and if you were here, I think you would tell me more. Maybe you're telling me a lot even though you're not here. Or are you here?

Love,
your grandson,
Randall

#2
August, 1986
Dear Grandaddy,
Lucio is the farmer here who really makes all the crops grow. He's about 40, I think. I didn't see you when you were 40 (I think you were 58 when I was born), but Lucio reminds me a little of you. He's not very big, maybe 5 foot 6 and weights about 130 at most. I think he's about your size.

Our mule lives at his house so he can have her to ride to work here every day. We discovered that the mule didn't have a name, so Lucio told us he'd like us to give her a name.

We named her Kate. It was partly because she seemed to like to sing, a lot during the day here, like Kate Smith. But the real reason was that I remembered how much you loved your mules, and I remember the last pair you had were named Kate and Nell. So we named Kate after your Kate.

You lived through the days when mules gave way to tractors, Grandaddy, but I can still see you with the long leather strap from the mules' bridles and running around your neck, plowing the garden, getting it ready for Grandmother to plant her vegetables. That plow cut such a nice furrow.

Some farmers here plow with oxen like your daddy did. That is, the few of them who own oxen or who have enough money to rent the few that are available when it's time to get the land ready for planting.

A good many have mules and horses to haul firewood or fertilizer, and I can sometimes see they enjoy having an animal as a co-worker just like you did.

They are poor folks, about the poorest I have ever seen. Even though I remember stories about you and Grandmother having to pick soy beans off the hay in the barn some in order to have enough to eat during the depression, most of these folks have been poor for generations, and many of them don't even think much about what it might be like to live a better life.

I think being poor makes it hard to love the land. I mean when a father here divides his land among his boys, and when the land you end up with is small to begin with, and on the side of a hill besides that, the land doesn't give you much but a lot of hard work to do, and I think it's harder to feel like the land is your friend, or even like a good mother who gives you enough to eat. The land here doesn't promise much. It's more like a tired and weak mother, who would like to be kind and give you plenty to eat, but who is so tired and overworked, who has been asked so many times to do things that she just can't do - well, I think it's hard to love land like that. And when it's hard to love the land, I think it's even harder to help the land be something better. Yet the people do love the land. I started this by talking about mules, didn't I? Another time, I want to tell you more about our mules and the other few animals we have around here.

#3
August, 1986
Dear Grandaddy,

I remember what Sunday was like at your house. Sometimes it was quiet, but most of the time you and grandmother sat on the porch and watched the road for company. Sometimes only a few folks would come, and they wouldn't stay very long. Sometimes the preacher would come for dinner, and there'd be cars and people everywhere. And sometimes relatives and cousins from as far always as Jackson and Memphis would show up, and the pasture would be full of ball games and uncles walking to look at the cows or somebody's new Chevy pickup.

There aren't any Chevy pickups here, and it's hard to find a pasture big and level enough for a ball game. But Sunday is a restful day here, too, and a time when people seem to walk the road a lot to visit each other.

We live a few miles from a place called El Salvador. They have a war going on there. I don't understand all of it, but it seems that a lot of the problem has to do with land - poor folks who need land and don't have any, rich folks who have more than they need but don't want to give any of it up, and a lot of folks all over the place who feel bad enough about the situation that they've started shooting at each other. They even had a small war with this country, Honduras, back in 1969, because El Salvador keeps needing more land than it has, and tried to take some from Honduras.

One quiet Sunday not long after we got here, we were sitting on the front porch with company, a boy named Michael (they call him Miguel, here). We started hearing something that sounded a little like thunder but not quite, so we asked Michael if he knew what it was. Speaking Spanish, he said "bombas". In Spanish that word can mean everything from a water pump to a balloon, so we asked him what kind.

This boy, about 10 years old, said "the kind to kill people." We couldn't see it, and we were miles away but we were hearing that war in El Salvador. It was the first time I had heard a war going on.

I remember when I was a boy, I would ask Daddy why he didn't fight in World War II. You see, all my buddies seemed to have fathers who had fought in wars and who were very proud about it. I must have felt a little ashamed that neither you nor Daddy had fought in a war. It made me afraid that I too would grow up without getting a chance to fight in a war and that I would also have a son who would be ashamed of me because I didn't either.

224

I don't feel that way now. I almost can't think about what it would have been like if bombs would have fallen on your farm on a Sunday afternoon when all the relatives were there enjoying each other. What it means here is that even though we have peaceful Sunday afternoons here at La Granja on Sunday afternoons, the people over in El Salvador don't have hardly any of that. Many of them have had to leave their farms, and some of those who stay have to hide in holes and caves when they hear the planes coming with the bombs.

My friends back in school when I was a boy talked about soldiers and people who fought in wars as the greatest heroes anywhere. So did the television, my teachers, my coaches, the preacher, Sunday School teachers -- everybody. At times it seemed like everything and everybody around me was getting me ready to go and fight and be a hero in war.

If I had done that, if I had gone ahead and signed that piece of paper that might have made me a pilot in the Marine Corps, I guess all the relatives might have been proud of me. And I'm sure they'd feel that what I was doing was a good and Christian thing to be doing for my country.

But you know what? If I had gone ahead and done all that, I might well be one of the people in the planes who are now dropping bombs on the poor people in El Salvador and blowing up what little land they have, instead of being here with the people of Honduras, especially those that want to do a little better with the land they've got. If I had signed that piece of paper, I might never had met or been willing to listen to the people who could help me come home again, and I would probably feel that it was sometimes more important to blow up land than it is to help the land grow more food.

It's no fun to hear bombs falling on a Sunday afternoon but what I feel toward these who are dropping is not all anger or condemnation. They just got led off track, somewhere, just like I could have. It'll be hard for them to get headed toward home. I think it'll be even harder for them than for the poor people whose land they are bombing.

On a lot of peaceful Sundays here, we still hear those bombs falling. They sure haven't run out of bombs to drop.

I don't really know why you and Daddy never fought in a war, but I am glad you lived your life taking care of land rather than destroying it.

Love,
your grandson,
Randall

#4
August 1986
Dear Grandaddy,
Even though I usually went to the barn with you at milking time, and I remember how you could squirt the cow's milk directly from the tit into the cat's mouth, I never learned to milk very well. You'd let me try a few squeezes that didn't produce much, then you'd look up at the seven cows still left to milk. I'd sit on a spare milking stool and watch in awe as you held that metal bucket between your knees and milked with both hands until the bucket was full.

Cows cost too much money for all the poor people here in Honduras, but a few of them are starting to own goats. I only remember you having one goat. And I remember you teaching me how to let the goat eat shelled corn out of my hand when I could not have been more than 5 or 6. I remember that I was scared and excited about it all at the same time. I remember how good it felt to have a goat eat out of my hand.

I have learned to milk the goat here. I cannot do two hands at once yet, but I'm doing O.K. And our goats also will eat out of our hands. And any time they do, I think about you, and I think about how much more you must have loved your animals than you ever told us.

Love,
Randall

#5
August, 1986
Dear Grandaddy,
Last night before I went to sleep a firefly flew in over our bed again. I'm starting to wonder if it's the same one who comes every

night - just to give us a little light, a little sign of hope in a country that has had so much more than its share of darkness.

It does seem to me that we have to be patient in the darkness if we want to be there when the fireflies come.

Love,
Randall

#6
August, 1986
Dear Grandaddy,

I remember what it felt like when we used to kill hogs at your house around Thanksgiving. I don't remember anything about anybody worrying too much about how much it hurt the pigs to be killed, but I remember that the weather would be cool and people like Mansel Tomlinson and other neighbors would come. Grandmother would come out with all of her butcher knives and you would sharpen them on your sharpening stone until they sparkled.

The big pig carcasses would get hung up by the hind legs and you would all shave their hair off with the knives and hot water. The men would make jokes and laugh when it came time to cut the testicles off of the male pigs.

Then Grandmother would put salt all over the big hunks of meat, and hang it in the smokehouse on a piece of wire. And we'd eat good things like ham and bacon and pork chops all winter.

The people here don't have any smokehouses. But most of them do have a smoke room to protect their corn from bugs. Sometimes their smoke room is bigger than the rest of the house put together. One of our neighbor families here has two rooms - one is a bigger smoke room where they keep a fire going on all the time to send smoke up into the attic where all the corn is kept. The other is just a little corner room where they cook, eat, sleep on their one little bed, and hang the hammock at night where small kids sleep. It's also the room where folks stand and sit around when company comes to talk awhile.

I bet there are a lot of folks here who would like to have a smokehouse like you and Grandmother had in 1954. But they don't.

They mostly eat little flat pieces of cornbread called tortillas. We heard that nearly half of the whole country's food comes from corn. And that means every little house has to keep a fire going in the smoke room so the smoke will keep the bugs off of the corn in the loft.

They do kill pigs here sometimes, but not very often and the pigs aren't very big. Most folks seem to think that one or two days a month is about as often as the country people here have any meat to eat.

I did love Grandmother's cornbread, but I don't think I'd like eating just cornbread all the time.

Love,
Randall

#7
August, 1986
Dear Grandaddy,

They build fences here out of barbed wire, probably more of barbed wire than anything. But they also build them out of rocks. What I mean is they stack up rocks, a stack that can be as much as 3 feet across, until it's high enough to keep cattle in or keep most varmints out of a cornfield. They don't have to go far to get the rocks here where we live because all the land is so full of them. Here the rocks are so bad, they can't plow with just one mule like you did. It always takes two oxen to break soil so full of rocks.

They work hard, and they do it without having all that much to eat.

They have to carry rocks to make fences. When I first saw these rock fences, I thought they were mostly left from some other time before barbed wire got here, but now I've seen that at least a few folks still build fences out of rocks.

Love,
Randall

#8

Dear Grandaddy,

When I was young with you, there would be jokes about the juicy cow piles. With flies buzzing all around them. The jokes must have been about the same that most every generation and probably most cultures make about manure - something with a strong unpleasant stench, something that even the smallest children would recognize, often with a giggle. In all corners, there seemed to be a light acceptance that this was something --- well, something base.

Something base.

Something like a base.

Something to use as a base.

Something basic.

I must admit, grandaddy, that I remember the flies and the stench more than I remember the times when we would hitch the mules to the wagon, load a large pile of manure onto the wagon, and then take it down and spread it out on the fields, so the corn and the cotton would grow better.

Something base

Something basic.

The roads and trails of Honduras are lined with manure. People here accept it with the same lightness that you did in your time. It is something natural. It is something base. It is probably something basic.

I remember thinking sometime along a misguided way that that image of the smelly cowpile with the flies all around it was something bad, something to get away from, to escape. So we turn to suburbs and plastic-coated little short-term delights which probably made it harder for us to see the basics of things.

A grouping within the culture less-inclined to matters delicate might have said that we didn't have all our shit together. Perhaps they, and you, and the country folks of Honduras are closer to more truth than was realized - that to be close to the manure of life is to be close to the basics, the earthy goodness of it all, the smelly, revolting deadness which alone can give rise to new life, and make things grow again.

I've often thought that when they put me in the ground they won't wrap me in too many vaults and boxes and that what's left of this part of me will be accessible to the worms and other creatures that make some part of the earth more fertile, more life-giving.

From dust to dust.

From cowpile to cowpile.

From basics to basics.

From earth to earth.

### Wednesday, August 13, 1986

It's mid-morning here. I've been picking beans with Lucio and wrapping them in a string from some plant so they'll dry in the sun. While we were doing this there in the bean field, Lucio asked me if I heard something. I did, but thought it was only light thunder in the distance. Later I listened again. It was not thunder. Lucio was right. We now seem to have a new sound in our life that comes from the war in El Salvador, maybe 12 miles away. It is the sound of machine guns. And even as I write these words the sounds continue. The machine gun fire goes on in the distance. It is so far away in miles and in circumstance that it doesn't really make me afraid. But it does give me anguish - to know that something, or someone is really being destroyed today. How long can the land, the plants, the animals, the property, and the people endure this?

### Sunday, September 7, 1986

*8:15 pm.*

Today:

Up at 7 or so - late

Breakfast- eggs pancakes.

Dish washing

"Church" with Kathy only.

Read in Luke 6 about Jesus and the poor. "Blessed are you poor."

What do you say if you are called to preach the good news to a crowd of downtrodden poor folks in the campo?

Then we read "Love your enemies - bless them that curse you."

A hard time now with the Honduran team. Hurt runs very deep.

Except good progress in a talk with Elmer last Wed. in El Sitio.

## Monday, September 8, 1986
*6:00 a.m.*

The campesinos who drop in and sit on our front porch often remark "how tranquilo" (peaceful) it is here, sometimes even when the porch is in disarray and has not been straightened up for days. The interesting thing is that we so often feel La Granja as not so tranquil, inconvenient, and is constantly full of people who don't understand our need for privacy, and a source of daily hard work from which it is hard to find a respite. I understand La Granja's meaning, and growing importance for the people here in the zone both as symbol and as place of growth and vision. But the struggles we have compared with the good feelings many visitors seem to have leaves me wondering what kind of struggles are involved in keeping Trappist or Benedictine monasteries the havens of silence and tranquility that they always seem to be.

The struggle for us here is not easy, for many reasons. It does seem to be an important one. I think we will keep at it.

## Tuesday, September 9, 1986
*6:20 a.m.*

Obaf (the goat) - licking me on the face while I was untying his rope. Goats like to eat awhile and then wander. Being tied, to keep them out of the corn, they can't do that. I'll be so glad when we get a pasture built.

Being here - an effort - a struggle – yet it is an answer to an urge to touch life in the places where it is fragile, wonderful, and sensuously close to what the world is really like.

Andres and the "grabadora" (boom box/radio) - Miguel Angel wanting to buy my 98-cent pocket knife. Technology is here to stay.

The trail to La Florida: What is it like?

Enrique in the meeting yesterday - his almost aggressive style - I was sitting on the bench with him. The bench seemed to be almost constantly moving because of his type A energy.

As I write, I worry a little that it seems that so many of my reflections are about me, my needs, my/our experience, instead of getting into what life is really like for campesinos in western Honduras.

I don't seem to be one of those people who can just forget myself in responding to the needs of others. I am constantly aware of how much time I spend thinking about and giving time and energy to taking care of my own needs. Maybe this is not all good or all bad. Maybe it just is. Sometimes I think the images that others have of us here ("sacrificing, serving the poor, etc.) is a rather long way from the reality - especially the inward reality as I experience being here.

When Bruce and Gro (Kathy's brother, Bruce Williams and his wife Gro) were here, they described our house as being like someone's "rustic summer cabin." Oh what a blow - after hoping that we could impress family with how rustic and simple is our lifestyle, we get told that there is something hinting of the middle-class about our life here. They might feel differently after a few months here.

But the fact is that this is true, and that there's more integrity in accepting it than pretending otherwise. I need to just laugh and accept that what they observed at least has a lot of truth in it.

## Thursday, September 11, 1986
*2:00 p.m., La Granja*

> *2020 notes: The following is the only time I can remember while we were at La Granja that we had a visit by anyone from the Honduran military, (soldiers did come on one other occasion while we were away which I will describe later) but one felt their presence all around. Having been at La Granja about nine months by this time, we had learned to keep our calm with soldiers. The military also served as ad hoc police officers some of the time. While our own government has plenty of ways to maintain surveillance over us I still marvel at the ominous feelings that arise when I think of armed soldiers at the door.*

Honduran soldiers came to our house today. I counted 27 of them. The early months of car searches and requests for documents were a bit difficult for me, but with this one I seemed to maintain a time-tested sense of acceptance and even calm.

To get from the road to our front porch one has to walk about 100 yards, after crossing the creek by stepping on rocks.

They were at our porch before I noticed them. Friendly, pleasant, no hard words at all. *"Are you the owner here?" "No,"* I explained. *"I am a volunteer working here."*

*"May I see your documents please?"*

Sure you may see my documents, I thought.

The exchanges were pleasant. Our documents were in order. They took their leave courteously, apologizing for bothering us. In the normal flow life in western Honduras, it was not such a big deal.

But then, when 27 soldiers, each carrying a submachine gun, arrive at the front door unannounced, and ask for documents – it is a bit strange to realize how unexpected this was, and how normal it felt for our life here.

## Monday, September 15, 1986

Independence Day - Central America

Parades speeches, flags, floats being blessed.

Children marching - children who learned their lines well.

The celebrations were not just sentimental patriotism. Many times the facts of ongoing dependence were mentioned. But at no point did I hear anyone even hint at criticizing the U.S. massive militarization of Honduras.

Nothing much comes to my mind to write. I've been sick with a cold. I got over it just as the latest edition of diarrhea hit.

I was ready to leave La Granja for a few days. The place was kind of getting to me. Now I'm glad to be back, the moon is full, the porch is swept - all is well. I feel peaceful - ready to get back to work.

How can I write anything that would be that helpful to anyone? Are there not hundreds of people with my convictions who understand Central America better than I? Would I not serve God better by forgetting about this need to write, and spending more time with the people all around us? Does this not stand to put me distant from the people with whom I work, the campesinos?

*2020 notes: Still more comments about my hopes to write a book. It is embarrassing to see how much this was so foremost in my mind during that time. The truth is there were and are plenty of good books on Honduras. Another truth is that the hard life at La Granja just did not leave any spare energy to take on such a project there. Now I feel fortunate just to see that I got this much written in my journal. My ambitions to publish something from Honduras now appear as just one more unconscious aspect of my colonial psyche. A professor in Central America doing research for his own writing for publication back home once told me about a local person saying to him, "you researchers come down here and 'study us', ask us questions, and then you go back and write your articles and your books. You get recognition and money for your effort, but we get nothing out of it.*

I have moments when I think the most faithful thing I could do in response to Central America would be to support a number of the more honorable leftist guerrilla movements here. In the final analysis, I have been touched deeply enough by some committed pacifists to know that that's not where I belong, but I also recognize that any resting in the middle often feels like a kind of sell-out to the ugly forces that perpetrate violence with little or concern for the meaningful development of the people. With violent leftists, one can certainly see the dangers of ideology of the left and dictatorship of the left. It would have its own ugliness to be sure. Yet living in a real world, where ugliness is here to stay, it sometimes seems to me that if the choice for the present is only between violent forces, then perhaps we need to be at least free and open enough to look at the violent ones who demonstrate movement toward a vision of better days for the poorest people.

I think I must struggle in the direction of nonviolence and pacifism. Who knows what in the final analysis is the greater effect of one's witness?

*Doña Alcaria and Don Esteben*

Don Esteban, our closest neighbor, died this morning at 9:30. We did not know him well. He was an older campesino who seems to have been sick for a long time. Many seem to be grateful that his suffering has ended.

235

The custom at the time of death rural Honduras is for family and friends to come and sit up all night with the body. We arrived at their house with a flashlight and a Coleman lantern to lend to them at about 9 p.m. Usually campesinos have been asleep at least two hours by 9.

The night sky has begun clear almost like daylight with a full moon. Still we had to feel our way along the path to the simple adobe house virtually hidden in the trees.

The house was elbow to elbow with people. We made our way in, exchanged greetings with people we knew, and then went into the room with the simple wooden box and a body completely covered in white cloth. Candles burn on all sides of Don Esteban. And dozens more candles brought by friends wait on a ready table. He will have no problem being surrounded by warmth and light until the light of morning signals the time to hoist the box onto shoulders for the two-mile mile walk to the cemetery. Honduran law says a body must be buried within twenty-four hours after a death.

The atmosphere feels gentle. – Conversation, food - a table spread in the moonlight. Tamales and coffee are served. Campesino men sit with their ever-present hats on to enjoy the food.

Women are hard at work tending food, and counting plates.

A light rain softens the nights as the people keeping watch over the body begin to sing simple choruses. Clouds blur the moonlight. Those who were sitting outside edge toward the covered porch area. The house is more full than ever. No one is hurried or pressured. There are sad faces, but no one is overwhelmed by the death. The people know the meaning of presence. Few will go home before dawn.

The campesinos of Honduras need no help in learning what it means to care when someone dies.

### Tuesday, September 23, 1986

Went back last night to the house of Doña Alcaria whose husband Don Esteban died a week ago.

The custom here is for friends arrive every night for nine days after the death So friends have gathered there each of these nine days.

Doña Alcaria was curled up in her bed asleep as we talked on and on in the shadows of fire provided by pine resin sticks.

I felt at peace there. Relaxed, very sleepy - but in a sense more with the people here than I have at any time in the past. It was a good gift.

There were tensions in the meeting of our entire CCD San Marcos team yesterday. I'm sure people felt the tension in my voice. It was difficult to talk about our needs for some privacy when the house at La Granja is in fact a public place. Hondurans do seem to laugh a lot when I would normally feel a sense of sadness, even tragedy.

We'll have to see how this one keeps unfolding. Enrique, our team supervisor did decide that we should meet for a longer time this Friday to have time to work through some tensions that people have been feeling for some time now.

*2020 notes: Apparently, I did not write anything in my journal after the "come to Jesus" meeting we had on Friday to try to resolve conflicts among us many were feeling, but I do remember it. Our supervisor, Enrique, did a good job of taking the leadership that was needed. Some hurts and unhappy feeling were gotten out on the table. We did not solve everything of course, but I do remember it as a step in the right direction.*

Last night a group of Mennonites dropped in for a few minutes just to see La Granja and how we work here. We had a good visit. I have much appreciation for the work of Mennonites here and elsewhere.

## Wednesday, October 8, 1986
*3:00 a.m., La Granja*

It's pushing 3 a.m. I sit in the pure silence of the wee hours after a midnight incident with our giant donkey, Solomon. Paloma (our farm dog) started barking at about 12:30. I got up to find the burro doing wind sprints across an open stretch down in the cornfield. He had gotten loose from being tied in the stable and decided to go for a little moonlight exercise. And I am quite aware that if he decides that I won't catch him to put him back to bed, then so it will be. Or even if I do manage to get a hand on his rope and he decides we'll go somewhere other than the stable, then that's where we'll go. His six

237

hundred pounds of good Kentucky mule muscle is more than my skinny body can overcome.

My toes feel around on the gritty cement floor for my shoes while one hand reaches for a flashlight. I leave across the front porch, and amble sleepily down the little hill to the field. There a very liberated jackass is living it up, doing wind sprints across the field, kicking his hind legs in the air, and making sustained snorting noises through what must be dozens of out-of-tune organ pipes somewhere down in his lungs. My first thought is that I have no hope of catching him. Paloma barks and chases ever faithfully, but she too is without the physical powers or speed needed to arrest this ecstatic beast of the night. I watch the spectacle continue with a kind of entranced resignation.

But after a few more wind sprints, the donkey comes to a calm stop, with that gentle demeanor that I like best in him. I walk slowly toward him and he allows me to take hold of his rope without a struggle. We walk slowly back to the stable where I retie him. He goes back to sleep like a good donkey, and I am back here in the bedroom now with urges to write about it all.

Because of the present limitations of our facilities the donkey has to live most of his life being tied. He is a beautiful animal, with those miraculous rippling - large muscles that could not be content to stand still and tied all the time. In time we will have a pasture where he can run free all day.

Because of the "limitations of the facilities" here in this part of Honduras, most of the Hondurans we know live most of their lives standing still and tied - and one feels that the present conditions give them less chance than a spirited donkey of realizing that self-expression which alone can give a certain quality of peace.

Henri Nouwen has spoken well of the need to "create loving spaces within which growth can happen." I am tempted to say we need more open spaces in the cornfield, but that metaphor goes against the need for more cornfields, better use of space to grow crops.

Finding those open spaces does not come easy for the people of Honduras. There are times when the only choice is to break free from the rope, and run hard toward whatever open space is available at the moment.

Our hens are about at the end of their two-year laying cycle. Egg production gets lower every week, and we are noticing that some of the eggs have thinner shells lately than the sturdier eggs in earlier months of higher production. Soon it will be time to slaughter them and allow these chickens to become food rather than sources of eggs.

The papers are full of news this week of changes within the Honduran armed forces, the real power in this egg of a nation with a military yoke and a thin democratic shell-at least as it relates to government.

It seems that a number of colonels are rather continuously engaged in some degree of power struggles, the majority of the details of which are not likely to be known very well by the public. The Commander of the Armed Forces, Gen. Regalado Hernandez holds the most powerful position in the country. He rather suddenly has decided that two of the higher-up colonels would serve Honduras better on a foreign assignment. So one was sent to Chile, apparently on about a week's notice. His house was guarded during that week.

The President of the country, allegedly the Commander-in-Chief of the armed forces and the country's democratic leader, found out about the charges only after the decisions had been made.

## Wednesday, October 15, 1986
*San Pedro Sula*

I think the truth is that the splendor of grace is just too much for me. Mostly, I know only how to do a little of my duty. This is not bad, and grace is splendid enough that not even the duty-bound escape the snare of its magnificence.

I think that if I were ever to allow grace to have me, I would be a fool of great power and impact. If I could renounce that which clings so tightly to the image, the duty; instead of the free-falling passion, and the discipline that sends it home, then the universe would receive from me all that it deserves to receive.

Meanwhile, we do our duty, probably without seeing many of the grace filled promises being placed into our care.

And yet may duty too know its own grace-filled moments.

*2020 notes: While I had professed "Grace" as primary in my faith for a long time before we went to Honduras, I acted as if Christianity was about "works" much more of the time then. That struggle always seems to be present in some form. This makes me relieved to see a moment when I remembered how primary Grace is in any way of wisdom/spirituality. I hope that at least a little Grace was evident in my life then some of the time. But the physical challenges of the time at La Granja, my own needs to "accomplish something" during our time there and lack of people who knew how to remind me of the primacy of Grace kept me living mostly in a "works righteousness" way of life. I do love the sentence: "if I were to allow grace to have me, I would be a fool of great power and impact." I have made deep contact a number of times over the years with the importance of the Holy Fool as one aspect of my life, especially in having been given a clown character that I lived inside of from time to time. I only remember one time when that clown showed up in Honduras. It was a very happy day. But Grace abides, always and everywhere, whether or not I am awake to it.*

### Friday, October 17, 1986
*10:00 a.m., La Granja*

"Summer" begins to peek above the horizon here. We now may go days without rain. Soon it will be weeks without rain.

Life will slow some in some ways. I will hope for more time to be still.

Life here is sometimes overwhelming with meaning. That means it hurts a lot. Tears do not come easily here for me.

I have not yet seen a campesino cry. There is for me both sadness and promise in the valiant acceptance of the people here of the hard life that is theirs. While I can feel myself rage at the injustices that keep so many of them from being all they could be, they simply live from day to day. One could call it resignation, or a too-submissive way of living, and I think there would be some truth in this.

But there is some colonialism in this view on my part. There is such dignity and beauty in the lives of the campesinos here. I do not see it often enough.

*2020 notes: Colonialism*

*In the years preceding and into the 2020s many White people in the United States have been coming to terms with widespread and unconscious participation in racism, especially in its systemic forms which have plagued our nation since Europeans first began to arrive in the Western Hemisphere. I believe the same can be said for colonialism, in which the "settlers" in the "new world" felt that they had a right to any land or other resources that they came upon. President James Monroe made this more explicitly in the 1820s with what came to be known as the Monroe Doctrine in which he declared that there would be no further colonization in the Western Hemisphere by European countries, Great Britain being the one exception. In other times, U.S. leaders would refer to Latin American countries as "our back yard."*

*I do not remember any frequent use of the word 'colonialism' during our time in Central America in the 1980s. But looking back now, its reality was present in a number of ways. It has been disturbing to see clear evidence of its unconscious presence in me in the writings from this journal.*

*It seems that national policies and assumptions often take form in very personal behavior.*

*One aspect of it seems to be an unconscious sense that as the U.S. citizen I am the "Give ER" and Hondurans are the "Give-EEs." In working with people who had little access to education, many of them unable to even read, it was very easy for both sides in any interaction to slip in modes of colonialism. There were times when I felt I could see it in a certain submissiveness by some rural Honduras in my interactions with them. My being white, male and taller than average certainly added to the reality.*

*The primary area of experience and expertise that poor campesinos (rural people) had that I will never have is the capacity to simply survive and raise a family in a situation of severe poverty. Since we were there as part of an agency to assist them in dealing with poverty and improving their lives, it was easy to fall into a "helper" mentality. I knew the politically correct language of people in our wider network about standing beside the poor and learning from them. But it was much more difficult to really practice this.*

*I do remember one experience when this reality did become utterly clear in a rare moment when I was left to be the "teacher for the day" with a group of campesino men. Our Honduran co-workers all had to be doing things in other places so I had been asked to serve as a "substitute teacher" for the day. I was with a group of about eight farmers. The Christian Commission for Development (CCD) had carefully prepared "charlas" or brief talks on various topics. They were neatly arranged on outer board, often with illustrations to make the words very clear and communicate with any who were unable to read. So as the substitute teacher for the day all I had to do was read the charla to the men. this seemed easy enough. I proceeded with a lot of confidence.*

*I don't remember exactly how it happened but early in my simple presentation there began to be a murmur with lots of smiling faces among the men. Here I was an urban gringo who had never raised a crop of corn serving as a teacher to men who had been raising corn for years. In this case, we all somehow "got it" about how ridiculous this was. It was a rare moment when my own colonialism was fully exposed. We were able to talk about it and have a good laugh about it. Then I continued reading my "lesson for the day" about which I knew almost nothing from direct experience.*

*In the case of Honduras with parallel realities in many other Latin American countries, colonialism on an international scale was much more serious. The clearest example had to do with land. The most fertile land in the country was located in the north coast area. With a predominantly rural population constantly short of food, it obviously made sense that the country's best land would be used to grow food for Hondurans. But this has not been the reality since the late 1800s when Honduras became the original "Banana Republic" and the best land was taken over by U.S. companies to grow fruit as a cash crop for export to the U.S. and Europe.*

*The Monroe Doctrine evolved over the decades and centuries, especially as the United States became a world power with the military to enforce its declarations, whether they were just or not. It*

242

*reached new level of imperialism in 1904 when President Theodore Roosevelt added the Roosevelt Corollary to the Monroe Doctrine which declared that "in cases of flagrant and chronic wrongdoing by a Latin American country, the United States will intervene in the country's internal affairs." It was this extreme version of colonialism that was at issue in U.S. policies toward Central America in the 1980s.*

*There is a lot of unconscious colonialism showing up in my attitude at many places in this journal. I am tempted to edit out anything that reveals parts of me I would rather not have others see. But it seems more honest to leave it in. Here I seem to be expressing some judgment because campesinos living on the edge of survival are not behaving according to what U.S. culture might consider emotionally healthy. I have never lived anywhere close to the edge of survival known by most Hondurans. I will never understand what that is like. As I write this in 2020 Hondurans by the thousand are trying to migrate north to the country that has had most to do with their long-term misery, my country, the United States. Survival for Hondurans today seems much more desperate than even what we saw up close in the 1980s. Two of the factors now are climate change, lack of rain and increased heat has made it impossible for campesinos to grow enough corn and beans to survive, and violence perpetrated by gangs, some of whom learned their ways of terrorism in the United States. The U.S. still bears much responsibility for the suffering of Hondurans.*

## Sunday, October 19, 1986
*Language Challenges Continue*

Went into a restaurant today to have a sandwich, and did not see as I entered a 17-year-old acquaintance who has been very friendly to us here. He saw me and greeted me with what was apparently a much-used greeting here. However, I don't think there was one word in his greeting that I learned during all those hours in Spanish class. I asked him to say it again, which he did graciously, but with that slightly disheartening sense that a greeting that he hoped would be cordial and complete never quite got to me.

He did say it again, but I still did not understand. I pretended I did, ad-libbed some greeting in return and then went on to my table to sit alone.

Language is such a treasure - and it is such an absence when the words are just not there for the communication that begs to happen.

Village La Majada - good leaders in the villages are hard to come by in the campo - excellent leaders even rarer. Gentle and full of service, Braulio is one of our best leaders. And yet he speaks of plans to move California where he has a brother. And how can we judge him for wanting a better life for himself and his family. But if he moves it will be a large loss for the village of La Majada, for Honduras in general and for us.

## Saturday, October 25, 1986

*Noon in San Pedro Sula, Noon (San Pedro Sula is an eight-hour drive from La Granja)*

Visit today with local Evangelical and Reformed Church people, activists in many ways. The "E and R Church" of Honduras is a "partner" of our United Church of Christ denomination the in the U.S. We don't see them often and our work does not directly intersect with them. But they had disturbing news of new and unpublicized political developments in Honduras.

For a few years now, Honduran campesinos have been being paid to fight the Sandinistas. Apparently, the pattern is: they work in the daytime like normal campesinos, then go off to fight at night so most do not notice. The payment received is reported to be around $10.00 per night.

In the same operation, recruiting is being done in Santa Barbara (one of Honduras' "departments" or states) among unemployed campesinos - offering them payment to go to the Nicaragua border area to fight.

Last February a new battalion of special forces was organized, dressed in plain clothes, who are reportedly killing people in the night - union leaders, others suspected of being communists.

Another scenario, talked about was a comparison of Honduras to Cambodia back when Cambodia was neutral in the Vietnam War. When Cambodia became a staging area for the U.S., all sorts of communist infiltration began to happen in Cambodia, until finally the U.S. began bombing Cambodia.

Thus, if the war here increases, and people in Nicaragua begin to flow into Honduras, it could well be that the U.S. will begin to fight the Sandinistas in Honduras, and the next wave of refugees for the U.S. will be Hondurans. A sad scenario, but possible.

## October 1986

I remember the Assembly of God pastor in San Marcos in whose home I visited. The wall between his living room and the bedroom was only a sheet. His unmarried teenage daughter was in the next room with her 18-month-old daughter. He was busy doing something while I sat there.

The little girl began to call out to him.

"Paapeeeta" (Papita is Spanish for Grandpa)

He answered by singing her name right back at her:

"Aneeetaaa."

"Paapeeeta"

"Aneeetaaa"

"Paapeeeta"

It was so beautiful.

## October 31, 1986

*8:00 a.m., La Granja*

The pen moves openly, easily this morning. I want to think that this writing is akin to praying if not praying itself. If the Love Greater is helping me to see me, and if this writing is the medium, then prayer it is. When I say I want it to be prayer, I mean that I want to touch into the depths of love that are certainly available to us.

It was just last Sunday that I was weeping, and Kathy was comforting me because Irv had died. Dr. Irving Goldberg was a respected Seattle psychologist who was very helpful to me during four years of seeing him weekly. He did so much for me. It was interesting that with the grieving that came quickly, there was also a sense of strength. Irv left parts of himself with me which helped me to realize strengthened parts of me, or maybe even parts that did not exist before my time with him. Those years - January 1981 until June

245

1985, were not spectacular - they were years of steady, day to day, week to week, growing. I finished them wondering sometimes if I might have grown just as much without all the therapy and the money. I have a hunch that this was due to the lack of spectacle in the process rather than to the lack of growth. Many wounds remain, but I am a person now who can be generally at ease in the great majority of relational situations into which I enter.

It is a bit odd, that I think of Irv by talking about the new strengths that I have. He would like it this way - although his compassion, his capacity to remain tenaciously committed to very hurting people, and his great gift of a mind that lived in his heart but in doing so never lost its sharp insight, its wisdom in knowing when objectivity and diagnosis should preclude the drifts of feeling of any one moment.

I think Irv was a quiet genius. Perhaps he knew this but simply never needed to say so.

It's funny - I just stopped to sit here in silence for a few minutes. I must admit that most of this sitting, although it is very important to me, leaves me with thoughts more negative than positive, with a head achy from conflicts unresolved. Perhaps there is some kind of catharsis in dealing with life's difficulties in such a manner in silence. I do believe this. I trust it. I need the silence. Yet I seldom experience the breakthrough of the catharsis directly. Nor does this breakthrough happen very often or very directly.

*2020 notes: In the early 1990s I would learn a practice of quiet prayer called Centering Prayer. The person best known as a teacher and spiritual guide in the Spiritual Prayer movement, Father Thomas Keating, speaks of "the unloading of the unconscious" that can happen in the practice of quiet prayer. By this he meant that, while we may hope for a sense of peace in the practice, often its "fruits" may be a surfacing of unpleasant feelings and memories, which is a way that Grace offers us some healing and release of old wounds and burdens. When this happens, it will not feel good. It will not take the form of the inner peace that we hope for in a quiet prayer practice. But it is a form of healing. I suspect and hope that this is what was happening here.t*

## November 1, 1986
*La Granja*

Kathy fed soy beans to the rabbits today. They didn't eat them but did eat the plastic lid she put them in.

## November 3, 1986
*Monday, 1:30 p.m.*

The refrigerator has been here about 3 weeks now. Our supervisors noted that we have been having a large increase in the number of groups come here for week-long seminars ("cursos" or courses). So the need has increased to begin to go and buy food and store more of it here. Since there is no electricity, this one is gas-powered. And of course, we get the benefits also. It sits in "our" kitchen. We must be the only house within ten miles in any direction that has a refrigerator.

## Wednesday, November 3, 1986
*3:00 p.m., La Granja*

Luke 8 - Women with Jesus.
"Seven demons driven out"
Feel need today to accept that grace that has already driven many demons out of my life.
A brief general conscious examen of my life into Jesus has loved me into many new freedoms and horizons.
And I made it (with him) to Honduras. Such a gift.
Day to build the fence - or help a little which is all I will do - at most.
Don't seem to feel much guilt about not doing more manual labor here, even though there is plenty to do. Seems not the center of why I am here.
Recalling the Oct. 8, 1986 dream about the open, juicy sores I have on their way to healing, but open and juicy.

## Thursday, November 6, 1986
Walked today with a bright young worker with the Honduran Ministry of Health. His program is a "sub-project" of the Ministry

which includes building latrines, strengthening water access, and in other ways providing cleaner water and better sanitation. I was pleased to hear that the program has been funded by AID. I was not pleased to hear that in this next year the program may be cut.

This is the same week in which we are hearing the news that the U.S. will offer to Honduras somewhere between 18 and 24 F-5 fighter planes. Another story suggested that 12 planes would be purchased at a total cost of $100 million. The juxtaposition tells its own clear story of U.S. priorities in Honduras.

*2020 note: Once during our time at La Granja, a fighter plane from the Honduran Air Force crashed somewhere within ten miles or so from where we were. It was big news, of course, and many people in the area found ways to go look at the crash site.*

## Sunday, November 9, 1986
*La Granja*

Peaceful Sunday afternoon. Sitting quietly with Kathy, we hear what is certainly submachine gun fire, or the firing of some larger weapon, in the El Salvador distance.

Later in the afternoon I walked up the hill with two boys visiting us. We could see an airplane in the distance circling a specific spot about 10 miles from us over the Chalatenango province of El Salvador, an area where the civil war there has been heaviest. It was flying in continuous circles. With each circle, when it reached a certain point we would hear the machine-gun fire again. It seemed obvious that some specific place was being fired at over and over and over. As we watched we saw that it flew to a second location, perhaps ten miles from the first and began a new circle and a new round of shooting at some group or place below.

The sound of gunfire is a familiar one in this area. Seeing an airplane doing the shooting is unusual. But it was not immediately alarming in the sense that the war is still securely in El Salvador only, at least 12 miles away.

It was surreal to sit on a quiet and peaceful Sunday afternoon, feeling safe and secure, and hear a war going on and people getting shot at and probably killed as we watched and listened.

## Sunday, November 30, 1986
*9:00 p.m., La Granja*

Reading "Managing Your Private World" by Gordon McDonald. Finding some of the theology alien to me, but I keep staying with it, interested -- I have about finished the thing in not much time. I think it's the discipline he speaks of that touches me. I think I know many good things would have been possible for me if I had just been able to clear out the space.

But good things still are possible. I am always starting from where I am now. There are yet rich things to create.

I think discipline for me for so many years meant a drivenness. I have been liberated from much of that drivenness I think. I seem to be a freer man in recent years, able, competent, yet not so inclined to wear myself out.

Perhaps I can in small but effective ways, recapture the parts of those driven days that were better steeped in intentionality, and especially in creativity.

There are many basic themes that MacDonald does not face - justice, redemptive suffering. He seems to make an idol out of controlling his schedule - not allowing it to be altered. If Bonhoeffer had done this, if he had hid in his office and written twelve volumes of theology, we would have more books on the stuff - but we would not have the powerful, faithful witness out of that era that we'd still need.

Yet Bonhoeffer spoke of discipline as the first stop on the way to freedom "control of sense and self" he called it.

It is time for me to think about and deal with discipline in my life.

I think it is a matter of time - of what are the elements that help me to be more of the free and creative person that I want to be - and then claiming the time.

There are two clear non-negotiables

- one is an hour of silence and prayer every day. I won't accomplish it every day, but this is a freeing gift that is now clearly a fundamental in my life.

- the other is a regular exercise - probably yoga stretches and jogging at least 3 times per week - sometimes more.

There are some other ways I can be kinder to myself by being firmer with myself. - one is to get up when I wake up - get into a posture in which I can make better use of precious morning time.

In spite of my struggle not to come off too pious, it still turns out that I'm inclined much of the time more to talk about spirituality than to pray. I had the thought today that maybe until I'm 50, I need to talk as little about praying as possible and spend as much time as possible trying to deepen my prayer life -- do it more, talk about it less -- then when I'm 50, I might be qualified to begin to say a few things.

I'm 38 - crowding 40. I've had 9 good years as a minister. I think it's possible that I could have 30 more, up until around age 70, if I don't dry up early and stop the juices from flowing. I think the best years are yet to come. I want to deepen the silence in order to know better where they will take me.

This sitting down to write before going to bed is a restoration of discipline for me. It is a certain assurance, proof that I can restore, regain some things that were connected to destructive things (i.e. drivenness) but which were good and deserve restoration.

I feel just a little teary-eyed now writing this - like something good, an old friend is headed toward me.

### Monday, December 1, 1986
*7 a.m., La Granja, Advent*

Awoke at 5:30. Was here in the "casita" soon after 6 for prayer. I pray that that's what it was.

*"Te alabo, Padre, Señor del cielo y de la tierra, porque has mostrado a los sencillos las cosas que escondiste de los sabios y entendidos."* San Lucas 10:21 (I thank you, Father, Lord of heaven and earth, because you have hidden these things from the wise and intelligent and have revealed them to infants. Luke 10:21).

### Tuesday, December 2, 1986
*4:15 p.m., La Granja*

*"Porque nuestro Dios, en su gran misericordia, nos trae de lo alto el sol de un nuevo día, para dar luz a los que viven en las más*

*profunda oscuridad, para dirigir nuestros pasos por el camino de la paz.*" San Lucas 1:78-79

(By the tender mercy of our God, the dawn from on high will break upon us, to give light to those who sit in darkness and in the shadow of death, to guide our feet into the way of peace. Luke 1:78-79)

## Saturday, December 6, 1986
*4:00 p.m., La Granja*

Today I walked to Cololaca to arrange some help for Braulio who is in bad shape with his eye. I see now that I could have been a little more patient, but I think it was best that I did go just to get things moving on his behalf.

## Thursday, December 11, 1986
*4:15 a.m., La Granja*

Woke up to pee, then decided I wanted one of chocolate chip cookies that had been sent to us. I ate three. Was it the chocolate that inspired me to get up and write a little?

I feel just wonderful in this moment - Not too tired, although I'm sure my body needs more sleep. I feel happy to be here, In Honduras, in life.

A truck passes on our road which is about 100 yards from the house. Looks like it could be a load of corn headed to market .

Gregorio Henriguez is one of our neighbors that we see often. We had enjoyed his harmonica music and asked him to come a play while Kathy's parents, Walt and Marie Williams are here visiting. Last night he came as he had promised. Gregorio never went to school even one day. His father bought him his first harmonica when he was a boy. He has taught himself to play all the tunes that he knows. I think we were touched and delighted by it. After he had played and we had visited for awhile, we hoped that he would take the hint that would come more naturally in U.S. social customs that it was time for him to go home so we could have a family dinner together. But for campesinos there is no such custom nor knowledge. We probably also felt some embarrassment that we were about to have a meal, and ordinary one for us: chicken, rice and radish leaves from the garden, food that he did not have much access to. We always live with some embarrassment at the food we eat compared to the campesinos around us. This night the contrast was even more accentuated.

The music was simple, joyful, lively. It was good music, moving music when I think of the springs of joy from whence it came, the heart of a very poor campesino who has never had a chance to go to school even one day, much less have a music lesson.

We finally decided we'd just ask him to stay for supper - I think at least partly as our only escape hatch from having to stay up too late or put off dinner any longer.

We had recorded his music on our little cassette recorder, so as we sat down at the table we had the sounds of Gregorio's harmonica as dinner music.

So we were five, four from the colossus to the north, and a gentle campesino with a soul saturated by God's best music.

The food was not all that extraordinary, chicken, rice, a salad of radish leaves from the garden, water to drink, tortillas bought earlier from Gregorio's wife Antonia, fresh papaya for dessert.

The kerosene lamp gave us light and its now familiar and steady burning sound. Conversation was simple. Faces in the shadows touches something good.

Sacrament - God's heart leaving in our direction, and we would have missed it if we had not been impatient, and hungry. When he finally did go home I was glad that he kept hanging around until we finally invited him to stay for supper and wondered why we hesitated at all to invite him. After the meal I wrote the following poem about the evening:

The poor and not the poor
I stood sideways
waiting
To go either way
When a poor man
Moved in on my left flank,
Smiling,
Loving

And I wanted to run.
If this poor man should find me,
If I should be found,
What then would I do?
Would I know what to do with myself if his foundness
Were to find me?
Could I make it in a world where suffering is simply part of the
Joy that is,
Where resting with the simple would turn out to be too much for
me
So magnificent that I could not stand it?
I can now see the poor man in the
distance.
His face has welcome, but he is not calling me;
He is only living.
If I too, were only to live,
And do it well,
Would I do it best if he were my teacher?

## Sunday, December 14, 1986
*6:30 a.m., Roatan, Bay Islands, Honduras*

*2020 comments: After their visit with us at La Granja, Walt and Marie treated us to a few days at a well-known scuba diving resort hotel on the Honduran Island of Roatan, a short plane ride from the mainland. Roatan is a popular tourist destination, especially for scuba divers and snorkelers. It was such a welcome experience, warm sunshine and aqua-blue, warm Caribbean water. It was luxury all around.*

*I have never been a strong swimmer, and I had never been snorkeling before, so going out to snorkel in water that was thirty feet deep was a bit terrifying for me, but I gave it a try. I was embarrassed after a while when I got shook and had to find a place where my feet could touch the bottom. We were not far from shore here and Walt found a rock that I could stand on. I was still embarrassed but relieved.*

*I did fall in love with snorkeling in water that was only 10-12 feet deep, not far from sandy-bottoms only 4 feet down where I could easily touch the bottom. I had never experienced anything like swimming with spectacularly colored tropical fish only a few feet below me and seemingly undisturbed by my presence. They seemed exceedingly generous in sharing their ocean with us. It was among the most beautiful things I had ever experienced. I remember that as I flipped my frog feet along I just kept saying to myself, or to God or to Something, "Thank you! Thank you! Thank you!" I don't think I will ever forget it.*

*Our room was on a tiny island about 50 yards from the shore that we reached by a small motorboat, always available to us with a man to pilot us in either direction. It was unlike anything I had ever experienced before. We would return to Roatan two more times. It remains one of my favorite places of all the places I have been able to visit in my lifetime. I was glad that our son Andrew was also able to visit Roatan in 2006 while he was a high school exchange student in Panama.*

*I also enjoyed some good reading time on Roatan.*

*"The seventy returned with joy, saying "Lord, even the demons are subject to us in your name!" And he said to them, "I saw Satan fall like lightning from heaven. Behold I have given you authority to tread upon serpents and scorpions, and over all the power of the enemy; and nothing shall hurt you. Nevertheless, do not rejoice in this that the spirits are subject to you; but rejoice that your names are written in heaven." -- Luke 10:17-20*

Today this passage seems to me to say: "I have given you a means to see the world, to love the world, with new insight, and I have given you powers to participate in the world's reconciliation with itself. You may find yourself in the presence of conflicts that seem beyond your power to solve. You have my power in addressing those situations. But don't take it too seriously. Let your yes be yes and your no be no. Let your sacrifice and your actions be many, and your words be fewer.

"Rejoice not that you have things all figured out, because you don't. Your humanness, (your "frailties) are very much intact. You will be reminded of this when you try to live out of your ego instead of out of my Spirit.

Don't put yourself in some high place as if you are superior to others simply because I have touched you in a unique way. For when you do, you are likely to come off like a fool.

Rather rejoice, and rest in the peace that you live out of the power of grace, and not out of the need to know all and control all."

## Monday, December 15, 1986
*7:00 a.m., Roatan, Bay Islands, Honduras*

Conscious Examen, Grace during our days here:
Where has God been present?
- all over the place in being easy with myself.
- in enjoying good family time with Walt and Marie.
- moments of playfulness with Kathy.
- magnificence of the snorkeling.
- kindness in the faces of Black people here.
- Rev Cleveland Tennyson in his sermon so full of love yesterday at the African-Honduran Church we attended.
- the ocean, the ocean, the ocean.
- Walt's wonderful authentic and natural inclination to connect with people wherever they are.

## Wednesday, December 17, 1986
*Roatan, Bay Islands*

I don't think doing God's will necessarily means living by majority rule even though I believe in democracy. I don't even think reaching a consensus necessarily means that a group or community has heard the word of God, because there have been so many times when the consensus was clearly not the way of God's love and justice.

I simply believe God's will is God's will, and that we do have access to it as a community struggling to discern. It does not mean that we will always discern correctly. But I do believe we have access to knowing that will, and that if we earnestly try to know it, we have good opportunities to do it.

Thus it is not just in the majority vote or the move to consensus that God's will is to be found. It is in the genuine search for God's presence specific situations touched by our common life.

*Sunset on the island of Roatan*

### Thursday, December 18, 1986
*9:00 a.m., Roatan, Bay Islands, Honduras*

Gentle water splashes onto jagged rows of coral. Slight breeze on my face. Blue as far as I can see. Coconut palms bowed in reverence.

Yesterday, Wednesday writing most all day - at least 7 hours -

It interests me that at this $85 per day resort I am enjoying it. The scenery is spectacular. Good food. I have learned to snorkel. Good, good relaxed days for Kathy and me.

But there is something not quite all-together connected about being here. I think it may be that I feel a little embarrassed at the juxtaposition of working beside someone like Alvaro and then coming to a place in his own country which he has no access to.

It is not a heavy trip I want to do on myself. It is just that I feel here the way in which the world's economy scene leaves out a lot of hard-working, astute, enterprising people from enjoying its first-fruits.

There was a time when I might have been critical of myself for feeling uneasy in a place so full of beauty and comfort. Now I think I appreciate myself for this. I think I'd rather be in an authentic friendship with someone like Alvaro than be too determined not to feel uneasy in the midst of luxuries that are out of the reach of so many.

There are moments when I do wonder why I remain in this world of so much affluence.

Life is being very good to me. God is very good to me in a thousand ways. I want to be able to give good things back to God.

## Friday, December 19, 1986
*San Pedro Sula*

San Pedro Sula, City of heat. People on the sidewalks, full and narrow. Buses speed past as if there were not people walking the streets. Beggar on the curb kneeling. He can only walk on his knees. Big pieces of old inner tube cover his knees. The main square is full of crafts, made by Honduras hands. Handmade dresses and shirts. Exquisite wood carvings of mahogany wood, now becoming rare in Honduras. Marimba band with sweat dripping off the noses of the musicians in the Sunday heat.

The cathedral is now gleaming white the upper reaches. A new paint job has spoken a needed 'I love you' on behalf of a supporting city.

A mother barefoot, aggressive-looking in her 30s with 3 children begs in front of the hotel where all the rich foreigners stay.

Factory-lined boulevards - the country's one show of industrial strength – a deceiving one for the strength is minor and does not touch many.

Paintings for sale in the town square, the kind that say Honduras is good, Honduras is real. Oils painting of the country scenes, tile roofed houses and simple roads that seem to be headed somewhere.

Posters for sale in the square. Big colorful posters, all from the U.S. it seems, all with white faces, none with faces that look Honduran. Nothing of the Hondurans rich, brown and earthy - only the whiter skins from the north - leaving one to fear that many Hondurans do not love the good earth brown that is theirs.

San Pedro Sula, where Coca Cola is writ large in lights on the side of a mountain, perhaps the only thing visible from anywhere in the city - like a sign, an omen, not necessarily cruel, just a reminder of the reality, "Hondurans, you are finally owned by someone outside of you."

*2020 notes: With very little going on for CCD between Christmas and New Year's Day at La Granja we went back for a second visit to the Abadia de Jesucristo Crucificado in Guatemala.*

## Sunday, December 28, 1986

*9:00 a.m., Abadia de Jesucristo Crucificado, Esquipales, Guatemala*

5 days of varying sore throat, cold, lack of energy. Spent Friday night and all of yesterday here just lounging around, reading. I think I'm some better. Still don't feel great, but I am glad that I'm here.

## Thursday, January 1, 1987

*Noon, New Year's Day, Abadia de Jesucristo Crucificado, Esquipales, Chiqimula, Guatemala*

We slept awhile last night, then got up for the midnight mass in the basilica. The place was filled with people, most of them standing - probably two thousand. The well-trained boy choir was at its best. The priest presiding seemed to be talking to each person present. One of the memorable worship experiences I've had recently.

Then we went into the dining room and had delicious tamales, bread, and eggnog. Everyone was so full of joy, monks in long black robes hugging each other and hugging friends from the community on this special day and moment of sharing.

*2:30 p.m.*

Had lunch and then watched the first half of the Cotton Bowl. I enjoyed it, but I was not all the way there. I am here with a commitment to write. While watching that game, always seductive for me, I felt urges to be back here at the desk writing. It is unusual for me to walk out of a football game.

For some blessed moments there, commitment became "hunger." I found that when the half ended there was no sense of tearing myself away from the television to come back here and write. It was what I wanted to do.

When commitment becomes hunger – this is a sure gift of God, and a gift of freedom.

Reading from Thomas Merton's, *Contemplation in a World of Action* here in the abbey library: he writes:

*There are certain forms of exhausting and meaningless servitude which are characteristic of "the world." It is of the very essence of the monastic life to protest, by its simplicity and its liberty, against these servitudes."*

*Monastic obedience exists not to make yes-men and efficient bureaucrats who can be used in institutional politics, but to liberate the hearts and minds into the lucid and terrible darkness of a contemplation that no tongue can explain and no rationalization can account for. (p. 44)*

## Friday, January 2, 1987
*7:00 a.m., Esquipales, Guatemala*

Dear God, I seem to be here in prayer wanting you to bring me something - an insight, a powerful inner sensation. I seem not quite confident to just be here with you, to simply trust this ordinariness, to let it be with you, trusting that all I need will be given me.

Help this child within me, God, who does not wish to grow up all the time. Help my heart to reach for you.

Help my heart to wait for you. To even trust that somewhere in the being is all the knowing I need.

## Saturday, January 3, 1987
*8:15 a.m., Esquipulas, Guatemala*

Last day of 8 days here in the monastery. Here I have:
- Been quiet
- I have done more thinking than writing in journals, although I have written an immense amount.
- I have walked on the grounds
- Eaten well
- Read some in journals and books here
- And other things.

I don't feel like writing now. I feel like trying to be quiet and pray.
In years of activism
The 80s
When nuclear weapons multiplied like rabbits
And when my heart began to see a little -
Our motives were not all pure, Jesus.
And we did not have answers -
We only knew that something was very wrong.

We wrote statements
We had forums and conferences
We organized groups and committees
We had demonstrations
And we urged people to study.

It was a busy time,
Sometimes an exciting, hopeful time,
Sometimes a time given to the
expanse of ego, of becoming "known" about town.

This was not all bad.
It just had its times of temptation,
And of ego.

We got frazzled at times.
Felt we should do more, tried
But couldn't.
We wanted peace, earnestly.
We did our best
We tried to pray.
and we trusted that you were with us.

Jesus, in looking back on
these years of my "peacemaking" work,
I remember the moments of seeing what an angry,
even violent man I could be.
So another "peacemaking" effort
By necessity
Took off in a parallel manner
The more difficult effort,
The one that had to do with
Facing the capacity
(sometimes the danger)
Of the violence in my life.

By thy grace alone,
It never came out in a disastrous
Manner,
Although I think it did do some damage.
But you saw me, Jesus.
You saw the struggle and you were
With me in the struggle,
With me, I believe, even when I
Could not really say that I
Was with you.

So I was working like hell, Jesus,
In two parallel peace movements.
They were not unconnected,
But neither were they integrated.
One was outward, activist, exciting

With momentary glimpses into the need
For inner work.
One was inward, private, more difficult
-and its struggles sometimes made me question the authenticity of
the outer.

And so the struggle for peace
Goes on
In so many ways known
And unknown
I think that now the struggle for peace
Is more than anything
A struggle for authenticity,
Integrity
A visible,
Substantive,
Efficacious struggle
That always reaches with
More impact
More power
Then could the inward or the outward
Struggling alone.

So Jesus,
You have been what integrity I have known.
You have been the authenticity
That touched me with some wholeness.
So now too,
And always,
Be thou my integrity.
Be thou my authenticity.

## Monday, January 5, 1987, back at La Granja

*Behold my servant, whom I uphold*
*My chosen, in whom my soul rejoices.*
*I have put my spirit upon him,*
*He will bring forth justice to the nations*

*He will not cry or lift up his voice.*
*Or make it heard in the streets.*
*A bruised reed he will not break,*
*And a dimly flaming wick he will not quench.*
*He will not fail on to be discouraged until*
*He has established justice in the earth,*
*And the coastlands wait for his law.*
*(He will faithfully bring forth justice)*
--Isaiah 42:1-4

Remembering that back on Dec 26 - 6:45 a.m.

Father Richard (the American Capuchin priest who is pastor for the church in the area) told us about a Christmas Eve in Cololaca, when a drunk young soldier fired his submachine gun at the front of the church. It happened in early evening I think, the night of church services.

Richard found out around 6 p.m. on Christmas Day and was in Cololaca by 9. He slept in the car in front of the military office until early morning when he could talk to the people.

Apparently there was a disagreement between the military and the Catholic Delegates of the Word.

Remembering:

Yesterday, Sunday Jan 4, 1987 in San Marcos-

Waiting 2.5 hours for a ride that never came. Children from Cololaca noticing in our bags a package of 8 tiny plastic cars we had bought for the neighbor children at La Granja. Their value was around 49 cents each.

They were enthralled with the little cars. We were embarrassed by what cheap toys they were, yet they were a hit, perhaps a luxury for these children.

Sitting on the dusty ground, playing little finger games - very, very close to each other in a certain way.

Coffee "cutting time." Children, women, others are all away cutting coffee. The red husks are taken off and the beans are then laid out to dry. Sometimes it seems like wherever we see a sheet of cement anywhere, it is being used to dry coffee.

263

## Tuesday, January 13, 1987
*La Granja*

Meeting on animals cancelled for today. Unexpected time on my hands. Wrote much in the dialogue journal - feeling more quiet than usual - more centered.

Perhaps there is not much to write here.

Reading again *Brother to a Dragonfly* by Preacher Will Campbell a native Mississippian who decided to become an activist in the Civil Rights Movement in the 1960s, including serving for a time as the chaplain at the University of Mississippi. I realize, in the gutsy personal writing of Campbell, what a coward I am in writing. I write, constantly protecting myself, even though I am known as an open person. I write ever carefully not to offend certain people, especially liberal friends. If this manuscript is to ever make it to book form, I will need to find some new guts to write. I will need to take the lid off - open the doors and windows, let it all be seen.

## Thursday, January 15, 1987
*La Granja*

We have had a series of days of not much official CCD work - no meetings etc.

More time than usual for silence. I have been getting the quiet time.

Last night I noticed moments with Kathy that would have, I think, been cause for an argument, had I not lately been more in touch with the silence, quiet time with God.

Today I am feeling that I have reason to believe Henri Nouwen's words than an hour of contemplative prayer per day will take care of most all psychological struggles, will overcome the need for therapy, and I would add, while teaching the person to function more under his/her own power.

But even if I were to continue the grace of daily prayer and still have hard psychological struggles, it would still be perhaps the central experience of relationships in my life - the relationship that cares for all my relationships.

*I waited patiently for the Lord. who inclined to me and heard my cry, who drew me up from the desolate pit out of the miry bog, and put my feet upon the rock, making my steps secure. Who put a new song in my mouth, a song of praise to our God. May will see and fear, and put their trust in the Lord.* Psalm 40: 1-3

## Tuesday, January 20, 1987
*6:30-7:00 a.m., La Granja*

On Sunday Felipe dropped in with his mother, his father and his nephew. We were pleased to see them. Had not seen them in many weeks. Felipe arrived with a rash all over his body from a week "of cutting coffee" up in the hills above us.

They shared with us about the completion of the water project in Junigual (a village about two miles down the road from us) but with little joy. Every house in Junigual now has a tap for water, except Felipe's, his brother's, and his father's. Felipe had a certain cold, distant look on his face as he told the story.

There has been some kind of division in Junigual over the project. Felipe's story is that he was behind on some of his own work and could not participate fully in the project, even though he is president of CCD's group in Junigual and has been the key organizer of the project.

Felipe's father also had a cold, angry, smiling expression on his face, saying that he did not want to be part of the project.

They asked us about the possibility of CCD funding a project just for them, a separate project just for the houses who did not participate in the community -wide effort.

Just as Felipe's family was leaving, another friend from Junigual, Mario Paz, arrived. He also had stories to tell, about the project. From his perspective the problem the principle conflict was Catholic-Evangelical. He didn't really have many details, but I had hunched that this was at least part of the problem and I was not surprised to hear him say it. But maybe I was a little too-inclined to believe it. Maybe it is not as simple as that and to reduce it to that would be wrong-headed.

We had long talks with Mario. He stayed for supper, helped us in the effort to get our sheep tied with ropes for shipment to La Majada (we did not succeed), and had supper with us. We learned much about Mario, his concerns, his family, and a little of his work with the National Party of Honduras.

(Even as I write of this division, I hear the sounds of another division - it seems to be another very heavy day of bombing in El Salvador.)

*2020 Comments: It was heartbreaking on a number of occasions to see the harsh divisions between Roman Catholics and Evangelicals even in remote villages. Felipe, an Evangelical Christian, had moved from being a friend that I enjoyed to being an angry person about the water project in Junigual which was certainly intended to serve everyone. CCD's commitment was always strong on behalf of helping Evangelicals and Catholics to work together, especially in the villages where survival itself sometimes depended on it often. The Christian Commission for Development was founded as an evangelical Protestant organization, but it was unusually progressive compared to other evangelical groups in the area such as World Vision. We never fully understood all the issues of the conflict in Junigual. But it was clear and unsurprising that the religious divisions were somewhere near the center. The sad result was that all the Catholics in the village had water running to each of their houses but the Evangelicals would have to wait for some other organization to provide the support needed for access to water. It was a sad and unnecessary segregation.*

## Wednesday, January 21, 1987

We went to the wedding of Blanca Edith and Hugo Serafin Nuñez in Guarita. Blanca Edith is the teacher of the one-room school in Coyolillo, a village nearby. Long sermon. Formal service. Couple sits at the front. Recessional is slow - couple is available to be greeted and hugged by everyone.

Dancing in a circle at the reception with Kathy and two 10-year-olds boys was fun. I had the sense they wanted to dance a lot more freely but felt too self-conscious in doing so.

I was enjoying the dancing and got into be my very free self, moving about the dance floor unselfconsciously. I had become unconscious of how the sight of this tall gringo dancing so joyfully might impact others there. Two very young soldiers were in the room as they would be in Guarita which is very close to El Salvador. Both were carrying the usual submachine guns. Both were obviously teenagers. Both of them appeared to be 15 or 16 years old One of them motioned for me to follow him into another room. My guess is that my dancing made him feel anxious and that he should check my papers. But Hugo intervened vigorously, telling them that I was one of his guests and there was no need for them to talk to me. I was grateful for his intervention, although I doubt if anything serious would have come of it.

Slept at Maria Isabel Quejada de Mejia's house. Single bed, with Francisco's brother Magno in the other bed. When she invited us to stay there, proud gringos that we were, we saw the two single beds in the room she pointed us to and we assumed we had two beds at our disposal. But when we came in after midnight and the late party into the dark room, only the lucky beam of the flashlight waved around the room revealed a male body curled up in one of the beds. I was glad I had a light and saw the man in the bed before I crawled into it with him!

A piece of conversation I remember from today:

*"Magno - "Are your parents evangelicals?"*

*Yes, gracias a dios. "Catholics believe in idols."*

White-haired man at the table, full of joy from San Salvador-waved his arms wildly - cigarette in hand, talking of politics in El Salvador.

Later, he danced with Kathy, a little too closely, maybe. But he was a charming man, the only one at the wedding wearing a coat and tie.

I pray God that you will help me be present to all of my moments, whether it be squeezing the puss out of a worm-infected goat's leg, listening to a friend, being present to a friend at the death of her 24-year-old brother in law, or helping a campesino child with her abc's, help me to be there - Help me to be there, or better - be the presence in me, especially when my presence is prone to things selfish.

## Friday, January 23, 1987
*10:30 p.m., La Granja*

Could not sleep. Urges to get up and just write about today.

Up by 6:30 - slept 9 hours. maybe 10. Animals to care for. It happened quickly. Oatmeal and the banana bread I cooked for breakfast. Kathy is cheerful. Cold, windy day. The wind blows on now as I write in flannel shirt.

Lucio arrives with news that's upsetting about having to get a bus to Conguacota.

Off to Junigual afoot, trying to reflect as I walk. Martia and Lazaro, young children, sitting beside the creek. I almost walked past without seeing them.

On to Andreas' house - no one home. Told one of the little girls that we wanted more firewood. She seemed to understand.

On to Junigual people in the road. Lots of action - a group cutting leña, staking it by the side of the road.

Arrived at Felipe's house in Junigual. Antolina is welcoming - maybe lacking in some of the enthusiasm I am accustomed to with her. Felipe and I could not have our "goat class" because he had made a commitment to work in the coffee fields. I expect that Felipe is very short of money these days.

I tried to understand. I hope that Antolina felt that I did.

I walked on to Guajiniquil - taking the first right turn off of the road, but missing the one that would have taken me there directly. I walked around stone fences, over them, through thick bush until I finally came upon one of the 7-8 houses there. Margarito was outside barefoot in his yard hitting his maisillo (sorghum) with a big stick, breaking the grains loose. I was so warmly and so completely welcomed. The wind continued to blow. Thelma snuggled their young son in a thin piece of cloth - not enough to keep him warm on this cold day. Margarito asks me if I like to "suck cane". I say yes, so he goes and cuts a sugar cane for me to suck on. He expertly slices off a piece for the children, while I take the machete and have to hit and miss a few times before I get it to work. I'm still not getting to the tender core of the cane where the good sweet juice is. After a while Margarito, ever gentle and courteous, cuts me a piece out of the "blandito" (tender) center. It is good.

Thelma talks of parents who died when she was 2, growing up with a brother whose wife was cruel. She seems happy.

Margarito tells me about the history of Guajiniquil, and shows me pictures of his father and mother, old pictures, faded. His father, he says, was a big man.

Margarito is proud when he shows me the tap that now brings water directly to their house. They will no longer have to walk to the creek to get the water they need. They share the good news of a cow who will deliver in August.

*Water Project construction. When we arrived at La Granja, we had to carry all of our water from the creek about twenty yards downhill from the house. These men are digging the trench for the pipes to bring water directly into the "pila" or water tank high on La Granja property making water available anywhere it was needed on the property*

*2020 notes: Water Projects and Understanding What Development Is and Is Not*

*One of the Christian Commission for Development's frequent projects for rural villages is to give support for the installation of a water project for the village. A water projects also provides a good example of how CCD attempts to practice development in ways that foster self-sufficiency rather than dependence.*

*Water is a challenge just about anywhere you go in Honduras. In the area where we worked, the norm for most villages was carrying water from the nearest stream to the village, often involving carrying a heavy container, with this work usually done by women and girls. Successful water projects enable a village to have water arrive by pipe to a central source in the village and sometimes to each individual house.*

*There are a number of requirements before a village is deemed ready to take on the installation of a water project.*

*The first requirement is enough cohesion and commitment to a common purpose within the community. The people in the village must be ready to take this on.*

*Another requirement is to find a water source, some underground spring usually, that is located at an elevation significantly above the village because gravity is the only power available to move the water. This usually also requires getting permission of whomever is the landowner where the water source is located.*

*Then the people of the village, usually the men, must be willing to commit to many days work to dig a ditch from the water source to the village, which sometimes can be a few miles. In one of the villages CCD served, 22 residents committed to give 26 days each to dig the ditches and lay the pipe.*

*The vinyl pipe for this village cost about $2,000, far out of reach of the village economy. CCD provides the funds for the pipe.*

*Once the project is in place the village elects a "water board" to be responsible for maintenance and any other problems that might arise.*

*The U.S. Army had a massive presence in Honduras in the 1980s and loved to publicize how many wells they dug for villagers in Honduras. After the wells were dug there would be photos of army trucks driving away as the people cheered. The problem with this is that no time is invested in helping the villagers work together and take a sense of ownership and pride in the project. It was something done "for them," not development that they were able to do for themselves.*

*In addition, we have read of many wells dug in developing countries that after a time became useless because villagers did not have the technical training nor the money to buy parts when repairs were needed.*

*CCD's method of supporting villagers in building their own water projects attempted to use affordable replacement parts when they are needed and to keep the project's maintenance within the capacities of the members of the village. And, of course, the intention in this is that villages learn how to work effectively as a community for the good of everyone.*

*One more telling example of how even well-funded development can miss the mark showed up on a visit to the U.S. Embassy in Tegucigalpa. We were welcomed into the office of the U.S. Cultural Affairs Officer. She told us about one program being offered to Hondurans - a well-funded book program in which just about any library or local school in Honduras can receive books originally published in English and translated into Spanish. There were long lists of the books available and local people needed only to check off the books they would like to receive. As a book lover, I was very impressed with this at first.*

*Then just a few weeks later in the countryside we came to understand how few people can read and the lack of accessible schools. I also began to notice the pictures/images available to Hondurans. Almost none of them contained anything that was distinctly Honduran or that reflected local culture.*

The maisillo (sorghum) harvest is in - enough to sell some in order to pay back the loan from CCD.

Hot coffee arrives as we talk.

When it is time to leave, Margarito walks with me down the trail for awhile. We pass by the home of his two sisters where a new granero (sheet metal grain bin) is standing. Margarito walks briskly, his bare feet seem to be of the same substance as the dusty path on which we walk. We pass by two piles of maisillo, look down onto rare green grass, and hear of Margarito's success with his corn crop.

Finally, we say farewell where the trail from Junigual meets the trail to the road. I take off toward the road, hoping to be there before the bus arrives, but first need to find a private place in the bushes. After walking a few hundred years I find the privacy I need inside a thick grove of trees. Luckily, I had toilet paper in my pack.

272

I passed by Jose Mejia's house, so I dropped in for a brief visit and heard about how his water is doing - not so well. I see the pup we gave them, now almost a big dog like our Paloma, his mother. His name is Tiburon (shark).

Further down the path I meet friends from Guarita getting sand for the construction of the new high school there - but the building will have to be built step by step because funds are so low.

Back on the road I cross a bridge with a good section of concrete, a perfect place to dry coffee beans. I joke to a young man sitting on the bridge that I'd like a cup of coffee.

On to the village - to Don Juan and Doña Enusia's house, but they too are "cutting coffee" in the mountains. I leave word about our planned meeting.

I looked for Mario Paz, but could not find him.

Back to Antolina's where she had served me rice, beans and hot tortillas, along with a cup of coffee. A feeling that she is discouraged, feeling poorer than usual. I thank her for her kind hospitality and continue walking.

Going over the hill to Doña Carmen's house, I see her headed for the road to meet me. She greets me enthusiastically and we have much to talk about: the wedding, the soldiers there who "acostared" me (stopped me) for my papers, goats, babies born in two adjoining houses the same day and hour, and her grandsons who live with her.

Her daughter from Terlaca, walked to the gate with a coke for me. We talked more.

And then I walked on home, stopping a bus headed in the wrong direction only to find out there is not one today going toward home. I stopped when I saw Candido beside the road, glad to see him, telling him he has not been to La Granja, lately. He answers, "there was no time. We were busy working."

I dropped in at his house for a moment and then came home by the path because the dust in the road is awful with all the wind.

*2020 notes: This day just described seems to capture better than any other entry in the journal the best of our life in the "campo" (countryside) in the region near La Granja. I cannot remember many specific days during our time there but I can remember this day. It was so full of the extravagant hospitality that was so much a*

273

*part of life there. It was not unusual for a family to have less than a dozen eggs that needed to last a week and for them to offer us one of them during a visit. Our inclination was always to say, "oh no, you need to keep this for your family," but we were instructed and we learned how important it was to them to accept this hospitality.*

*The visit to Margarito and Thelma's house says a lot about the variety of work CCD did in the region. They have water running directly to their house.*

*Grain Storage Bins – For hundreds of years the crucial supply of grains, mostly beans and corn, were stored in an attic area for preservation during the months after harvest. To control insect this storage required keeping enough fire going in the house all the time so the smoke would keep the bugs away. These fires were very costly in a number of ways: They caused a huge drain on the firewood in the area. Deforestation was at crisis levels.*

*It meant that the house usually had smoke circulating which caused endless vision problems and sometimes pain in the eyes. Finally, this process at times was not fully effective and the bugs would still destroy some of the grain.*

*The Christian Commission for Development's response to this reality was to teach local men to use sheet metal. They taught them how to bend, shape and enclose it so that one ten-foot high metal storage bin could store enough grain to last an entire year. While we were there training programs were held with the plan of teaching at least one man in each village to build these bins whose responsibility it would be to teach others the same. CODE provided access to the metal and tools that would be needed.*

*The local leader in this work was a gifted campesino named Emigdio. We got to visit his home once. Not only did he have excellent storage for corn and beans, he also had a few cows and had learned how to make use of the fumes from cow manure. He had learned how to harvest the gas from a pile of cow manure and run a pipe from there into the kitchen where he had made from sheet metal a burner on their stove that could be used for cooking. It was very inspiring to witness how this man had made all the parts from pipes to burner and more to make life better for his family and serve as a model for others.*

*Coffee - There were no large coffee plantations near us, but even poor farming families would often have enough coffee growing to produce one bag that could be sold at the market, and enough left over for them to drink. On more than one occasion we were served a cup of coffee that had been grown, picked, dried, ground and brewed within one household.*

## Saturday, January 31, 1987
*3:00 p.m., La Granja*

Sounds of shovels straining sand for the new dormitorio (dormitory, a simple structure that will house double bunk beds for use during our five-day seminars). A spider crawls across my Bible. The wind blows. Kathy feeds the goats. Matilde and Lazaro laugh loudly at hearing their own voices on our little cassette tape recorder. Peanut butter with honey on bread goes down well for lunch. Francisco arrives wanting to sell wooden beams for our new animal shelter. Alvaro arrives, ever efficient, with many chores already done, and others left to do.

## Monday, February 2, 1987
*La Granja*

*The gringo gives plowing with oxen a try.*

I could never be a campesino. One of my definitions of a campesino is "a farmer who farms with a machete as his only tool," but some do have other tools and a few have a mule or a horse. They work heavy with large muscles. They rest easy with no misgivings. I work heavy with small muscles. When I work hard with large muscles in this setting I get very tired. I do not rest as easily as they seem to.

*Co-worker Lucio sowing in newly plowed ground*

Sometimes I give the instructions, tell them what work needs to be done today around La Granja, as if I am "the boss." It's a little of the pattern again I'm sure, the gringo comes south with a weak back and money in the pocket, enough to buy the privilege of telling Hondurans what they must do if they care to earn a pittance of money. But it is not so simple as that here. The money I dispense belongs to CCD. And I am not making anything off of their labor. Our intention is that they and others like them will become the primary beneficiaries of this work.

Gregorio and Francisco are carrying lumber, just about all day today. It never stops. I did good work also, at my desk, work that is me, that I can do. I am not them. They are not me. They are treasures - but then so am I.

Lord bless the campesinos who walk in funny rubber shoes with no shoestrings.

Bless the shoes which walk beneath
Pants patched over many dozen times.
Bless the patches,
Which are worn beneath a shirt
That is worn and still worn most days of his working.
Bless the much-worn shirt,

Which is wrapped around a campesino heart, simple, often
Steadfast, ever beating for the labor of the day.
Bless the campesinos beating heart, worn
beneath a face, authentic with pride
Bless, Lord, the pride, and the heart,
And the feet, and the steps and the path
Of the campesino,
And lead us all in the way everlasting.

## Tuesday, February 10, 1987
*La Granja*

Hard today to know how to pray
For a world
Helped
But not bound
By ideology
Hard to find Jesus
In the spinning
swirling
Confusion
Of everything
I see the mission
In a glass darkly,
Not quite face to face.
Perhaps this is enough.
I am where
And who
I am
The child of God,
Seeing the vision that matters,
Hurting for what cannot
Soon
Come to pass.
God, help us to love you.

## Saturday, February 14, 1987
*Tegucigalpa, in the Cathedral*

Walked here from the hotel at 7 a.m. Found a church packed for a Saturday mass. Sat in a side chapel from which I could see the priest presiding. A good silence to sit a little away from the praying crowd, touched by it, if not really a part of it.

*"Asi que, si all llevar tu ofrendar al alter te acuerdas de que tu hermano tiene algo contra ti, deja tu ofrenda alli mismo delante de altar y ve primero a ponerte en paz con tu hermano. Entonces podras volver al altar y presentar tu ofrenda."* Mateo 5: 23-24

"When you are offering your gift at the altar, if you remember that your brother or sister has something against you, leave your gift there before the altar and go; first make peace with your brother or sister, and then come and offer your gift." Matthew 5: 23-24

Cast us O God into the shadows where our brothers and sisters wait for reconciliation. Put your hands upon us there, where staying is not easy, where saying the words of healing begins our journey into wholeness.

O reconciling Christ, ever beside us, broken for our reconciliation, show us the way - and show us the places in the shadows where darkness will revel our hope.

## Tuesday, February 17, 1987
*Esteli, Nicaragua*

*2020 notes: This is a return visit we made back to Esteli described above in the July-August 1984 section of this journal. This trip back to Esteli gave me the opportunity to visit the family I lived with. The matriarch and head of the household was Silvia Diaz. Her husband had been killed during the 1979 war/insurrection to overthrow the dictator Anastasio Somoza whose family had been brutal rulers in Nicaragua for decades. Silvia was a woman of great dignity and courage. Living in that household had sure given me a deep experience in what grass roots democracy can look like and what it can mean when even the poorest people in a society have some voice in and control over the day to day realities of their lives.*

*Silvia's house (see entries above for July and August 1984*

In the summer of 1984 when I had been a guest for five weeks at Silvia's house, the dirt-floored house of walls, half brick and half used lumber, had been full of all manner of life. A daughter and son-in-law with their four young children lived there. Also in that household were five more of Silvia's children, a couple who had no other place to live, three youth from rural villages who needed housing in Estelí in order to go to school, and one pig who roamed freely from room to room (sometime he would lie calmly by my bed before I got up and I would scratch his back). It was so good to be back for a brief visit.

By how North Americans measure well-being, the house was a sample of severe poverty. But in Nicaragua the house represented many advantages that most poor Nicaraguans did not have: It had a courtyard in the back and a latrine. There was running water. Sheets hung from the ceiling made partitions for many rooms, most of them not much larger than the small bed in each. I had a room all to myself that was slightly larger than the space to hold a bed. I had room for a suitcase and a few things. Food was cooked over an outdoor adobe stove under a canopy in the back.

The living room fronted onto a dusty street full of similar houses. There was a mud hole just outside the front door that was difficult to get dry because of frequent rain. But the living room was also the center of everything. Silvia worked daily there at her treadle sewing machine and made beautiful clothes that she sold. Adult education classes were held in the room weekly for adults who needed to learn to read or to improve their reading. There was a constant coming and going of people.

Silvia made money from having students from rural villages live there, from her sewing, and from visitors from NICA such as me.

When I went back this visit, all but Silvia's two youngest sons had left. Teenage son Donald was in the army fighting at the front. William was still in Bulgaria on a scholarship studying engineering. Rosa Maria and her husband Francisco, had started a fruit stand, converted to Christianity in the Pentecostal church, and the youth who had been staying there for school had moved on. A young adult son Rodolfo has emigrated to Canada.

Silvia was wearing a new dress she had just made for herself and was as welcoming as ever. She spoke proudly of Rosa Maria and Francisco's new success. She as a Catholic had been the one to influence Francisco to become an evangelical Christian. I didn't ask about the pig but assumed that by now it had become food for the household.

Silvia looked weary and seemed to have lost a lot of weight. From talking to her I suspected having one son fighting at the front and another in a foreign country had been difficult for her.

Being back there helped me remember how privileged I had been to be a part of that family for a few weeks. I had been welcomed then and was welcomed back now so extravagantly.

Eugenio *(see entry for August 4, 1984)* was one of the students who was living at Silvia's house when I was there in 1984. He is a lively and warm 16-year-old. He told us his story of being in an explosion and almost dying as a 10-year-old in the 1979 insurrections. With shrapnel in his abdomen, 2 Russian doctors somehow got him through two national guard (enemy) checkpoints to a hospital in La Trinidad about 20 km to the south. He survived, but with only half of his right arm. I had attempted to arrange for him to get a prosthesis in the United States but that proved to be too difficult. He had also talked to some doctors from Bulgaria who had been in Nicaragua and he still hoped this might be an option.

On this return trip, we asked about him and found him living in a new government housing project with three sisters, his mother and a house full of his nieces and nephews.

When I walked in, he was sitting at the table, eating a breakfast of meat with sauce and tortilla. He greeted me warmly, got me a little stool, and asked me to sit beside his mother. He had no shirt on and his right arm with no hand was apparent as ever.

We visited as he ate, then he got up to get ready to go off to work. He put on a perfectly pressed long sleeve white shirt. Then he walked out with a right hand coming from the right sleeve that looked almost real. Obviously, he had been able to get the artificial arm. He looked tall and handsome. His face was full of new pride and confidence. I was so happy for him.

With no embarrassment, and with much satisfaction, he showed me that he had not just one but two artificial hands. One was just for appearance. But a second one was equipped with a strap across his left shoulder and could be used to pick up small items. An older sister stood beside him to help him demonstrate how it worked.

It was a brief visit, not more than twenty minutes. Then he had to leave for a job he now had selling vegetables on a regular route. I was so grateful to get to see him again.

Rev. Leon Zelaya was the new pastor of the Alfa and Omega Baptist Church in Estelí, with whom we had worked out a partner relationship with our Seattle church, University United Church of Christ. We had met during 1984 but I did not get to know him well then. He seemed to be a reserved man. But this time was different. We talked over a long lunch and heard him speak of his convictions about the revolution, his opposition to the Sandinistas and his respect for them, his dreams for the church, his sense of the role of the church in the current Nicaraguan situation. It was his view that the church should not identify with any one political party. It should be a place for all to come. His views were quite different from mine and from those of many other Nicaraguan Baptists who were certainly in disagreement with the new Sandinista government but who still respected the humanity in the new government that carried out policies to serve the poor that had been unknown in the days of the dictatorship.

Rev. Gilberto Provedor, Marta Provedor and their young adult children, also named Gilberto and Marta.

We had a number of happy visits with the Provedor family. Gilberto was also a Baptist minister but now worked in the region around Estelí as the Regional Director for CEPAD, an ecumenical church-funded program for assistance and development, especially in the rural areas. In many ways its work was similar to the work of CCD with whom we worked in Honduras.

## An Earthquake Story

Marta shared with us some of her experience during the massive earthquake in Nicaragua in 1972. Younger Marta was only four when it happened and Gilberto was away working. "Walls were falling all around us," she said. Dust was everywhere and so thick no one cold see across a street. For fear that something would fall on them the children were told to clear out. There was no time to think, no time to cry, no time to try to understand the reality of what was happening. She was separated from her daughter Marta and did not find her until the following day when she found her with hair full of dust sitting with caring local people eating a tortilla.

## The Lights Go Out

During our visit, we were in an evening service at Alfa and Omega around 8:30 p.m. when suddenly all the lights went out. We had been through a program of dedication of a new educational building. It was a humorous novelty at first, children screaming, people laughing, finally filing into the dark streets where we saw that all of Estelí was dark.

The next day, the news was spreading that a light tower had been bombed a few miles out of town by the "Contra" troops, the counterrevolutionary soldiers funded by the United States government to fight the new Sandinista government. Not only Estelí, but all of the north-central zone of the country was without electricity because of the substation that had been bombed. It was not only lights and other critical machines dependent on electricity - in Estelí the water system functions on electric pumps so that for up to a week, the people of this city of 40,000 would walk to water, sometimes up to a kilometer away and more.

That evening we spent the night in the Provedor home. During and after supper we sat by candlelight and heard happy stories from all of them about the good times they had had in recent years with American Baptists who had come to Nicaragua to help them build their church building. Daughter Marta, now a beautiful young woman in her early 20s, got up and with enthusiasm went and got a box of photos so they could show us pictures of the people they felt such love for.

It later struck me that while we were having to sit without lights because bombs and other weapons provided by the U.S. government had put out their electricity, they were at the very same time telling us stories about American that they loved dearly. For me it seemed to be a cruel irony. But Nicaraguans, like people from many other nations who have had to live with U.S. atrocities, are always clear in how they distinguish the people of the United States from the government of the United States.

### Thursday, March 5, 1987
*Back at La Granja*

> 2nd day of Lent
> Matthew 4:1-11
> Jesus in the wilderness. He said no to all three temptations and then "angels attended to him."
>
> Is there not a promise inherent in this that when we say no to things that are tempting, but less than who we are, - when we move through appropriate no's in order to get to the deeper "Yes," can we not count on it -- that "angels will care for us." -- that forces from beyond us which are also within us -- forces which are made of love -- will we not be helped and held by this love.
>
> How can we know it is there? When the no's have been said until we reach the place of yes -- and all we feel is desert, loneliness, and private hunger, how can we know that the angels will attend to us?
>
> Many no's have brought us to La Granja. I have also felt many moments when it seemed that no angels were nearby.
>
> Today is different. A new struggling pattern of inner peace has taken me.
>
> There is some new trust in being about what should be done -- some new acceptance of all that won't happen soon. So we feed the goats, write the reports, stumble along with our Spanish, help out as best we can, try to be helpful companions to the campesinos and we get and receive mail. Angels - caring for us in the desert moments.

### Tuesday, March 24, 1987
*6:30 a.m., La Granja*

> Just remembering some images of life in recent days:
> La Majada – March 12 - Purificacion is one of the leaders for CCD's group in the village. We had been able to get a latrine project moving in La Majada in which each household would have access to

an outdoor toilet, which would be a great mark of progress of La Majada and for CCD. But we were horrified to hear that one of the village leaders of the project, who name was Purificacion, had threatened. the people with military presence if they did not finish their latrines.

Good leadership was essential within the villages to make some progress possible for everyone. Purificacion's threatening ways here were horrifying, of course. Fortunately, this was a rare exception rather than the attitude that we knew mong most village leader

March 25 -- Trail Corrizalitos - return trail. Walking with no shirt. La "derechiera" the short-cut. Much sweat. Very hot.

March 25 -- Went to Guarita for lunch and to deliver a letter. The coolness of the hammock in the living room. Good food.

I had a good talk with Alvaro about schools in Honduras. The "Basic Plan" (Plan Basico) is the most common level of school in Honduras and goes through grade 6. Of those who go to school in Honduras, many go only through the sixth grade as is the case with Alvaro.

"Colegios" sounds like it could refer to college, but it is the name here for school that go from grades 7-9. There are relatively few such schools at this level. For many, going beyond the sixth grade requires living with someone in a distant town and paying them some room and board, out of the question for just about everyone living in remote rural areas.

High schools ("secondarios") are even more rare and generally require a second relocation in order to attend.

Illiteracy in Honduras in the mid 1980s is around 50%. In our meetings with campesinos, there is sometime some joking around about who can read and who cannot. But beneath that joking there is always some sadness and probably some shame about not being able to read.

We had a visitor named Karl from Sweden with us today. I had a good visit with him as we rode in the pickup.

## Wednesday, March 25, 1987
*La Granja*

Sorpresa, ("surprise" in English) the little female goat – rearing, jumping up on me like a dog. A promising goat for the future.

Our neighbor and frequent hired worker Geronimo is the new president for the new CODE group that just began here in Ana Sanchez, the very small village closest to us which also includes houses that are even closer.

Geronimo seems to be showing new initiative and creativity lately. He repaired the pasture fence in the quebrada (creek). And he just seems a lot friendlier.

*2020 note: Geronimo lived nearby and was often employed to do work at La Granja including taking care of the animals when we were away. His five-year-old daughter Matilde was also one of our most frequent visitors.*

Moments with him and his son Reyes (Spanish for kings. Reyes was born on Epiphany) in his house. Lots of father-son tenderness. Reyes is starting to grow from a child constantly in tears to a child with a ready smile in his eyes. Geronimo showed up singing the children's song about the pollitos (baby chickens) today.

We had some less than happy moments in our early days working with him. It was difficult to communicate requests and instructions to him. this was probably as much our problem, especially with the language, as it was his. He once cut our clothesline because he had a better use for the string. Maybe we all have changed and grown some, but I think more of the changes are within us than within him.

So my good question or set of questions- how do campesinos change? And how do campesinos effect change in the lives of non-campesinos? What changes have we seen in particular people here? Dec. or Jan. - when was it? The wedding in Guarita - returning to find that Feo and the evangelical pastors group members who were there had been quite offended by the fact that a "missionary" was dancing. It is too easy to dismiss this as just unfortunate legalism. But it is important to know how our choices are impacting local people.

## Thursday, April 2, 1987
*La Granja*

Dionisia arrives, as ever, ready to work in the kitchen as we start another five-day course, and with 5-month-old Antonia in arms.

She finds a place on the simple bench in the dining room to sit and gives her breast to her daughter.

In the morning greetings to all, Antonia is filled, satisfied. Her smiles, to all comers are evidence that she is lacking in neither love nor nourishment.

The work begins. Dionisia's children are growing up around a tireless worker to the point that at times we must urge her to go home at the end of the day. She wants to work overtime on her own.

Today's work is cooking the meals for the group. the large adobe stove stands in the middle of the room, Rosalina, Paulina, and Dionisia moving busily on all sides.

Antonia lies on a simple cloth on the cement floor beside the door. Sister Marta, age 7, is now the one giving her baby sister attention and care. A colorful discarded Colgate toothpaste box is today's toy. Dionisia adds firewood into the front opening of the adobe stove. Marta attends to tiny Antonia. The day of work is under way. The children are in the middle of everything going on.

But Marta's patience has its limits and it is not long until Antonia is wailing. Marta does not want to help anymore. Dionisia places a four-gallon pot of water on the stove, wipes sweat from her forehead with her forearm and heads resolutely for Antonia. The tasks of preparing the lunch have increased and there is less time for children. The hammock is the only reasonable alternative. Strung from one rafter on the dining room ceiling to another on the other side of the room, the strong net hammock is well-secured. Antonia is wrapped in an old piece of synthetic cloth that is easily accessible to campesinos here. Dianisia places her in the small hammock on her back and ties the hammock above her. The effect is that of a baby in a see-through net sack. But she is secure. And she is as cool as one can get in this hot climate and in this setting. And the hammock swings back and forth to offer Antonia some comfort. But the contentment lasts only as long as mother's eyes are affixed to her eyes and mother's voice close enough to send soothing sounds her way.

The soothing presence of mother must end even if the gentle swaying continues for a time. Dionisia returns to the work in the kitchen, a lengthy fifteen feet away and a wall between them now. Antonia cries out her protest from inside the hammock net. Her cry sounds desperate to me. She kicks her legs and moves her tiny arms. Now there is no one to come to the rescue, Sister Marta has gone off to play. Dionisia is busy in the kitchen.

Antonia swings, yells, kicks and then yells some more, until all the energy of her morning is spent, and she goes to sleep, wrapped and suspended, loved and sustained, upheld by the meager but dignity-saturated supports that are possible in her world.

*2020 notes: During the early months of 1987 there was some new construction going on at La Granja all the time.*

*A new "galera" to provide shade for outdoor classes and a place just to relax..*

*A new water tank that ended the need to haul water from the creek.*

*New flush toilet, with each flush requiring a bucket of water..*

*Addition to the chicken/rabbit house.*

*Packing down the dirt outside the new kitchen-dining hall.*

*Gregorio was known as a master carpenter in the surrounding and did much of the building at La Granja. On one occasion when a baby died Gregorio built a casket on about two hours' notice.*

*Mixing sand and clay for adobe construction. Good adobe construction requires careful selection of the right soil, and mixing it well with straw and water. Some adobe structures last a century or more.*

*Adobe blocks made from the mortar.*
Photo credit: "Hombre cargando leña y su sombrero - Making Adobe; Santa Bárbara, Honduras" by Lon&Queta, CC license 2.0. See photo credits at end of book for full details.

## Palm Sunday, April 12, 1987

*6:30 a.m., Abadia de Jesucristo Crucificado – Esquipulas, Guatemala. We have come back to Esquipulas for Holy Week.*

Morning Peace
Awaiting a savior on an ass,

Comic redemption for a world
Heavy with parts unhealed.
Sounds, cars, shower dripping,
A beating in the distance,
Somehow cannot break into the
Solid quiet of Palm Sunday morning.

Headed for a week over-heavy,
He arrives light,
Conferring hope on all failures,
Conferring power on all weakness,
Conferring weakness on all power.

I too want to cheer,
I too strain to shout an
Irrational noise for the
Uncompleted victory of the humble ones.

## Monday, April 13, 1987
*Esquipulas, Guatemala*

*Tests for genuine dialogue*

1. Am I truly opening myself as an act of love? Or have I been simply ventilating my own
emotions, manipulating my partner?

2. Have I truly wanted unity, to know and to be known, or have my efforts at dialogue really been a pursuit of my own happiness and satisfaction?

3. Do I invite the openness of my partner only through my own openness, or do I pressure him, poke with probing questions into areas that he has not voluntarily opened? Have I driven him into a defensive posture by my frontal attacks on his privacy?

4. Do I have a sense that we are collaborators or competitors? Do I want my partner to open up for his sake or for my own? If he did open up, would I feel that it was a victory for my perseverance or his victory over his own inhibitions?

5. What suppressive techniques might I be using without even knowing it? In general do I look so depressed and fragile that no one would dare tell me the truth? Or do I look so domineering that no one would want to risk his individuality with me?

6. How have I received my partner's attempts at openness in the past? Have I ever used her self revelation to "hit back" in an argument?

7. Have I exposed my own needs, deficiencies, and incompleteness in such a way that my partner knows he does not have to fear me? Does my partner know of my need to know him, to share whatever she is and whatever is in her?

8. Am I, in general, the type who is always ready to give advice? Do I usually feel that I know what is best for people even when they do not realize it themselves?

9. How do I speak to my partner of the confidence I have received from others? Would she see in me a judgmental, harsh, or condescending person? She may have seen the dried blood of others under my fingernails, and not wanted to risk his own tender flesh.

10. Am I too filled with my own emotions to be truly present and available to my partner?

## Maundy Thursday, April 16, 1987
*Esquipulas, Guatemala*

It's Holy Thursday, and I'm not sure if I have anything profound to say.

*2020 notes: Apparently within two weeks we left Esquipulas in Guatemala, went back to La Granja, and then went all the way to Tegucigalpa for something, probably for a meeting of all the personnel working for CCD or for a week-long course. It appears that we were on the move a lot during those weeks.*

*Horses and mules are crucial to rural life in Honduras, yet where we lived owning one was very much the exception rather than the rule for local farmers.*
Photo credit: "Hombre con su mula - Man with his mule; cerca de Sulaco, Yoro, Honduras" by Lon&Queta, CC license 2.0. See photo credits at end of book for full details.

*(In May 1987 the Memphis, Tennessee daily newspaper, The Commercial Appeal, published this op-ed article that I wrote during these months)*

*San Marcos de Ocotepeque,*

*Honduras May 24, 1987*

*Back in the 1950s in Alcorn County, Miss., my grandaddy still used mules to do some of his plowing.*

*I can still remember how he looked — those long, leather plow lines tied around his neck, sweat dripping down his face, his straw hat ever in place, and "gees" and "haws" shouted seeing Kate (the red mule) and Nell (the black one) on course. He was in the twilight of his working years as a farmer when folks mostly used mules either for nostalgic reasons or because they were too poor to own a tractor.*

296

*Mules seldom are signs of the lowest levels of poverty in the dry and hilly countryside where we live and work in the western Honduran department (state) of Lempira. They are very much a part of daily life.*

*A lot of farmers here can't afford one, even though mules are the critical means of transporting meager crops of corn and sorghum from distant fields to homes where they eventually become about 50 per cent of the diet of Hondurans in the countryside. A mule is also a means of hauling firewood, adobe bricks for building houses, clay roof tile, and even cases of Coca-Cola into remote villages inaccessible by car.*

*A mule is a sign that the owner is a step above the most desperate poverty, sometimes many steps above.*

*While the Iran arms-sale debacle makes it a little less likely that the Nicaraguan "contras" can continue their brutal, but generally ungainful war, Honduras are mostly unaffected by the situation (save for the charges that a number of Honduran officials also were involved in the dealings).*

*Honduras, touted as the United States' staunch ally in the region, continues to languish in many poverties. The sufferings of this population, 80% of which is poor, remained unmoved and unlikely to change significantly until there is a viable movement for reform within Honduras or a change in Washington's policy toward the country.*

*Philip L. Shephard, Honduran scholar at Florida International University, has written, "the lowest priority of U.S. policy toward Honduras is Honduras itself." Seen from here inside the country, Honduras shows all the signs of being a steppingstone in the higher U.S. policy goals in the isthmus— namely, overthrowing the Sandinista government in Nicaragua.*

*In the area where we live, we see communities without even a one-room schoolhouse while the U.S. offers new fighter aircraft for the Honduran air force.*

*We see teachers who labor against immense odds: expected, for example, to use their meager salaries to buy chalk, paper, pencils and other supplies for children who cannot afford them, while a military exercise provides a new airfield near the Nicaraguan border.*

*We see remote villages accessible only by foot or horseback, while the United States comes and builds road based on strategic military criteria.*

*We have noted the figures for U.S. economic aid over the years to Honduras, along with the phenomenal increases in same during the 1980s. Were they not accompanied by proportionately even larger increases in military aid — not a help to the country's economy — the figures might be impressive.*

*Instead, what remains negatively impressive is how few signs there are of progress in Honduras in spite of so many dollars coming in.*

*There are many poverties here*

*One is the poverty of economic failure. Honduras was to have been the Reagan administration's model of how free-market capitalism can get a poor Third Word Country back on its feet. It has not happened. Aid and advantages sent toward the Honduran private sector have not resulted in new growth and certainly have produced nothing better for the nation's poor. The national debt remains a crisis with no solution in sight. Wealthy Hondurans are reported to have more money in dollar accounts abroad than the total of all personal accounts in Honduras.*

*Another poverty is militarism. Its nationwide impacts include creating a climate of fear and war along with making the country unattractive for investment. At the local level one senses the quiet but heavy hand of the military keeping the lid on any serious reforms that might upset the status quo.*

*We had a company of 27 soldiers come to the front door of the farm where we live just to check our papers. They were courteous and went on their way when our papers proved to be in order. It was a reminder, however, that the close eye of the authorities steadily discourages anything that might look like significant dissent. This also means that any sentiment of reform is put down with the blanket and seldom-substantiated charge of "Communist."*

*One Honduran friend experienced the ways of politics in the countryside told us that anyone speaking publicly against the government's current policies could be picked up, questioned, even threatened or tortured. The evidence of the efficacy of this work is that in this part of the country, no one does it. And everyone remembers stories from earlier years about what happened to those who did.*

*Closely related to this is the poverty of democracy. Even though the United States points with pride to recent elections in Honduras and contends that it has made the transition from military to democratically elected governments, local facts tell a different story. Any minimally literate Honduran knows that the bottom-line power in the country is held by the military, in spite of massive participation in elections (probably one of the more misleading measures of democracy in Central America).*

*Recent years evidence of this has been two changes in the powerful position of chief of the armed forces, with the country's president (allegedly the commander in chief of the military) not a participant in the changes.*

*But the greater barriers to authentic democracy in Honduras have to do with a population that is 50 percent illiterate and unable to understand the decisions and processes by which the ballot box might be a means to a better future. This along with a weak and often nonexistent media make the logistics of carrying out a democracy almost impossible.*

*Members of the Honduran Congress, for example, do not customarily communicate extensively with constituents after being elected because lack of communication systems makes it difficult and because of political custom in the country.*

*Finally, there is the poverty of leadership. Prof. Shephard has also noted the essential Catch-22 of current U.S. policy toward Honduras; If the U.S. is to maintain Honduras as the primary base of its anti-Communist crusade in Latin America, it must work through the military-economic power structure which is really in command of the country. Yet if it does work through this group— largely composed of people either corrupt or uninterested in economic reform—it guarantees that the economic progress the United States would like to see will not happen.*

*Current conditions here solidly confirm this thesis. Militarization continues by leaps and bounds. Yet the country is an economic disaster.*

*One of Honduras' daily newspapers recently reported that President Reagan has sent to President Jose Azcona Hoya of Honduras a gift of a Cadillac valued at $150,000, complete with almost every imaginable electronic extra, including explosive-detective devices on the underside of the car. The car stands as one more symbol of how U.S. excesses are missing the mark for the long-range economic development of Honduras, and possible for the intention of helping Hondurans to feel that the United States is an authentic ally.*

*But I do have a suggestion for President Azcona. He should send that Cadillac back to Washington with a cordial note saying, "thank you very much, President Reagan, for the offer of the Cadillac, but in the best interests of the Honduran people I feel that I must return it. I would, however, like to request another gift in its place, something that will address some of the real needs of the country, help us get moving from the place where we really are instead of the place from where you or I might like to pretend that we are.*

*"Could you take the $150,000 that would have been spent on the Cadillac and use it instead to send us few planeloads of good Mississippi mules?"*

*(N. Randall Mullins is a graduate of Westwood High School and Southwestern at Memphis (Rhodes College). He is a former teacher and football coach at Booker T. Washington High School. He and*

*his wife, Kathryn, serve as co-managers of the Model Farm and Capacitation Center in Cololaca, Honduras for the Honduran Commission for Development and Emergency).*

## May, 1987
*El Hatillo Conference Center, Tegucigalpa*

Dear God, You whose everlasting arms strain to include where we your frightened children have hidden in our exclusivism-- be present now with all who bear the beams of love reaching across crumbling old walls of separation.

Give patience and wisdom to those whose passion to do the right thing blurs the beauty of the person in front of them.

Grant that our fear of conflict not overwhelm our courage to do the good you have placed in front of us.

In the harsher moments of the growth of your church, when sisters and brothers in the faith become our enemies, give us, more than ever, love for our enemies.

Be thou the balm of healing for your people at First Congregational Church, Berkeley, that the howling winds in the breath of your changing, may move them to the land of gentle breezes, where time and love mold scar tissue into new hope, and new reconciliation.

Be thou the constant companion of all your homosexual children who have sure suffered long in ways others cannot know.

Be thou the constant companion of all who feel excluded by those who say gay people should be included.

Eternal Spirit whose love still spins Jesus into our midst, show us how to take his hand

Loosen the soil of every heart that growing we have not imagined may yet begin.

*2020 comments: The Church in Honduras in the 1980s*

*Honduras in the 1980s was still a predominantly Roman Catholic country, both culturally and by belief. The majority of Honduras still claimed Catholic identity. But evangelical churches, "Iglesias evangelicas," were growing fast then, as they were throughout Central America.*

*While in the United States we are used to the majority groups of churches being Roman Catholic, mainstream Protestant, and evangelical, Honduras basically had only two, Catholics and evangelicals. Even the remaining groups who had come into being by the work of mainstream church missionaries were generally considered evangelical. Tensions between Hondurans Catholics and evangelicals were frequent and sometimes intense. It was not easy to get the two groups to work together, but our Christian Commission for Development worked hard to serve both populations, even though we were an evangelical organization, probably one of the most inclusive and progressive in the country. Funds for CCD's work did come from more progressive churches in the U.S., Scandinavia and Europe.*

*The Catholic church in Honduras suffers from a shortage of Honduran priests. During our years there, probably over 50% of the priests were from Spain with another large group from the United States.*

*Since the region around La Granja was so remote, a priest came only once each month to say Mass at the nearest church in Cololaca. On other Sundays the service was led by trained lay leaders called Delegates of the Word, who were trained to take leadership to cover some for the shortage of priests.*

*Among our co-workers in San Marcos and at La Granja, all of them were Roman Catholic except one. But in our other regional offices evangelicals were in the majority.*

*We felt the Catholic-evangelical tensions locally in Cololaca where there were two evangelical organizations working on behalf of improving the lives of the rural poor there. One, called CEPAD, clearly refused to work with Roman Catholics. Their work included trying to convert Roman Catholics to evangelicals. The other, our CCD, attempted to work with both groups and to bridge differences that were common in many local villages.*

*Once while I was in Cololaca for a Spanish lesson with the local school teacher there, the brother of our friend and co-worker, Alvaro Melgar, a Roman Catholic, dropped in. The teacher, an*

302

evangelical, promptly began to criticize Roman Catholics saying they did not respect the "word of God," the Bible. He did a little dramatic presentation talking to me in front of this kind Roman Catholic man. He put a Bible on the floor and walked across the room stepping over the Bible, commenting that Catholics just step right over the word of God. It was difficult to watch.

CCD also had initiated its own program to train Roman Catholic Delegates of the Word, which at first seemed an appropriate and helpful thing to do, given that our work was in villages where we wanted everyone to work together. then one day the priest from San Marcos, an American, came for a visit and questioned us about this program, saying it had not been cleared with the area Catholic bishop. This needed to be attended to.

*The Bishop's Visit*

If a priest came to Cololaca and the area around La Granja only once each month, a visit by a bishop was much rarer and only happened once every decade. We were told it had been twenty years since the last time a bishop visited the area. But during the months that we were there word went out that the bishop would be coming to visit.

Bishop Luis Alfonso Santos was the bishop that we had heard most about in Honduras. His Diocese of Santa Rosa de Copan included our area near the El Salvador border as well as Mesa Granda, the United Nations refugee camp in San Marcos which was home for hundreds of refugees from the war in El Salvador. Bishop Santos was respected because he considered everyone as members of his flock.

We were honored when Bishop Santos stopped for a visit to La Granja as he traveled farther west into the remote countryside. He was a tall, charismatic and gracious man. He did wear a robe but he clearly was not a man who needed to speak down to the people.

## May, 1987

*La Granja, the Bishop's Visit*

Just about every village we work with has a church building, most them simple adobe structures built by the people of the village. Evangelical churches are growing all over Honduras, but this part of the country remains predominantly Roman Catholic, both religiously and culturally. But the Guarita district of the Diocese of Copan is a very remote area. The bishop's headquarters in Santa Rosa, Copan is a four-hour drive from the area around La Granja. So back in August when it was announced that there would be a visit to this area by Bishop Monsenor Luis Santos, the area began to buzz with excitement and preparations got under way.

One aspect of the preparation appeared when one day ten-year-old Andres came to our house and with great excitement, and without the slightest hint of shame, he announced to us that his parents were getting married. The practicalities and poverty of life in the remote countryside makes it normal for couples to come together and raise a family without getting married. We never got all the details about the wedding and marriage, but in preparation for the bishop's visit his parents wanted to get married. Andres was so excited about this. He did show even a hint of shame about his parents being unmarried. Everyone understood how nearly impossible getting married was in the countryside.

This would be the first visit by a bishop in over 20 years and aroused more excitement by far than anything we had seen or heard of during our time at La Granja.

He was scheduled to arrive at 11:30 in Cololaca about two miles from La Granja and the site of one of the larger church buildings in the area. The streets were full of people from many remote villages in the surrounding hills. Women dressed up like I have never seen them, and men wearing the jeans saved only for dress-up occasion probably many of them bought just for this.

The bridge at the edge of town was neatly lined in green with coconut palm leaves and an archway had been built of various other branches. There were signs saying welcome and with Bible verses on them. A popular guitar group had been brought in from somewhere to provide music for the occasion. The church building itself was decorated with greens and streamers hanging everywhere, with most of the benches removed because a larger crowd could be accommodated standing than with seating for some.

Three cars appeared up the road in the distance but it was not clear which one Bishop Santos was in. They rolled across the bridge under the archway and turned left under a second archway toward the central plaza and the church. A crowd of about one hundred, a large crowd for a village so small, many of them children, ran along beside the cars, their heads bobbing up and down as the multitude moved up the hill to the church.

As the cars came to a stop someone with a portable microphone tried to get people to "make room! make room!" but no one seemed to obey. Monsignor Santos got out of his four-wheel drive vehicle which he had been driving and walked slowly to the front of the church accompanied by two priests from the area, one of them Father Richard who comes to say Mass once a month in Cololaca. The crowds followed and seemed so fully connected to their bishop and all that he symbolized for them.

Everyone processed into the church for a simple ceremony of welcome. People were elbow to elbow, most of them standing. The training of Delegates of the Word by the Catholic church in Latin America has become well-known. "Delegados" are lay men and a few women who are trained to lead Sunday liturgies and provide other church leadership in the absence of a priest. Fidel Guardado is the presiding delegado in Cololaca. He spoke opening words to the crowd through a specially arranged loudspeaker. After being in church with him a number of times I had never heard Don Fidel speak with such fervor and pride. Father Richard then introduced the bishop and gestured permission for the people to do, what they were going to do whether he gave permission or not, and give the bishop a hearty round of applause.

Monsignor Santos then stood to speak from the chancel, using no notes, holding the microphone in front of him with both hands. His manner was formal but gentle. He obviously knew how to communicate warmth and well with a crowd of people from the countryside.

He greeted the people and began to speak about peace within and peace between persons. I hoped he might say something about the wars going on in two countries bordering Honduras but he did not. He did speak of the need for peace as it related to some difficult conflicts between the Roman Catholic Church and evangelicals in Honduras. He shared an experience in which a zealous evangelical had showed up at the meeting where the bishop was presiding and began to interrupt to the point of slandering the Pope and speaking hostile words against the bishop himself. After recounting that his reaction to this hostile situation was to accept it without responding and then to simply request that the man allow them to proceed with their meeting. It was yet another sad but typical story.

He went on to say that for those evangelical Christians with an openness to receive him, he intended this pastoral visit to be for them as well as for Catholic Christians.

Later in the afternoon, he said a Confirmation Mass and accepted a few dozen new members into the church.

Yesterday, the bishop continued his tour of the more accessible villages along the main road. We knew that he would stop at La Granja for a one hour visit. We had been nervously making our own preparations for this, especially trying to decide how we could keep the coffee hot and be sure we found someone who could cook sweet rolls good enough to be worthy of the bishop's visit.

The Christian Commission for Development comes from Evangelical and Protestant roots. Much of our funding comes from more progressive denominations in the United States, Europe and Scandinavia. But our ecumenical and cooperative stance has been clear. Our work with people in any village was never limited to one group or another. Our effort was always to help everyone in each village to work together on behalf of the good of the whole community.

But there was one point of tension between the Catholic Church and our work. A few weeks ago, a priest came out from San Marcos to visit with Kathy and me about CCD's work with Delegates of the Word. Since these leaders played an important role in the development work in the villages, our leadership training programs were often directed at Delegates of the Words as well as to evangelical pastors and other leaders. The priest spoke his concern that CCD was working with Delegates of the Word without any real permission or understanding with those in authority in the Catholic church.

*Bishop Luis Alfonso Santos, Bishop of the Diocese of Copan talking with friends on his visit to La Granja.*

We had strewn palm branches in the path from the road to the main meeting house at La Granja for the bishop's arrival. When the bishop drove up, he came upon someone he obviously knew well and was glad to see who probably had heard he would be at La Granja and came there to greet him. The bishop greeted him warmly and enthusiastically beside the road as he got out of his car. I noticed that he gave his full attention to this friend and did not appear to be rushed at all to be "on time" for meetings. I appreciated this about him. He also took off the skull cap often worn by bishops and put on a wide-brimmed hat that gave him a local, country look while also protecting him from the sun.

He came down the hill and across the creek into our meetinghouse where about 25 people had gathered from nearby villages. We served him the coffee and sweet rolls which seemed to be agreeable with him.

Our conversation with him was cordial and he was very supportive of the work we were doing. But obviously, word about CCD's training programs for Roman Catholic Delegates of the Word has reached him and he spoke very firmly and clearly about how he felt about this. I remember his specific words so clearly: *"De ninguna manera puedo acceptar que sea un programa para los delegates due es parallelo al nuestra."* (There is no way I can accept that there is a program for delegates of the word that is alongside our program for them).

CCD staff in each of our four regional offices generally includes the same staff: a Coordinator/Supervisor, a nurse or someone in charge of health programs, an agronomist to take the lead in agricultural support in growing food and raising farm animals, a woman who takes the lead in working with women in the villages, especially in issues of nutrition for children including breast-feeding and who takes the lead in "Reflexion" (reflection) which includes Bible study and occasionally adds literacy training to respond to the many who have never learned to read. Elmer Reyes is our co-worker for Reflection and he and I took note of the bishop's concern about our programs for Delegates of the Word without any consultation with those in authority in the Catholic church.

*2020 notes: Soon after this meeting with the bishop, we wrote a letter to Daniel Medina in our main office in Tegucigalpa. Daniel was in charge of the area of reflection for all of our various regional offices which included work with Delegates of the Word. Daniel responded by making an appointment with Bishop Santos in his office in Santa Rosa. He made the long drive across country this this meeting and asked Elmer and I to join him. We had a very friendly meeting in the bishop's office, with good sweet rolls and coffee, but the details of how we all would work with Delegates of the Word in the villages was not discussed in much depth. Daniel seemed to have his own strong opinion that there was no reason for CCD to change its programs of working with Delegates of the Word. The meeting ended cordially, but I did not fully understand what had been accomplished there nor what any next steps might consist of. In retrospect, I think there may have been a lot going on culturally that as a gringo, I just did not understand. I wondered if Bishop Santos needed to meet CCD representatives and thus have his own authority acknowledged and respected more than he needed to make any changes in the programs. I'm sure I was seeing the situation from my experience of the very easy and comfortable Protestant-Catholic relations I had known in Seattle, but this was a very different place.*

## Friday, May 8, 1987
*1:00 p.m., La Granja*

Unfinished silence,
Marcel Marceau builds kingdoms for us,
and we see how much we can see
and how much really does exist
  for us to embrace,
  to delight in,
  to dance with
  on the horizon.
The work of just seeing is almost enough,
  but it is the step into sacrifice
that keeps us earthy.
This courage to see and create
to put self on the line
because truth and duty so order it
to see and create
because the seeing and the New Creation
were placed in front of us,
this is the path.

*2020 note: Here I tried writing a poem in Spanish.*

Niña, con cara mirando adentro de mi,
con sonrisa rodeada por manchas de la buena tierra,
ensename,
lo que tu sabes de la vida
(sin saber que tu sabes).
Ensename el camino,
la verdad delicada

que tienes en tus manos.
Niña,
Con pies bien bronzeados por las buenas tierras,
pies que toca a la madre tierra
sin nada separandoles,
ensename niña
porque yo tambien quiero
conectarme a la tierra
yo tambien necesito
ponerme los pies
en buen suelo.

Tu niña,
en tu humildad,
supuestamente desposeido,
eres el camino.

(translation):
Little girl,
with your face seeing inside me,
teach me
what you know about life.
without knowing that you know.
With your smile surrounded by spots
made by the good earth ("dirty face")
teach me
what you know about life.
Teach me the way,
the delicate truth
that you hold in your hands.

Little girl,
With feet well-bronzed by the good earth,
With bare feet touching Mother Earth
With nothing separating you from the earth,
teach me
because I also

want to be connected to the earth.
I also need to place my bare feet
on good soil.

You little girl,
in your simplicity,
supposedly dispossessed,
you are the way.

*Kitchen crew at work.*

## Wednesday, May 13, 1987
*1:20 p.m., La Granja*

We were to give out fertilizer in Cololaca today to the people from Las Flores. But the written notice that was sent had tomorrow's date on it, so we did not work. We came back home. After not working very hard yesterday, I slept well last night, but found myself sleepy this morning. I slept an hour, then took this hour to pray, reflect, and write.

La Granja is full of work, new construction — building an adobe oven in the new kitchen, a new bridge across the creek, cleaning land, a new small house for guest teachers, and more. It is a busy time. La

Granja is growing. I hope it is a growth that is connected to the growth of the people in the region. Usually I think it is. Sometimes I wonder.

*2020 notes: When I read that final sentence, "sometimes I wonder," it struck me as having some unconscious colonialist mentality in it, as if I were somehow in a position to judge what is best for a people that has known how to survive against many odds for centuries. It is humbling to notice such, but I do notice that growing in consciousness takes time and that we live by grace, not by being perfectly awake all the time. The adobe oven was a memorable piece of work. It required a special blend of good clay soil, sand and a few other ingredients with the right amount of water added to get the right level of consistency and strength. Mixing these ingredients required our walking around on top of it in our bare feet. It reminded me of people pressing grapes in Italy. We had some fun with that.*

## Sunday, May 31, 1987
*Noon, La Granja "Casa arriba" (in the new house up the hill)*

The new house for instructors up the hill behind the house is nearly enough finished that we can now use it for a reading and praying getaway. The cement floors are dry. The walls and roof are up. And we have brought up a temporary table and chair. It has a great view, looking across these Honduran ridges to the nearest mountain of El Salvador. One looks down on freshly ploughed ground and our new grass-top shelters here in La Granja. A breeze blows. Birds sing. Roosters crow. It is peaceful. And today, unlike most Sundays, there are no sounds of bombing from El Salvador.

Moments from recent days:

New roadblock in Cololaca -- Living here as we do between the continuing civil war in El Salvador and the United Nations refugee camp in San Marcos for Salvadorans escaping the war, this is a sensitive area. There is now a military roadblock just two miles down the road in Cololaca, and we just learned UN workers are not allowed to enter the frontier area. One friend suspects collaboration between the Salvadoran and Honduran armies so that when the bombing increases in El Salvador and thus more campesinos seek to leave as refugees, there will be no UN personnel to assist them into the camps in Honduras.

We also learned that two San Marcos area soldiers (Honduran) were jailed for having sold weapons to Salvadoran guerillas.

Clowning in the parade in San Marcos --There was a carnival and parade in San Marcos so I decided to have a little extra nerve and put on my clown face that I brought with me. There was a man with a microphone and he really took me right into the action. It was great fun.

Three little girls on our front porch. One with a "switch" the other two playing like they are cows. They are having a ball. Sometimes I have felt that children aren't as free to imagine and play here in the campo. Perhaps I am wrong. In any case I was glad to see it happening and glad it was happening on our front porch.

Martina, a 5-year-old who would sit without moving for two hours in earlier months, now is a bundle of playful energy when she comes to accompany her mom on washdays. She teases me, takes the initiative in interaction, hugs me around the legs, and does little things trying to be helpful. Such a joy to see the change.

*One day-long workshop brought mothers and children to La Granja to learn about getting better nutrition from the food available in the area.*

Canned peaches are expensive in Honduras. At Enrique's house last Thursday (the 28th) we each had a peach half from a can of peaches, which is a hard-to-get luxury in Honduras. He mentioned that his family would not be eating them were his brother not in the army which provides discount commissary prices. Makes me wonder how many people are "pacified" by such perks who otherwise might comprise a significant political opposition movement in the country. When the military leaks its favors in many directions, there is less danger of significant opposition, especially when the favors are complemented by widespread terrorism and fear.

Incident that happened in April 1985 an area of Valladolid, a few miles west and south of us. A Mennonite worker was arrested with a group of campesinos and all were taken to the nearest military post for all-night interrogation and torture. They were thought to be collaborators with the guerrillas in El Salvador.

The Mennonites wondered after this if their work was more of a threat to the people than a help. They took two polls, one among the Honduran people with whom they work, and another among people in the communities in general. The people with whom they worked overwhelming voted for them to stay. 60% of the larger community, however, felt that the Mennonites were communists and should leave. They decided to remain, but with the addition of a US couple in residence in the area who would hopefully provide more security.

That couple Ray and Sonja, who live in San Marcos, (forgot last name) told us this story. The Mennonites are still at work in Valladolid.

Brad and Doña Alejandra dancing -- This happened during a workshop on raising rabbits here at La Granja. Dona Alejandra is barely 5 feet tall, a slight woman, toothless, kind of bouncer in her personality and always has something to say. Brad is one of our CCD co-workers, a gentle guy, late 20s, warm with people, a caring and fun-loving person. We were playing a game in which various people have to do "penalty." His turn came to do penalty during recreation time at the rabbit workshop. He had to dance for the group in order to do his penalty. He demanded music (we made marimba music with hard-clapping and mouth sounds) and a partner. He had not more than requested a partner when Doña Alejandra was on her feet. They danced to hand-clapping and the good music of uncontained laughter. A great moment in the life of La Granja.

## Monday, June 1, 1987
*La Granja*

Sometimes I wonder what are the secrets I know without my knowing that I know them. That is to say, what authentic wisdom do I unselfconsciously put into practice in my life. But then I come to decide that it's better that I not be too aware of all that I unknowingly know. For thereby I have less danger of becoming a totally pompous ass.

## Sunday, June 7, 1987
*La Granja*

(See 31 May) Speaking of the roadblock in Cololaca. If the activity of the Honduran army increases at the same time as the activity of the Salvadoran army against the guerrillas, and if at the same time the UN is not allowed in the area to help refugees, then it seems more than likely to me that the Honduran army and the Salvadoran army are cooperating. That is to say, the army of Honduras is quietly involved in fighting the guerrillas of El Salvador.

In today's prayers, the words came to me - "if I do not tell the story of the people in Lempira, Honduras, who will?" Perhaps that is stating it with a bit of over-melodramatic urgency. Perhaps not. I think it is time. I don't know of many, if any, US writers who have lived in this part of Honduras who have seriously tried to write of life here. I need to be about it -- day by day -- experiencing, capturing images, trying to love and tell stories with my pen in my hand. It has not and will not be easy. I cannot do it forever. But I can be about it.

*2020 notes: Once again, that book I was going to write other than this journal never came to be. But rereading this journal has reminded me of how much I learned during those eighteen months at La Granja.*

*In June 1987, Kathy and I had flown to Memphis for my sister Margaret and fiance Chip's wedding. On our return to Honduras, we landed at the San Pedro Sula airport and rented a hotel room to spend the night before returning by bus to San Marcos and La Granja the next day, or so we planned. The headquarters of the Christian Commission Development was in Tegucigalpa, a four-hour bus ride to the southeast of San Pedro Sula. San Marcos and La Granja are a much longer bus ride to the Southwest, toward El Salvador and Guatemala. From the hotel room in San Pedro Sula I decided to call our main office in Tegucigalpa just to check in and say we had returned and ready to get back to La Granja. Our friend Tim Wheeler, an American Quaker in charge of agricultural programs, answered the phone. I opened with my friendly voice but there was an uneasy silence before Tim responded. Then he said, "We want you to come to Tegucigalpa. Do not go back to La Granja." I could hear something in his tone that told me not to ask any questions. So I said, "it sounds like that's all you want to say right now and that we should not ask any questions." He replied, "that's right."*

*So we went to the bus station and caught a bus to Tegucigalpa where we learned why we should not return. While at La Granja just a few weeks previous we had had as guests for dinner at La Granja two young men from Great Britain, Carl and Frederick, who had come with an interesting and important mission: They traveled from village to village throughout the countryside to record the natural medicines that the country folks had learned would bring some relief to various ailments. They were friendly and interesting and we enjoyed our visit with them very much. Carl had as a side interest trying to detect the presence of bats in our part of the country. Since bats give off some kind of unique sonar signal, their presence can be detected by a simple "radar" detector. He had one, showed us how it worked, and, according to this detector, we did indeed have bats flying about around La Granja. Not surprisingly we had never seen one.*

*Carl and Frederick had a carefree and adventurous spirit about them. While we were back in the U.S. for the wedding they were walking along our road on the other side of San Marcos doing no one any harm, but they did not have their papers, their "documentos" about why they were in Honduras, with them. With*

316

*the extra military patrols now in the area it was not long until they were stopped by two young Honduran soldiers carrying submachine guns. We never learned exactly how the conversation with the soldiers evolved, but we did learn that the soldier had told them to kneel and take off their shirts, a typical preparation for minimizing a bloody mess when soldiers are about to execute someone.*

*By sheer good fortune the bus came along before this happened. The bus stopped. Bus drivers are used to communicating with soldiers. We imagined that the driver may have talked the young soldiers into getting on the bus and driving to some place that might allow for other alternatives. We had met one or two Honduran soldiers carrying submachine guns who looked to be as young as 14 or 15.*

*The bus stopped at La Granja. By even more good fortune the Executive President of the Christian Commission for Development, Dona Noemi de Espinoza, was there at the time to show visitors from European funding agencies our work there. Noemi was experienced in the ways of the Honduran military having been a "person of interest" herself in the past for her leadership in agencies that served the needs of the poorest. (In Honduras anyone engaged in work that helps the poor can be suspected of being a "communista").*

*Even more seriously, I had left in our bedroom at La Granja a few articles and other literature that was clearly written in support of the Sandinista government in Nicaragua, already identified by the U.S. and Honduran governments as a communist enemy. We don't know exactly how it all happened but Noemi went through our room, found these papers, and managed to burn them before the soldiers came to search the house. Otherwise my privileges as a U.S. citizen having this literature in my possession could have gotten our co-workers into some difficult trouble.*

*There was a five-day workshop on raising goats going on at La Granja during all this, so there were people there from a dozen or more surrounding villages. The incident came to a close with no one being hurt or even detained, but it had the effect of spreading a new level of fear and paranoia throughout the countryside.*

*About two weeks after we had relocated to Tegucigalpa, we were able to go back to La Granja and get the rest of our things. On this trip, we were required to stop at the main regional military headquarters in Santa Rosa, a four-hour bus ride from La Granja, and get special clearance, something we had never had to do in the past. We met with a colonel who seemed to be the person in charge of this outpost. He was very courteous to us. There were no problems, but it was clear that "security" measures in the area had expanded.*

*When we got to La Granja, we had time to visit our nearby neighbors. It was then that we learned how rumors and fear had moved about the countryside. Many thought we had gotten into serious trouble and had been forced to leave the country. We did as much correcting and reassuring as we possibly could, then packed up all our things and headed to our new home in the capital city.*

# CHAPTER 5
# TEN MONTHS IN TEGUCIGALPA
## JULY 1987-MAY 1988

**Saturday, July 18, 1987**
*Joy and Eric's House, Tegucigalpa*

Weeks have passed since writing here. Those weeks have included so much- Margaret's wedding, the return to Honduras to find that we could not go back to La Granja, backaches, prospective children to adopt, meeting the abandoned babies at Leonardo Martinez hospital in San Pedro Sula - it has been too long. We are

319

living in the apartment of two friends from the U.S. while they are away.

So we now live in Tegucigalpa. Many details have been passed over in saying this. Honduras no longer feels like the relatively secure easy place to be that it has been for us during all of our time here. It probably never was as free as we felt it to be. I think we wanted it to be and did well at convincing ourselves that it was freer. Now we know differently. I would like to write more here, but it seems now that we must take precautions even in what is written in the privacy of a personal journal.

Yet while unfreedoms flourish, hope also takes off in new ways. And these days it is in the form of a tiny baby boy in the hospital nursery room for abandoned babies, Leonardo Martinez Hospital, San Pedro Sula. He could well become our son, or something may prevent it. But he has already had an impact of hope on me, and I think on Kathy also.

On Wednesday of this week, I was sitting outside Dr. Joyce Baker's duplex in San Pedro Sula talking with Susie Briggs about our adoption plans when Jaime, Jimmy, age 23 walked up. He is an adopted child of U.S. missionaries, and now lives here in Honduras. When he heard that we were talking about adoption, he opened the La Prensa newspaper in his hand to an article which said there were eight abandoned babies at the Leonardo Martinez Hospital. After some moments of talking about it with Susie and Joyce, I took off to the hospital to speak with the Director himself, Dr. Guillermo Florentino. At the front entrance of the hospital, they told me he was not in and that I should come back the following morning. I walked away reluctantly, then wandered down the sidewalk beside the big wall at about the point where I thought the Director's office might be (hoping, I think, that there might be a back entrance, and that I might by chance run into him. Instead, an employee of the hospital, perhaps a maid, noted my curiosity and asked me if I was looking for someone. When I told her of my interest, we started to walk together, naturally, and she seemed like a messenger placed in my path on our behalf. She had completed her shift of work for the day, but was going back into the hospital to get a shot. She took me back to the main entrance, through the door, and walked with me all the way to the maternity department where she called the nurse in charge by name. The nurse waved us on to the nursery where I was most warmly received by a young woman intern doctor and two nurses. They directed me to wash my hands, put on a robe, and then I could go in and see the babies. So I walked in. There they all were. Tiny, some not looking so well, others looking better, none of them looking like the healthiest babies I've ever seen.

One of them was very ill with encephalitis, his head at least three times its normal size. I cannot get him out of my mind, and I wonder about the deep suffering of his mother (and perhaps his father too) knowing that they have left a child with so many needs, while they must have also thought heavily about the difficulties that would have faced them in raising him.

The nurses told me I should come back the following day to meet Dr. Saenz, the pediatrician in charge. We were hosting a group of students the following day, so we could not, but on Thursday, I brought Kathy to the hospital. Dr. Saenz was there, and we went in so Kathy could also meet the babies.

We tiptoed a little, looked around with great wonder, and after a while the doctor said, *"cargelo! cargelo!* (pick him up!) when he saw our interest in one of the little boys.

When we left, Dr. Saenz walked with us to the social work office where we were promptly directed to the Tribunal de Menores. There we talked with the woman in charge who sent us on to the social worker. A strong Mennonite, she took down all our biographical information and then admonished us rather strongly about the problems that have happened with adoption processes.

This was in San Pedro Sula. Within a few weeks all of our efforts toward adopting children were transferred to Tegucigalpa, the capital city, where we would live for the remaining months of our time in Honduras.

*2020 notes- Adoption*

*A few months before we left for Costa Rica in September 1985, Kathy and I had come to terms with the difficult reality that having children by birth was not going to be an option for us. I had put most questions about children out of my mind before we decided to make the move, although we had begun to make some inquiries about adoption. I do not remember mention of adopting children in our conversations as we made plans to move to Central America,*

*In the early months of 1987 we did begin to talk about adoption with our Hondurans co-workers in San Marcos/La Granja and we instantly began to learn about how many children in Honduras were in need of and available for adoption. My impression was that in the culture of Honduras adoption was not a widespread practice and of course in a place of such widespread poverty, adding a child who was not born into a family would be an added burden.*

*We were still living at La Granja when one of the early pieces of information we received was that there were four birth siblings who had been orphaned and needed parents. We were intrigued, but taking in four children at once just seemed more than we could take on. After we moved to Tegucigalpa our conversation became more serious and we found that a lot of help was available. We learned that Honduras had a steady flow of adoptive parents from the U.S., Canada and Europe seeking children. For most the process required traveling to Honduras and living for at least a few weeks to complete all the requirements. We felt that in living there already we had a distinct advantage.*

*When we spoke of our interest to our co-workers at the Christian Commission for Development (CCD) possibilities began to grow very quickly. Noemi Madrid de Espinoza, our Executive President and an attorney, put us in touch with Sister Teresa Gonzalez who was a part of the School Sisters of Notre Dame community in the city of El Progreso, and with another attorney Lisette Sandoval, who had assisted many parents in the challenging legal requirements for adoption. Sister Teresa ("Hermana Teresita") was widely admired for her work with children in Honduras, including children who lived much of their lives in the streets. She was also an advocate for adoption. From our first meeting with her we felt a sense of trust in her understanding of the needs of Honduran children as well as in her experience with adoption.*

*I imagined from one piece of news that many Hondurans had mixed feeling about so many of the country's children being adopted and taken out of the country. After Sarita had come to live with us but before we had completed all the required paperwork for adoption, a bill was introduced in the legislature of Honduras that would terminate all adoptions of Honduran children by foreigners. At first reading, this caused us some anxiety but it turned out that the bill had little chance of being voted into law. But it did send a message that some Hondurans were not enthusiastic about foreign adoptions.*

## Monday, July 20, 1987
*Tegucigalpa*

We are still living at Joy and Eric's place. They are a U.S. couple here doing short term work but they have been away and were kind to allow us to stay here. We are nomads without a home at present.

I don't remember the exact date of Nancy Webber's death, but we are at the one-year anniversary. I think of her often, with gratitude.

Today began with a letter under the door. We do not know who wrote it, but it was not pleasant. It had words of threat for someone but it was not clear to us for whom the note was intended. There was no signature. It was very unsettling, so we reported it to the Executive President of CCD Noemi Madrid de Espinoza.

Then there was a staff meeting, singing, brief meetings and a hamburger for lunch.

This afternoon we met Licenciada Mayra Torres at the Junta Nacional de Bienestar Social (National Board of Social Welfare). She explained to us the next steps in the adoption process. We shall be spending many days now collecting documents.

This is being written the week that the letters started arriving at the apartment. Two or three threatening, unsigned letters were left at our front door saying that some of our co-workers' names were "on lists," meaning that they could be in danger.

*2020 notes: The notes placed under our door were alarming at first. In a situation where abuses of political and military power were not unusual, a number unsigned notes under our door seemed to be significant threats to the people and work of CCD. We promptly took the notes to our Executive President Noemi de Espinoza and left it all in her hands. After some internal investigation, it became clear* who had been writing the notes and more or less why. A CCD co-worker whom we did not know well, apparently, had some significant mental and emotional problems was having an affair with an American volunteer working for a variety of organizations in Tegucigalpa. The experience must have been very upsetting to her to the extent that she responded by acting out — i.e. writing unsigned notes which named some of our co-workers as being on "hit lists." She placed them under the door of other "gringos" on the staff. Since we were mostly new in town we seemed to be the safe place to receive most of these notes. The result of it all was that both of them were dismissed. The man, whom we had only met once or twice, had purchased a pet bird in a cage that we had agreed to keep for him while he was traveling for a week or so. After he left CCD he also left Honduras completely so we were left being the involuntary "parents" of a charming tropical bird, some smaller species of parrot, whose name was Rosita.

## Saturday, July 26, 1987
*10:00 p.m., Home of Pat and Trish Ahern, Tegucigalpa*

*2020 notes: Until we finally settled in our own rented apartment, we lived in a number of places for a few months between June 1987 and sometime in the fall. We housesat for a "Christy" a friend of Noemi, for a time. We were living there when we finally brought Sarita home to live with us before the legal process of adoption was complete. We lived in a lower-level apartment in the house being rented by Joe Eldridge and Maria Otero and their young sons. They were in Honduras for a year after Joe left the Washington Office on Latin America which he had founded. He had become a respected voice on human rights and other issues in Latin America. Maria was the daughter of a Bolivian diplomat and was working then on arranging micro-loans to start small businesses among poor populations in Latin America. It was very fortunate for us that we were able to get to know these dedicated and knowledgeable people. Joe was well connected with higher-up political leaders, business leaders and journalists from all across Latin America. Because he was a frequent critic of U.S. policy in Latin America, he was also a known figure at the US Embassy in Tegucigalpa, which was located just a few blocks from their home.*

324

*Later we lived for a few weeks in the home of Patrick and Trish Ahern. Patrick was the Director of a Roman Catholic relief and development agency in Honduras whose primary work at the time was inside the refugee camps of Salvadorans living in Honduras. I visited one of those camps once and witnessed ten-year-old refugee boys learning to make their own clothes on sewing machines and with teachers provided by the agency. It was impressive and inspiring.*

*When we left the Ahern home, it was time for us to get an apartment of our own.*

We are at the next stop on our movement from house to house in Tegucigalpa. From Joe Eldridge's to Joy and Eric Olson, and now to the Ahern home. This one is easily the most embarrassingly and wonderfully immense. This study really has a way of calling me, embracing me, setting me down to work and write.

I just had an idea of forming a group that would buy a piece of land in Kitsap County near the Trident Base as a kind of retreat center. It would include facilities for private retreats, a library with all the anti-nuclear information that one could want. There would be adequate facilities to offer overnight stays. Perhaps a community might emerge who would do the cooking and maintenance. Or perhaps I might be a part of that community.

*2020 notes:*

## THE TELA RAILROAD COMPANY

*Of the four million people who lived in Honduras in the 1980s there were 20,000, most of them workers on the banana plantations, who lived well.*

*As one of the central "banana republics" Honduras has a long history with fruit companies owned by U.S. corporations, United Fruit, better known now by the brand name Chiquita, being the most prominent among them. Its presence in Honduras began around as the 1800s became the 20th Century. The company, known in the area as simple "La Compania," (la com-pone-YEE-ah) occupied a major part of the land in the north coast region, the most fertile land in the country near the towns of El Progreso and La Lima. This generally meant that this land, which could have grown food crops needed by Hondurans, was instead used to grow bananas which were exported to the United States and to Europe. The great wealth earned from the bananas likewise moved north.*

*Since the company is located far from where we lived during our time in Honduras, we only arranged one visit there for the visiting delegations that we hosted.*

*When I called the company to arrange for a visit they were prompt to respond and glad to arrange a tour. We were met at their headquarters by a charming Honduran man who spoke perfect English. He put us all in an air-conditioned van and drove us around the area. We learned that he was a graduate of Tulane University in New Orleans, no doubt one of many who profited from the steady traffic of ships between Honduras and New Orleans that had been constant since the early 1900s.*

*It was a very pleasant visit and, in its way, impressive visit. We learned that for the 20,000 Hondurans then employed by the company, all of them had access to the company's own private health care. Good schools were also provided. And as in the case of our host those affiliated with the company in any way had some access to travel to the United States, especially by way of New Orleans, home for the largest number of Hondurans anywhere outside Honduras.*

*We were taken into the highly-automated center of the banana plantation. We saw one good reasons it was called a railroad company rather than a fruit company. Railroad tracks ran throughout the fields. And automated conveyors take the bananas directly from the trees to the railroad cars and loaded, then to be taken by train a short ride north to Puerto Cortes and loaded directly onto a ship headed for New Orleans, and to European and other ports of more affluent countries.*

*At one point in his enthusiastic sharing about all the assets of the company, he said with real emphasis "I love this company." And*

326

*who could blame him for that? In a country of four million he was among 20,000 inside the company who were doing well.*

*The massive problem with the company for the overall welfare of Hondurans has a number of problems, all of them having something to do with Honduras being dominated by forces outside the country, and in the last century, mostly by the United States. In a country with massive hunger and malnutrition the best land in the country is being used to grow bananas to send to other countries.*

*The company pays some taxes but it always seemed to be a problem to get them to pay their fair share given how much wealth they are making off of Honduran land and taking out of the country. The Tela Railroad Company always had immense power and influence on tax policy, including connections with the upper levels of the military.*

*LAND AND LAND REFORM IN HONDURAS*

*Land reform is a high priority issue in Honduras as it is in every Central American country. Honduras is known as having one of the most progressive land reform laws in Latin America since it began to receive more attention as part of the Alliance for Progress initiative for Latin America during the presidency of John Kennedy in the 1960s. Its basic premise is that any land that is not being used for its highest potential may be taken over by new owners. It is a radically progressive law intended to address the massive gap in land ownership between the rich and the poor. Its great limitation has always been enforcement of the law. Powerful landowners in Honduras usually manage to prevent most efforts to take over such land.*

*Since we lived most of our time in the mountainous area of Western Honduras we had little contact with Hondurans who sought to use this law to increase and/or land ownership. But we did have a few visits with both people involved in "land recuperation," the people taking over unused land, and with those who had been the previous owners, who referred to this as "land invasions."*

*The most inspiring example we visited was a parcel of land of about fifty acres which was the site of a former garbage dump for the city of Comoyagua in Central Honduras. A group of women moved onto this land, somehow got a house built for each one of them, and began to farm the land as an agricultural co-op. It was an inspiring example of people with little power or influence makings of the law.*

*The Tela Railroad Company and other large fruit-growing corporation were mostly exempt from the law even though it could be argued that their use of land in Honduras was the most egregious violation of proper land use.*

## Monday, July 27, 1987
*Noon, Home of Pat and Trish Ahern, Tegucigalpa*

This house is a plush embarrassment and a great blessing. It does have a way of pulling me into its study, to get me closer to serious work. But I am not yet there. I allow too much to intrude. I am yet lacking in the appropriate "take myself in hand" day-to-day discipline that gets me seated and as focused as possible. I do hold out hope, ever trusting that I am turning out some things that in their own simple way, do matter to people. Mostly they are kittens. Yesterday I wrote to Koh Min Yung in Korea and to Trinidad Gutierrez in Nicaragua, two friends in struggling places.

Here in the quiet, new ideas start to move about the manuscript on life in Western Honduras. I still believe it is possible to turn out something worthwhile, maybe even good. Seems that most of the pushing must come from me. I have a sense that I need to be able to ask for a lot of help on the project, but that either I don't know how or am too threatened to do so. In any case I'm sure that I need to work at the project a lot more diligently while I take it a lot more lightly.

This is page 326-but how well I now know that there is more to writing than filling pages with words.

## Monday, August 3, 1987
*8:35 p.m., Ahern home, Tegucigalpa*

*2020 notes: Apparently, I wrote a sermon, or part of one, in Spanish. I wonder if I was hoping someone would invite me to preach in Honduras.*

La Debilidad de Dios y la Resureccion
The Weakness of God and the Resurrection
Todos creyentes bien saben que Dios es todopoderoso. Es una caracteristico fundamental de Dios. Sin embargo, el Dios de la Biblia, de Abraham, Isaac, y Jacob- de Jesus, Pablo, y Pedro-- este dios es un dios bien distinto de los demas dioses. Este dios dejo todas las caracteristicas clasicas de que significa ser un dios. Este dios dejo su propia creacion para desarollarse por sus propias fuerzas. Dejo su control del universo para que sea un universo de toda libertad. Dejo su control de todos los seres para que ellos sean creaturas de libertad. Dejo su contro de su querido ser human, la persona que creo en su propia imagen, para que el amor entre Dios y el ser humano sea autentico.

*All believers are well aware that God is all-powerful. It is a fundamental attribute of God. The God of the Bible however, the God of Abraham, Isaac and Jacob, of Jesus, Paul and Peter — this God is very different from other gods. This God left behind all the classical characteristics of what it means to be a god. This God left to his own creation the work of developing themselves from their own powers. this God left he control of the Universe so that the Universe could be a place of total freedom. He gave up his power to control all beings so that they could all be free creatures. He let go of control of His dear human beings, those whom He created in the Divine image, so that the love between God and human beings could be authentic.*

En este sentido, es correcto a hablar de la debilidad de Dios. Es una debilidad escogida. Es resultado de una decision permanente de Dios- a crear el ser humano con posibilidades sin fin.

*In this sense it is correct to speak of the weakness of God. It is a hidden weakness. It is the result of a permanent decision of God — to create a human being with endless possibilities.*

Nuestro Dios escogio el camino de la debilidad. Lo hizo por su fe en su creacion. Lo hizo por su fe en la persona humana.

*Our God has hidden the way of weakness. He did this because of his faith in His creation. He did this because of his faith in the human being.*

Esta debilidad no es una barrera al poder de Dios. Su poder, o sea, su amor, lo cual es toda libertad, y lo cual es amor, llena la creacion buscando las puertas abiertas, para que entre, y para que continue, la misma creacion, a traves del universo mismo, y especialmente a traves del ser humano, la persona. *This weakness is not a barrier to the power of God. God's power, which is God's Love, is totally free. This love fills all of creation seeking open enter into, places where the work of Creation can continue throughout the universe itself, and especially through the human being.* Entonces, que pasa cuando en su libertad el universo se cae en la destruccion? Que pasa en un terremoto, por ejemplo? El universo sigue siendo libre, y a veces hace mucho daño. ?Y como reaciona Dios en este momento? Con fuerza? Con debilidad? Dios no deja la libertad con cual creo el universo. Dios interviene en tal situaccion. Bien que si. Pero interviene con libertad y con amor, no con control, ni con el fin de la libertad. Y cuando la persona sufre como resultado de la libertad del universo, como reacciona esta Dios? Nuestro dios sufre tambien. Queda sufriendo en una debilidad. Dios llora. En la misma manera de que Jesus lloro al sentirse el dolor de su querido Lazaro, Dios llora cuando su gente sufre.

*So what happens when the universe in its freedom falls into destruction? What happens when there is an earthquake, for example? The universe keeps on being free and at times much destruction results. And how does God react in this moment? With strength? With weakness? God does not leave behind the freedom with which He created the universe. God does intervene in such situations. This is very true. But he intervenes with freedom and with love, not with control. And not by ending the reality of freedom. When a human being suffers as a result of the freedom of the universe, how does God react? God also suffers. God remains present in suffering and weakness. And God weeps. In the same way Jesus wept when he felt the loss of his dear friend Lazarus, god weeps when God's people suffer.*

Asi que puede hablar de la debilidad de nuestro Dios, aquella Dios que dejo las caracteristicas tradicionales de ser un dios para relacionarse con su creacion. La conclusion de nuestro Dios es la cruz. Otra conclusion es una cara de un Dios, sufriendo con su gente.

330

*In this spirit it is possible to speak of the weakness of God, the God who left behind the traditional characteristic of being a god in order to be in a real relationship with Creation. The final word, the conclusion, of our God is the Cross. Another conclusion is the face of God, suffering with his people.*

Un dios debil. Un Dios rendido a la cruz. Un dios con lagrimas en las mejillas. Un Dios debil, pero la conclusion final no es asi- porque la misma cruz, las mismas lagrimas, son los primeros elementos de la resurrecion. No es un evento antes de la resureccion. Son partes fundamentales del proceso de amor que siempre busca y llega a la resureccion.

*A weak God. A God surrendered to the cross. A God with tears running down his face. A weak God, but the final conclusion is not weakness — because the same cross, those same tears, are the first elements of the resurrection. All of this is not an event that comes before the resurrection. They are fundamental parts of the process of love that always seeks and arrives at the places of resurrection.*

Las lagrimas de Dios dan la humedad al alma del universo, y asi sigue la creacion con libertad, y con amor. Las lagrimas llenan los almas de las personas humanas, y asi ponen la resurrecciion en cada corazon que tiene una puerta abierta.

*The tears of God give moisture to the soul of the universe and from this there follows the freedom of creation, with love. These tears fill the souls of human beings and in this way place the resurrection in every human heart that has an open door to receive it.*

## Saturday, August 8, 1987
*Ahern home, Tegucigalpa*

Psalm 85:8 ff:

*"Let me hear what God the Lord will speak for he will speak peace to his people, to his saints, to those who turn to him in their hearts. Surely his salvation is at hand for those who fear him, that glory may dwell in our land.*

*Steadfast love and righteousness will meet; righteousness and peace will kiss each other. Faithfulness will spring up from the ground, and righteousness will look down from the sky. Yea, the Lord*

*will give what is good, and our land will yield its increase.*
*Righteousness will go before him, and make his footsteps a way."*

It is not a day when I feel particularly good. My back problems
are minimal, but they do seem to stay with me. I must take care. But
I also feel some worry, I think -- a bit of spiritual fatigue -- nothing
awful. The anxiety is about my future as a pastor. Doubts are all about
me. What will I do? Is there really a place for an experimental parish
in Seattle? I can only trust and go ahead. I believe I am a pastor. I am
nourished in the land of prayers and hymns, words and teachings,
covenants and plans. It is covenant out of which I want to live.

Within almost just weeks, we may have a child. He is much on
my mind. And so is she-- both of them. Sometimes I think, how will
we even have the time or energy to be parents with the way we live.
But then it is about to happen. It seems very likely. My heart is full
of fantasies of playing with children, laughing, looking at the stars
together, touching animals, building things. Ideas take off. I guess I
had better fantasize about changing diapers, getting up in the middle
of the night, and a few things like that as well. A tiring, magnificent
adventure is on its way to us.

## Wednesday, August 26, 1987
*4:00 p.m., Ahern home, Tegucigalpa*

Psalm 63
*"O God, thou art my God, I seek thee, my soul thirsts for thee; my*
*flesh faints for thee, as in a dry and weary land where no water is. So*
*I have looked upon thee in the sanctuary, beholding thy power and*
*glory. Because thy steadfast love is better than life, my lips will praise*
*thee. So I will bless thee as long as I live; I will lift up my hands and*
*call on thy name."*

We have just finished 2 weeks with the group from University
Congregational in Seattle. We are very weary but satisfied with the
results.

Life feels very unsettled for us -- living out of many houses.

We are not very close to each other at the moment. These times
of distance always concern me, but I lean into the future, wanting to

trust that a hope and grace beyond me is sufficient for a relationship that I often struggle with. I know Kathy must struggle with it also.

Yesterday we went to El Progreso and talked with Sister Teresita Gonzales about Silvia who may well become our daughter. It looks very promising. I look forward to having a chance as a parent, going through all the bumps and joys of sharing in the life of a child. I also know I am being naive about it in some ways, perhaps many ways. I naively feel that I will define my days in the future as I have been able to in the past. Yet I know that this is not so. God will provide.

*2020 note: I sure was naive about that. Becoming parents rearranged everything. Whoever Silvia was, we never got to meet her.*

## Saturday, August 29, 1987
*8:30 a.m.*

Today begins three days with two Congressmen and others here in Honduras. It should be a most interesting time.

*2020 notes: This delegation was one of the most interesting I hosted. It had been arranged by a much-admired doctor, Charles Clements, who had spent much time in El Salvador during the civil war there offering his services in any way he could. He had written an excellent book about his experiences and was a much-respected voice about issues in Central America.*

*The delegation included Clements, a congressman from Virginia who with Clements was a member of the Unitarian-Universalist community, an impressive member of the Texas state legislature and at least two more people who were very knowledgeable about Latin American politics. Clements requested that I make an appointment for the group with Everett Briggs, the U.S. Ambassador to Honduras at the time. So I called the embassy and learned that the ambassador would be willing to meet but only with the congressman. I was told that the ambassador's schedule was very full and that he was away up on the north coast. When I relayed this information to Charles Clements, he requested that I call back and let the ambassador's office know that the ambassador would meet with the entire group or there would be no meeting at all. Upon getting this news the ambassador had a helicopter fly him back to Tegucigalpa earlier than planned and arranged for the group to have lunch at the ambassador's residence. It was a great lunch and we had a lively conversation. It was also quite a lesson for me about what it means to know how to play one's cards well in the power dimensions of politics. I also arranged a meeting of the group with the Nicaraguan commanders of the U.S.-funded "Contras" who were based in Honduras at the time.*

## Monday, September 7, 1987
*7:00 a.m.*

On Saturday, September 5, we met Sara Patricia (or "Sarita" as she was known), her grandmother Marta Molina, and aunts Brenda and Cecelia. She was slow to relate to us, understandably so, but it was quite a visit.

She sat across the room from us, most in Marta's lap, but she watched us aplenty, I think. We certainly watched her until she must have felt our eyes burning into her.

We were impressed at her assertiveness. When grandma pushed her, perhaps a little too fast, to come to us, she said "no" with real gusto. Then when I took the little stuffed dog we had given her, trying to use it to get a message to her. She came promptly and took it from my hands. She would not be invaded without consent, nor without protest. We are sure that this could be a problem in the long run, but more likely evolve into a strength for Sarita. We both preferred to see this rather than a passive child.

She is very bonded to her grandmother. And it remains to be seen whether it will prove best for her to depart from grandma and bond to us. We feel that more of the decision belongs to Sara than to anyone.

Yesterday, I watched a friend with her two-year-old and the bonding that happens from the birthing process. Probably there is some bonding that will never quite be possible for us - one which we will sense is absent - since we cannot be birth parents. This is not a great negative. It is simply a reality that needs to be accepted.

## Monday, September 14, 1987
*11:30 p.m.*

Reflections on Time in Central America

These are the closing months. Pretend as I might that something strong and new may yet be lifted out of our time here, it is clear that we are accelerating toward the day of departure. Energies will reach toward the more distant future and our intentions and efforts to be creative and useful will not contain the same depth that we sought and often found in our earlier months in Honduras.

*2020 notes: In September, I must have been naively thinking that whatever the difficulties of the adoption process might be, that it could be completed within a month or two, especially since we were there in Honduras so that we could deal in person with any questions or complications that might come up. It all took much longer than expected. The Honduran requirements for stacks of legal documents were many, but it was the extensive delays at the U.S. Embassy in getting visas for Sarita and Andrew that caused the longest delays.*

This is good. It is ok. And I seem in this moment to be accepting the reality that more creativity will flow out of these closing months if we will, if I will, give in to the energies of closure and not pretend that something else is happening, that too much is possible.

A general strategy for these closing days is to write, to reflect, to evaluate, to put things into packages that can be passed on. It may be a time to be more quiet - to retreat more, to find days away, to send more pieces of mail, to pray more, to trust the silence and more fully into my "creaturehood."

Today, the question arises within me as to what depth of conversion has happened within me as a result of my time here. Probably very little in some ways, and yet some realities of the time here deserve reflection.

Kathy said in our first Vista del Sur (the newsletter that we sent out every few months) that our intentions in Central America would not be to "accomplish" anything. Well, we did not accomplish very much, and that may, in the end, work out to be okay, even though it was hard as hell in many moments.

I am remembering that among our Honduran coworkers, nobody, no one person had more formal education than either Kathy or I -- and yet we clearly had to function in the role of being generally dependent on our "less-formally-educated" Honduran co-workers for everything from how to get the cook stove to work to how to communicate with campesino pastors. This, I believe, was more painful for me than I was ever willing to admit completely, probably more than I was conscious of most of the time. We were in the hands of people much more humble than us much of the time. Just to what depth the Holy Spirit was able, allowed to make use of this in my own ongoing transformation, I of course cannot say, but I do now begin to feel that this reality, this being in the hands of humble folk, was a critical and valuable ingredient in this experience.

It has not been a quieting experience. It has mostly been upsetting, upending, disturbing, inconvenient, conflictive - not the sort of elements I would not rationally recommend to a person such as I whose metabolism has long been overly bent toward over-activity and a shortage of silence and centering. Was this God's will? Well, I think so, while I also know that it was God's will for me (both of us) to allow ourselves to be nourished by silence more. That upsetting, prophetic quality of spirituality is something that perhaps only friendship with the poor can give to us. It seems much more likely to me that whatever spirituality turns out to finally be, that its meaning for me required this contact with the poor ever so much more than it required a mustering of prayer technique and the discipline of silence, important as those are for me. I shall need to continue and to grow in the struggle for a deeper daily intimacy with Jesus through silence and prayer, but perhaps the time here has taught me that the starting place for any authentic spirituality is the doing of justice. The struggle for intimacy with Jesus, and the resulting creativity it seems to me, must follow the struggle for justice.

*2020 notes: It is interesting to compare this writing to my speculations about this time which I wrote above in the entry above for November 20, 1985.*

## Friday, September 18, 1987
*El Progreso Afternoon*

After a few days in Mexico for a meeting, we arrived back in El Progreso where Sarita and family were again waiting on us, surrounded by drums beating and a parade about to begin, for it was the week for the celebration of Honduras Independence from Spain in 1821. We tried to interact, again with Doña Marta pushing, probably a little too much, with not much success at first.

Then we went up the street to the parade where Sarita allowed us to pick her up. She even sat on my shoulders, kind of willingly but cautiously, to watch the marching bands go by. It seemed to me that she wanted to relate to us, but just was not altogether sure about the whole thing. We took some pictures at this time which we still have.

Before the parade we went to a small diner and had lunch. Everyone was there: Sarita, Dona Marta, Aunts Brenda and Cecelia, Kathy and me. I played finger games at lunch with Sarita. We all had a good time.

After the parade, we walked to Sarita's house in the Coracol (snail) Colonia, a long walk by foot, between one and two miles. She allowed me to carry her most of the way. Finally, we arrived at a tiny house on a dirt street. We sat on a little bench beside a wall/room divider made of cardboard. Doña Marta talked of the struggles of being poor, and hinted that she would like to receive some money from us, which we gave to her. Brenda was also present, and I think Cecelia as well.

Kathy assisted Brenda in a little changing and bathing process out back by the house's one faucet and concrete sink. Later on, we said goodbye to everyone and went back to our room at the Hotel Las Vegas.

## Saturday, September 19, 1987
*El Progreso*

As we had agreed the day before, we arrived back at Sarita's house at about 9 a.m. to spend more time with her. But when we arrived, Sarita was not there. Only Brenda was at home who explained that Sarita had been sick during the night and that Doña

Marta had taken her to the hospital. We were concerned, so we worked and got a taxi to the local hospital hoping to find the two of them there. But they were not to be found. We waited for an hour at the hospital and then took the bus back to mid-town. We went to the local health center. And then to the Instituto Notre Dame trying to track them down, but we never found them. Probably afternoon, we went back to Sarita's house and found them waiting on us. We visited a while and invited Sarita to come with us to buy some new clothes, with Brenda only coming along this time -- a little test to see how comfortable she would be without her grandmother.

It was fun. We bought new dress and colorful underpants at a children's store. We then found some sneakers for her and a few more items at the public market. I distinctly remember how Sarita began to walk differently, with pride, (well it was almost a strut), and it was a total delight to see.

We went back to the same little diner for some lunch. Brenda wanted more food than we ordered at first, but said she had "pena" (embarrassment) to ask for more. We ordered. Sarita also ate well. The place made good little tacos.

## Sunday, September 20, 1987 (written later from memory)

As I remember, we went for Sarita in the morning - as always, a very hot day, and on this day, as we had decided, with the family, we went "solo" for the first time. We, with the slowly-won approval of Sarita, took her with none of her relatives along.

We tried not to rush things. We went to the Hotel Las Vegas and had lunch, probably chicken, at their air-conditioned restaurant, usually saturated with hard music as well as cold air.

Later we made the long walk with Sarita to the El Progreso "POPS" ice cream store and had ice cream together. Somewhere in the day, we went back to our hotel room and lay down for a nap. I remember that they had already stripped our beds but let us go back with the room after checkout time, probably because we had Sarita with us. The mattresses were covered in thick, clear plastic. We had been told by Sarita's grandmother that she did not sleep during the day. And in fact, she at first said "no" to the idea of lying down to rest with us. But she did give it a try, and soon was asleep. I was there with Kathy under one arm (awake) and Sarita under the other arm (asleep) when out came the classic words for the good moments in our home, "living high."

We had been on again, off again during the weekend about whether or not to try to take Sarita with us back to San Pedro Sala, and on the San Marcos and La Granja. Somewhere in those three days, we had pretty much given up the idea, but that got turned around again until we decided that we'd go back to Sarita's grandmother's house and give it all a try. When we arrived, Doña Marta was not there. Said to be at her sister's house, Brenda went with us to see. Another bus ride back across town to the "compañia" area of old houses left by United Fruit Co (or one of the fruit companies). Doña Marta was not there, but we met Sarita's great aunt and great grandfather, both of whom were completely encouraging to us to take Sarita with us. I remember his emphatic words to us when we asked if he felt we should adopt her. He said *"llevela! llevela!"* ("Take her! Take her!). this was the strongest affirmation we had heard. We tried to explain our desire to go slow in the process, but their counsel was almost a form of pressure. We still did not feel good leaving with Sarita until we had checked with Doña Marta, even though for weeks the plans in the long run had been clear to all concerned.

We had a Pepsi-Cola in a plastic bag and then got on the bus again to go back across town, back to Doña Marta's house, hoping that by now she might be there, or to wait for her if she was not.

The latter proved to be the case. We waited. We wondered if Doña Marta was, in a way, purposely being difficult to find as a mean of avoiding the pain of separation that she was certain to face at some point. And we came face to face with the possibility that our well-intended plans not to push too fast could well be a prolonging of something extremely painful for Doña Marta. We talked with Brenda, Sarita's aunt some more, and we decided that we would take Sarita if Sarita herself was agreeable.

We asked her, and at first she responded with her very firm distinct "NoOO." I can still hear the inflection exactly as she said it.

She made no into a two-syllable word with the accent on the second syllable.

So we sat, and we waited more. Sarita and I gathered rocks and she threw them at a little puddle of water which was in front of her front door.

A little later, not more than half an hour, we asked again. This time Sarita's answer was an almost matter of fact "si." Brenda gathered many of her clothes together, and we walked off with her into a dusk that was quickly turning to darkness, past the ever-interested neighbors and their continuous stares. We did not know it then, but we were making that walk with Sarita away from her house for what would be (or at least has been up until this writing) the last time.

We got to the bus and made the ride back to San Pedro Sula, through La Lima, and checked in at the Hotel Terraza. It was not to be an easy night for Sarita, or for either of us.

*Sarita on the day she met Mary Ellen Smith and Nancy Hannah at La Granja,
who would become godmothers to Sarita and Andrew.*

*2020 notes: My memory is that on the next day we got on the bus
with Sarita and headed south to La Granja to host a delegation there
from California. But friends Mary Ellen Smith and Nancy Hannah
from University United Church of Christ in Seattle had also come
to Honduras for a visit at the same time and joined us on the trip to
La Granja. So Sarita went to La Granja with us and met Mary Ellen
Smith and Nancy Hannah for the first time. I cannot begin to
imagine what it must have felt like for a four-year old Honduran
child to travel by bus for six hours with us and be among strangers
for all that time. But under the circumstances with her grandmother,
aunts and other family members it did seem to be the best option
that we had at the time. I remain in awe of what this child who would
become our daughter had endured. She had lived through more*

341

*trauma in four years than most have to endure in a lifetime. She was an amazing survivor and an amazing human being.*

*A Memory from the Village of Coyolillo*

*While we were back for a visit at La Granja showing our visitors from the United States around, Don Juan Rodriguez, a campesino we had known from the nearby village of Coyolillo arrived by foot with anxiety and urgency all over his face. He explained that his daughter was in labor and that the birth was not going well and that the village midwife needed some help. Coyolillo was only a two-mile drive plus a half-hour walk from La Granja. Mary Ellen was at the time a Ph. D. nurse practitioner on the staff of the highly-respected Child Development and Mental Retardation Center at the University of Washington. She also had previous experience collaborating with midwives to provide health care to families on an Indian reservation. With much relief, I felt that by fate or Providence we had just the person to go and help. Mary Ellen was very willing to go and offer any assistance that she could.*

*I loaded Don Juan and Mary Ellen in the pickup and drove to the trailhead to Coyolillo. Don Juan walked very fast ahead of us, almost running to get back. We walked as fast as we could.*

*When we arrived at the house I went into the living room and could see into the bedroom just enough to note that the midwife had the head of the bed elevated very high allowing gravity to offer all the assistance it could in the birth. The midwife seemed calm and very much in charge. Mary Ellen walked in while I waited outside. I watched as she stood and observed, apparently sensing that she should not move in to help too quickly.*

*After being there about a half hour, Mary Ellen said, "the midwife is doing everything I would know to do. I think we need to leave it in her hands."*

*The urgency of the situation had subsided significantly and we reassured Don Juan that all was well and quietly took our leave. Later we got word that the baby was born and that mother and child were both doing well.*

342

*I hasten to say, however, that while this experience demonstrated the ability and experience of a local midwife, that area of Honduras would have been blessed extravagantly to have Mary Ellen available. There was almost no one in the area with medical training. For a population of around 15,000 in the area there was one medical student in training available. There were no doctors.*

*Perhaps there is nothing specific to be concluded from this experience, but it sure has stayed in my memory. I think of how many children are born into the world without any of what we call "professional" healthcare and how most of them do survive. This of course does not mean that people in in desperate situations all over the world can make it just fine without more medical support. Of course this is not true. But this experience did imprint on my memory how the poor majority in the world are able to live sufficiently without the health care that we in privileged settings take for granted.*

*I have memories of other moments during those weeks but I cannot fit them all into a clear chronology. Once in San Pedro Sula we had a meal in a restaurant with our Honduran friend and co-worker Alvaro Melgar and Sarita and he got into a wonderful game with her pushing paper back and forth across the table. He had her laughing and they were having a great time.*

*Back in Tegucigalpa with Sarita*

*Apparently, I did not write anything in my journal about the time after we got back to Tegucigalpa with Sarita. This is not surprising remembering how challenging it was to become parents for the first time and still keep up with part-time duties with CCD. We were invited to house-sit for a new friend Christy which provided a good place for us in our first weeks with Sarita. A primary memory from those days is how much she cried every night before going to sleep for her grandmother. I can still hear the anguish of her cry for "Mamita, Mamita, Mamita." It would go on and on until she cried herself to sleep.*

*It was also during this time that we were able to get Sarita to a doctor and begin to get her some help for her malnutrition and what we would learn were parasites in her stomach. When we realized how much she had suffered from just these two realities we were even more amazed that she had survived at all.*

*During the days at Christy's house, we hosted a Latino United Church of Christ visitor from California, Rev. Alfonso Roman. He was a Puerto Rican and knew some wonderful children's songs in Spanish. He would sing to Sarita and get her to sing some also.*

*Refugee Camp Visit - One of my duties during Alfonso's visit was to drive him to a Salvadoran refugee camp near the El Salvador border. While there I witnessed the most remarkable phenomenon of ten-year old boys on treadle sewing machines learning to make their own clothes. Many of the programs available for refugees in this camp were run by Catholic Relief Services, whose Director in Honduras was Patrick Ahern, in whose home we had stayed for a few weeks while he and his family were out of the country. I was very moved by the quality of the programs offered as well as by the initiative and creativity of the Salvadorans in the camp.*

## Thursday, October 8, 1987
*Tegucigalpa*

Sara Patricia Irias, 4 years old on August 29, 1987

Dates- thinking back a few weeks. We've been too busy to write in a journal. I will try to recap here.

Tuesday August 25, 1987- date of first meeting with Sister Teresita in El Progreso.

Saturday September 5, 1987 -- date of first meeting with Sarita at the Instituto Notre Dame, El Progreso, Honduras with Sister Teresita Gonzalez, Doña Marta her grandmother and guardian, and her aunts, Brenda, and Cecelia. A tender day - fear, uncertainty, Sara was sick, threw up, Doña Marta wanted to push interaction with us, but Sara would not accept it. Kathy helped with the cleaning up when she threw up. Sister Teresita brought a pair of pants which we still have. I tried to interact with her, but she would have nothing to do with me. We had taken a small stuffed dog as a gift. She took it with great energy, with very strong affirmations of "mi-a!" (mine). It had to be an upsetting day for Sarita.

El Progreso is located about twenty miles outside of San Pedro Sula. So to visit Sarita and her family members required a four-hour bus ride to San Pedro Sula, then another half hour on the bus to El Progreso.

We came back home on the afternoon bus to Tegucigalpa.

*2020 notes: We were invited and expected to attend a meeting of other United Church of Christ staff in Latin America in Guadalajara, Mexico in the days after we first met Sarita. We enjoyed our time there, which included Lloyd Van Vactor, veteran in international church work who spent many years in the Philippines, and Patricia Rumer, Latin American Secretary for the United Church Board for World Ministries.*

## Tuesday, November 10, 1987
*Tegucigalpa*

Matthew 24: 45ff. - Faithful and Unfaithful Servant
*Who then is a faithful and wise servant? He is the one that his master has placed in charge of the other servants to give them their food at the proper time. How happy that servant is if his master finds him doing this when he comes home!*

## Sunday Nov. 22, 1987
*3 a.m. Tegucigalpa*

Rooster crow
Insomnia, troubled.
Have I not the courage to even pursue the convictions that I say I have?
Do I seek consolation when the elements of my healing are decision and discipline?
Covenants
Vows
Like
Ordination- marriage
I carry them heavy.
If I could but be with my vows like this ever-faithful unquestioning cocker spaniel beside me, who brings me comfort in

the wee hours. Would that I could be satisfied by just bringing comfort and could walk away satisfied that vows thus have been fulfilled "yes, yes it's ok" Yes, you have that sense that there's something more redemptive that you could be, but that you just can't be, let yourself be it -- It's ok, because after all, you are saved by grace and not works. And maybe it's even a little bit arrogant for you to try to be something that might be as much due to your ego as to your callings.

Reading Wendell Berry, *Unsettling of America* with a sense of how we are ceasing to be a culture that interacts with the land -- a culture in which even environmentalists have a terrarium view of nature -- it is something that we admire but not interact with. We are not a part of it.

In retrospect, I know that I, like so many thousands, have simply had to work with what is -- a self that is not nearly as courageous as I would like be, and a world, a creation, that begs us to treat it with reverent action.

So here I am. I'm a loud-talking, go-do-it type, and a I'm a cautious, non-moving tip-toer. I carry on with it all only because God loves me, and I remember that well-enough only because people love me.

So where to? Where to from this moment?

## Friday, December 11, 1987
*11:00 a.m., Tegucigalpa Apartment*

Mt 11:16-19
*But to what shall I compare this generation? It is like children sitting in the market places, and calling to their playmates, 'We piped to you and you did not dance; 'we waited and you did not mourn.'*

*For John came neither eating nor drinking, and they say he has a demon," the son of man came, eating and drinking, and they say, 'Behold, a glutton and a drunkard, a friend of tax collectors and sinners!" Yet wisdom is justified by her deeds."*

Advent Dancing Mourning
To play to the music of life
To play
To be in the action.

To let oneself be taken in
You won't come out unscathed
But you'll come out healed, refreshed, hopeful.
So jump in the fire.
Jump in when the music starts,
but most importantly
Jump in there minute by minute
Care for the minutes
and allow the hours
and the years and
all in between
to take care of themselves.
Let there be quiet.

*2020 notes*

*REMEMBERING* ....

*Endless bureaucratic challenges of completing a legal adoption process in Honduras.*

*The tasks and difficult emotional work of completing an adoption seemed endless. We had a good lawyer to assist us but she lived a long way from us in San Pedro Sula. Documents had to be signed in El Progreso where Sarita had lived. One official in one of the social agencies there asked me to take a walk with him outside his office. When we walked enough to be reasonably private from others, it became clear without his actually saying so that paying him a bribe was assumed as part of processes such as this in Honduras. I had been advised by Honduran friends that the best option in such situations was simply to pay the bribe. So, I did. Later I thought of it as simply a fee that was part of the process. I believe it was about $20 U.S. It seemed very reasonable for the purposes being served.*

*Back in Tegucigalpa, we had to come up with a way to get approval by licensed social workers in the United States. This would require an interview to evaluate our competence to be adoptive parents. We thought this might require a trip back to Seattle for this, but it turned out that we were able to do it by phone. Our dear friends Gail and*

*Ed Crouch were both licensed and experienced social workers and knew us well. They agreed to do the interview for us by phone. I remember that phone conversation as the most pleasant step in the adoption process.*

*We also had to complete individual interviews with a social worker in the Office of Social Welfare in Honduras.*

*By far the most emotionally demanding task was to drive 225 miles one way from Tegucigalpa to El Progreso three times with Sarita's birth mother Angela Irias: go get her, drive her back to Tegucigalpa to get her approval of the adoption in person at the Office of Social Welfare and then take her back home.*

*Kathy and I decided that it would be best if I did this alone. We knew that Sarita had spent very little recent time with her birth mother and that she had been raised by her grandmother and two aunts. We had all the birth family approval and permission possible to claim her as our daughter, grandmother, two aunts, and even a great-grandfather that we were introduced to. Everyone involved, and especially our "adoption midwife" and spiritual guide Sister Teresa Gonzalez felt that the best option for Sarita was to become our adopted daughter. With some fear and trembling we moved ahead with it all. We knew enough about the realities of poverty in Honduras to realize how credible this option could be.*

*Angela wanted to have her boyfriend accompany her which seemed like a good thing to me, for her to have a companion during seven hours on the road with a gringo who was new to her. During the trip I was able to have some conversation with her and confirm that we had her support to move ahead with the adoption. We had had less contact with her in the weeks preceding than with any other member of the family. I remember the moment while driving when Angela said she was glad Sarita would be in "buenas manos" (good hands). It was a long day, nine hours of driving for one signature, but of course it was more than worth the cost.*

## Saturday, December 26, 1987

*10:00 p.m., Our Apartment, Tepeyac Tegucigalpa*

> *2020 notes: Our apartment in Tegucigalpa was in a middle-class part of town called the Tepeyac neighborhood, named after the mountain in Mexico where a pregnant, peasant Mary appeared to Juan Diego, the origins of Our Lady of Guadalupe, the patron saint of Latin America. It was a spacious place in a complex with about sixteen other units. It was multilevel with a kitchen and dining area on the upper level and a living room and bedroom on the lower level. The bedroom had a high ceiling with a beam across the top from which I was able to hang a swing for Sarita. We had no car but we were walking distance from the largest super market in the city. As I remember we did most of our moving around town by taxi which was not all that expensive.*

Christmas passed in joy and peace. Kathy's sister Wendy and her friend Phil came for a visit. Tia (Aunt) Wendy, Kathy's sister, touched us with her involvement with Sarita. They became friends very fast.

## Friday, January 1, 1988

*3:45 p.m., Tegucigalpa*

A quiet and cloudy New Year's Day, 1988. I am a parent. I think that no change in my life has brought such meaning. This is surely one of the big ones. Probably I will understand more of life from having entered into parenthood.

I am restless in some way. Perhaps my hunger for silence is not what it has been in times past. Too many little details have been to take me away from larger, most significant pieces of work. My growing edge spiritually in these days I know has something to do with this. For example, we take lots of pictures and I send them off in envelopes to be developed. I am spending more time doing this than getting the pictures and slides organized into attractive useable form. I am lacking some in the pushing of self into things that I know are good. It is like I am putting brakes on myself, almost going out of my way to hold myself back from creativity. I am not doing badly. I am just not doing as well as I could be.

*Tegucigalpa*

## Wednesday, January 6, 1988
*Tegucigalpa*

One More Adventure with the Transit Police

Honduras has a unique branch of its law enforcement administration called the transit police. They are notorious for making an issue out of something that is not an issue and expecting a bribe in the process. On one earlier occasion I was driving one of CCD's vehicles when I was pulled over and since we did not have bright orange triangles in the car, the car was impounded and taken to a large government car lot. I was so embarrassed. When I told our supervisors what had happened, they were not at all dismayed. I began to learn that this was not unusual. One of our experience staff members went and promptly got the car back. I assumed he did so by paying the customary bribe to the person in charge.

Today I was driving one of CCD's vehicles and a transit police office on one of the city's busier streets pulled me over. He told me I had changed lanes without giving a signal which was entirely possible. But my violation would not be easily dismissed with a traffic ticket and a fine to pay. The officer got into the car with me and said I would need to drive to police headquarters. I had been here long enough to know this was not as serious as it seemed. The young officer was courteous. I asked him if I would need to pay a fine and he said that I probably would. I began to assume this this "fine" would simply be the usually bribe expected by many local officers.

So I asked him, "is this fine one that must be paid at your headquarters or is it one that I can pay to you directly?" He first replied that it must be paid at headquarters. But a few minutes later he said, "it is possible for you to pay the fine directly to me."

We pulled over. I paid him my "fine" and went on my way feeling unperturbed.

I felt like this was some rite of passage and that I had made it to the inside of some community of understanding in the life of Honduras. I felt very proud!

*Hoping for a better life in the city many move from rural areas to crowded hillside barrios in Tegucigalpa.*

## Friday, January 8, 1988
*Tegucigalpa*

Focus in my life

Occurs to me today that it is not I who gives focus to my life but rather grace that reaches out to me and into me to accomplish this.

Being touched by peace.

Today I was touched in a phone conversation with Bishop Luis Alfonso Santos that he had remembered me and greeted me with such warmth.

Suddenly ideas start to flow on many fronts, and there seems to be new energy to do, new likelihood that things I have wanted to get myself into will happen. And we will have a son soon. I do believe this.

## Monday, January 11, 1988
*Tegucigalpa*

Today we went to meet our son for the first time. We will call him Andrew Alvaro Mullins-Williams. and he is a great blessing.

## Friday, February 26, 1988
*Tegucigalpa*

Days are filled with parenting and as the number of days between journal entries shows, not much reflection and writing lately. Days are good. Parenting is full of exhaustion, tenderness, at times hard-to-control anger and exasperation, and with more commitment and centeredness in it than I knew I had. I am already feeling I am being made a better person, able to see more and see more clearly, more able to struggle with patience, because of being a parent. But it is going to take me a long time to learn how to do this. At 39, I am getting a late start. My past experiences of enjoying nieces and nephews for an afternoon visit is a far cry from this twenty-four-hour regimen.

## Tuesday, March 15, 1988
*Tegucigalpa*

With reasonable, not always diligent, faithfulness, I read Scripture devotionally. I like it. I want it to speak to me. In its way, it has sustained me all my life. But this silence -- sometimes filled with gentle thoughts, or hilarious idea, or just gentle stillness -- and more -- I sometimes wonder if this silence is not worth more to me in my relationship to God. The scripture -- with my straining effort to connect -- often does not. But the silence is freer. It has no bounds. It can take in everything.

I believe God is in this silence in a special way. God sighs when the silence begins and knows that she can move a little closer to me, which she has been wanting to do all along.

Being with God is not something that can happen when one is too busy. Just be still. God will do the work that is necessary.

## April 21, 1988
### For Sarita

Is there a word worthy of what you bring? And yet I must search my tender and wonderful one. For the goodness that you are to me begs for lines, that the savoring may not fade into the petty struggles of days.

You are the color given to hope,

You are the warm here and now who holds me, while hope's reaching for us, and our reaching for hope, carries us on.

Your tiny hands loom large for me, Endless six-second neck massage. Eternity's own caress. Your tender days are replete with the finer things of love.

You are the lid lifted, the stops all pulled, on every goodness, Joy complete, joy ever remaking itself.

*2020 notes:*

*Sarita's Story*

*When Hermana Teresita first suggested a little girl who came to her mind that we might consider adopting, she was concerned that "Silvia" was more dark-skinned than we would prefer. We were a little taken aback that skin color was mentioned but apparently, it had been a concern for previous adoptive parents she had worked with. We assured her that skin color would not be an issue for us. A touch of my "liberal pride' almost wanted to say, "the darker the better," but some years later I would need to live through some difficult lessons about how adoptive parents with children from another culture are not immune to subtle forms of unconscious racism.*

*It turned out that we never got to meet Silvia. But news of a little four-year-old girl named Sarita followed close behind. The journal tells the story of our adoption of Sara Patricia or Sarita (sah REE tah) as she came to be known to all who knew her. Sarita is the Spanish diminutive for Sara. Not included was the astounding discovery through our Honduran attorney Lisette Sandoval that Sarita had a birth half-sister, a year younger, who had been adopted by a couple in Phoenix, Arizona. Lisette assisted us in getting the appropriate permissions in order to access the family's contact information. A few years later we made contact with "Amber Day" and her parents Mike and Phyllis. They had none of the knowledge of the birth family that we had, so they were even more amazed that Amber had a sister. It took all the parents some years to feel ready for the two of them to meet one another, but the day finally came when they first stood face when Sarita was about 13 and Amber about 12. It was, of course, an unforgettable sight to witness, two sisters who favored each other meeting for the first time at age 12.*

*It was sobering and challenging to get to know up close a human being whose early years were marked by malnutrition and poverty all around. Sarita was 4 and weighed twenty-five pounds when we took her in. She had about twenty-five words in her vocabulary by my count and I kept track until the number increased to fifty. After getting some medical care that she apparently had never had, she immediately began to grow and become more congenial. I never ceased to agonize over the conditions and timing under which we made the decision to have her come and live with us. We had permission from all the members of her birth family who had any regular connection to her. But the emotional agony we saw her live through in her first weeks with us left a permanent imprint on my heart and left me with many doubts about the wisdom of international adoption, even as I remain convinced that in so many situations it may be the best option available for children.*

*Kathy and I met six or seven members of Sarita's extended birth family, including two aunts, Brenda and Cecelia Irias, who had been a regular part of her life when she was a young child and her great grandfather. I can still hear his words in response to our recurring question of everyone, do we have your support in adopting Sarita? Is this a good idea.* His response was strong and unequivocal, *"llevela! llevela!"* *("Take her! Take her!")* We would not know what all was behind such strong words, but it did seem to be a strong affirmation.

The adoption legal process required an in-person signature in Tegucigalpa by the mother if she was living. We rented a car and I made the six-hour round trip with Angela Irias and her boyfriend at the time. I was grateful that he was with us as a support for her and to make for a more relaxed conversation during the trip.

While driving I was able to engage with her some in conversation that went a little deeper than just being assured that we would have her permission. I wanted to know if she was fully in favor of our adopting her and she assured me, that for reasons that were private to her, that she was. She said she was grateful that Sarita would be in *"buenas manos."*

When we returned to Seattle with Sarita, our house was less than a mile from the very reputable Child Development and Mental Retardation Center at the University of Washington. Our dear friend Mary Ellen Smith, who with partner Nancy Hannah became Sarita and Andrew's godmothers, had already met Sarita while in Honduras, was a Pediatric Nurse Practitioner there and became their pediatrician. So we had some of the best care for her anywhere in the world. Our house was between the clinic and Mary Ellen's house. She often biked to work and on a few occasions made "house calls" on her way home.

One of the outcomes of early malnutrition is deficiency in brain development which later results in learning disabilities. Sarita was blessed with wonderful teachers in two Seattle Public Schools. But her third-grade teacher was able to see clearly that Sarita was not going to be able to keep up with other children her age academically. We had spent many hours helping her with homework but it always seemed to end with Sarita feeling a sense of failure. We could not find in the public schools a program that would enable her to grow and succeed.

*A new school for children with learning disabilities had recently opened not far from our home and seemed to be made for just such children as Sarita. We were able to enroll her there and it was a great gift to her and to us also. Instead of coming home with assignments that were beyond her capacity and which left her with a sense of failure, she came home every day with a "report card" that she kept herself and which always showed progress and success. The system had screened out any sense of competition and we were overjoyed to see her self-confidence grow. She also became involved in gymnastics and took piano lessons.*

*As Sarita grew into her early teen-age years we began to tell her the full story of when we adopted her as our own daughter and about her birth family back in Honduras. We offered to take her back for a visit whenever she felt ready. She thought about this for a long time, but the trip never happened. She would sometimes say, "my soul wants to go but my body is not ready." I have wondered if it would have been in her best interests if we had taken her back to Honduras when she was younger.*

*When Sarita was ready for the seventh grade we were able to get her enrolled at St. Therese School, which had a strong reputation for its academic program as well as for being a caring community of learning. After three years in a school for children with learning disabilities she was back in a normal school academic program.*

*It was during this time that the strains on our marriage became very heavy as we tried to carry on two demanding careers while attending to all that was required of us as parents, especially for the unique needs of Sarita. Marriage counseling helped some, but our relationship had been deteriorating for so long that I decided that I could be a better person and a better father outside of the marriage. I also resigned from my position as pastor at Pilgrim Congregational United Church of Christ. There was no option that felt like "the right choice" for me.*

*It was also during her seventh and eighth grade years that Sarita first made mention of having thoughts of suicide. Kathy and I responded in all the ways we knew how, especially by getting Sarita back in contact with child psychiatrist Dr. Albert Reichert, who had already been such a help to us on behalf Sarita and our parenting. The principal at St. Therese School was also a great support and source of compassion and wisdom.*

*When it came time for high school, we did some hard searching. Kathy and I both had long-time loyalty to public schools, but we were not willing to put that loyalty ahead of Sarita's needs. We needed a program that was right for her. We found Eastside Catholic High School which had a good program for students who were unable to keep up with the regular curriculum. But the fact that it was part of a high school culture had endless social benefits. She decided to be a part of the cross-country team which turned out to be a group of young people who, even though some were very competitive runners, also had some remarkable sensitivity to people. Sarita was always dead last in just about all of her cross-country meets. When other runners would complete the 5k course in times ranging from twenty to twenty-five minute, Sarita's times were always over thirty minutes. But this did not seem to matter to her. She always finished and there were always teammates who were cheering for her as she crossed the finished line, including some senior boys when she was a freshman.*

*I was able to be present at some meets where Sarita was filled with joy at her own performance. Once in a West Seattle meet at Lincoln Park, she, once again, came in dead last but she finished with the best time she had ever had, and was jumping up and down with joy afterwards. I came to feel reverence for this amazing human being whose childhood realities had set her apart from other children, and yet who would learn to be such a generous friend to herself and in celebrating her own growth and successes.*

*One final cross-country story took place at the house beside Lake Sammamish. In one of the last meets of her senior year, Sarita began to come close to running a 5k course in under thirty minutes. The cheering throng of about twelve parents and ten or so teammates who had already finished got word that Sarita was running at a pace that in which she might break thirty minutes. So the crowd of twenty or so were standing on tiptoes as she headed toward the finish line in great suspense And she made it! She came in at 29:59, under thirty minutes for the first time and another new personal record. I still get a bit teary-eyed when I tell that story.*

*After her graduation from Eastside Catholic High School, Sarita was able to get her first job behind the counter at a Kentucky Fried Chicken Place and was proud to have that position. Doing enough math in her head to make correct change did not come easily for her, but she worked hard and learned how to do. Along with this she enrolled in classes at Seattle Central Community College where she could take remedial courses that could enable her to eventually attend regular classes there. During this time her interest in young men and discovering her sexuality came forth as it never had before. One challenge now was that she had nothing close to the social support system that she had known at Eastside Catholic High School. And when she became 18 years old, she was legally an adult and there were new limitations on supervision and boundary-setting by parents.*

*She made a series of bad choices, hanging out with people who were not a good influence on her and her life began to disintegrate in a number of ways. She had turned 18, a legal adult, and this limited our ability to get information about her from her teachers at the college. Except for a few days when we did not know where she was, we were able to stay in regular contact with her. But there was always a lot we did not know and could not find out.*

*There were many difficult and some very happy times with Sarita from age 18 to age 20. But her life descended into a very dark place until she took her own life at age 20. This was devastating to everyone who was close to her and sent us as her parents and other close to her reeling into the agonizing questions of "what did we do wrong?" There is of course very seldom a good answer to this question in the wake of a suicide, but the harsh wound and the agony never fully go away.*

*Sarita had found a home as part of University United Church of Christ in Seattle. She had made many friends there as well as at Eastside Catholic High School and in other setting of her life. The church was packed for her memorial service. Words written by Kathy and me were read. Faithful godmothers Mary Ellen Smith and Nancy Hannah spoke beautifully and truthfully about her life. Peter Ilgenfritz and Dave Shull were gifted and compassionate pastors and friends to Sarita, Kathy, Sharon and me. They led the service with compassion and with sober and straightforward words of healing.*

*There was a time in the service when anyone who wished to could come forward and say a few words. It pleased us that many did so, including past classmates from Eastside Catholic High School and even some former boyfriends. It was wonderful. But the words that I remember most came from our good friend Dr. David Hall, a child psychiatrist, one who had lived very close to the lives of children and youth in a lot of pain. He said two things that I remember well. He said, "please remember how many hurting children and out here are out there." Then he said, "twenty years may seem way too early for someone to pass away. But I encourage you to honor Sarita's life as a complete life."*

*Father-Daughter Dance, Eastside Catholic High School, 2001*

*The harsh pain of such a death never fully goes away. But Grace
does eventually find some space within us where it can reside more
comfortably. Its sharp edges become a little smoother and the many*

*blessings and graces of Sarita become visible alongside her tragic death.*

*I remain grateful beyond words that I had the privilege of being her father and learning all that she taught me. I honor and rejoice in the complete life that she lived in her twenty years.*

*A poem by a good friend helped us:*

*Black-eyed Pea*
*(for those who loved Sarita)*

*Uncommon life,*
*Peculiar muse,*
*A strong-willed*
*and fragile heart.*

*She grabbed all the sun*
*she could*
*and we trembled*
*that there might not be more.*

*In the middle of her olive flesh*
*Was her pearl—*
*Unavoidable.*
*An eye of black radiance*
*Announcing her power, revealing her rue,*
*Embracing our affections.*

*The days of a black-eyed pea*
*Disappear so quickly,*
*Before the fields can give her foundation.*

*She grew in our soil,*
*She fell in our soil,*
*And our same one condition remains.*

*We grieve as we have always done*
*Replanting her seed*
*And praying for the sun to be brilliant still.*

Kali Kucera

*2020 notes: January - May, 1988. Writing in my journal came to an end many weeks before we finally left Honduras in May. Those months were so very full with two young children and first-time parents, lots of trips to various offices in both Tegucigalpa and in San Pedro Sula to complete the adoption process and hosting a number of continuing delegations from the U.S. and other countries. Writing in journals or anywhere else moved way down on the priority ladder while I had a crash course, on the job training, in becoming a parent.*

*Andrew's Arrival*

*The call came to say we could come to the orphanage to pick up Andrew up and bring him home while I was a three-hour bus ride away hosting a delegation of church people visiting from Minnesota.*

*Of course we wanted to get him home with us as soon as possible. Kathy shared with me notes from her own journal of that time.*

*She lived through the endless challenges of Honduran transportation with hard-to-hail taxis, gathering needed supplies, and taking care of Sarita during one of the most emotional weeks we had known since arriving in Central America. News had just broken that two respected human rights workers were assassinated in San Pedro Sula, where I was at the time, the day before Kathy got the call.*

*After many hours of tiring trips back and forth across town, Kathy was finally able to bring Andrew home on Friday, January 15, 1988. I returned the following Wednesday.*

*After that we were able to settle into a somewhat stable routine, living further into the shocking realities of becoming parents of two small children at age 40. It was a time of joy, but also a time of exhausting work and for me, a time of great awakening to the demands of becoming the parent of an infant.*

*But I soon fell in love with Andrew and learned that being a father to my two beautiful children was the greatest gift of my life. One memory from those early months stands out: One day Andrew fell asleep face down on my chest while I also was resting. I could feel his heart beating next to mine. I'm not sure I ever became a great parent, but I did work hard to learn and do my part.*

*Andrew's Story*

*We chose the name Andrew because it has a beautiful sound in both its English and Spanish (Andres) forms. We chose Alvaro as his middle name after our good friend and co-worker at La Granja, Alvaro Melgar. We loved Alvaro and we admired him for how he had been raised in a humble farming family with limited educational opportunities yet had become such a graceful, compassionate and resourceful man against difficult odds. Our co-worker from San Marcos and La Granja were able to visit us only once after we moved to Tegucigalpa so Andrew and Alvaro were able to meet one another that one time. We took just one photo of Alvaro holding Andrew. I hope it is still living in some box somewhere.*

*Andrew's thriving has continued throughout his life. He did well in school and had what one grandmother called a "winsome" personality. My father said about him after meeting him as a toddler, "That boy never met a stranger." He was outgoing and made friends easily.*

*At age 5 his career in sports began with baseball (t-ball). Baseball was his first love among sports. He loved it and I loved teaching him what I could. I got to be his coach for one year of Little League.*

*Later his Little League team made it to the state playoffs. He played into his high school years.*

*He was also good at soccer and played from age 5 through high school when his team made it to the state playoffs. One of his teams made the city play-offs, which continued into the rainy, cold month of November. During his high school years, he once made a goal from what seemed to be an impossible angle near the sideline but almost even with the goal. I will never forget it.*

*In college he was sports editor of the college newspaper.*

*After some difficult days at the beginning of high school, Andrew made up his mind that he wanted to go to college and made good grades. His eleventh-grade English teacher required that students write poetry which Andrew loved. He wrote some beautiful poems and for a time enjoyed reading them to anyone who would listen. He also took piano and learned to play a very challenging arrangement of Pachelbel's Canon which he can still play from memory and will do so with some persistent requesting.*

*His record was good enough that he had a number of good options for where to attend college. I made sure he visited Rhodes College in Memphis where I went to school but had little expectation that he would go there. This was a West Coast man. But to our surprise, he chose to go to Rhodes after falling in love with the beauty of the campus. Then, even more to our surprise because we had never planned to live in the South again, Sharon and I moved to Memphis during Andrew's junior year when he was already very much in love with Lindsey Gibson, a fellow student from Kentucky. We lived in Memphis for 9 years and got to be there for Andrew's graduation, his wedding to Lindsey and for the birth of two of our grandchildren, Henry and Hadley.*

*After a year working for the Memphis Redbirds baseball team, Andrew took a job in a local bank and later got a job in another bank based in Memphis. Then in October 2019 a good offer to a position near Palm Beach Gardens, Florida resulted in a move to Florida where the four of them live as of this writing in 2020.*

*Andrew, Lindsey, Henry and Hadley in 2019.*

### *Doña Benita (DON-ya bay-NEE- tah)*

*The large unemployment rate in Honduras means that it is the norm there for many middle-class families to have full-time housekeepers. Our lives were so blessed in those months by Dona Benita who was with us many days during each week. I remember her as being everywhere for us. She cleaned our apartment. And she always seems to be nearby when we needed to hand off either Sarita or Andrew. And the best fit was that she loved them and they took to her right away. She became an adopted Honduran grandmother during our final months there. I have a memory of her on our small front porch with Sarita in one arm and Andrew in the other.*

### *House Church at Joe and Maria's*

*Another great blessing during those months was a weekly house church at the home of Joe Eldridge and Maria Otero. Joe was an American United Methodist minister but was better known as one of the important voices on human rights and development in Latin America. His voice was respected by many political leaders in both the U.S. and throughout Latin America. As a critic of many U.S. policies in Latin America Joe was at times a persona nongrata at* the U.S. Embassy in Honduras. Maria was Bolivian by birth and grew up in the home of a Bolivian diplomat and official in the World Bank. They were very good teachers for us. The also had two young sons and they also adopted a Honduran daughter during those months. Sarita and 3-year- old David Eldridge enjoyed playing together and Andrew was instantly friendly with anyone, allowing himself to be passed around to anyone without protest.

### Anti-U.S. Protests at the U.S. Embassy, May 1988

In April and May 1988, for the first time that anyone we knew could recall, there were strong anti-U.S. protests at the U.S. Embassy. It was an intense time. Honduras had been one of the few Latin American countries that behaved almost totally as a loyal U.S. dependent. Anti-U.S. protests were usually mild and carried out by a small minority. It could be dangerous to protest too vigorously. But this time was exceptional. Many Hondurans were tired of being used as a U.S. military base and staging area for its war against Nicaragua to the south when Nicaragua with U.S. presence posed no threat to Honduras.

By March of 1988 we were finished with all the Honduran legal requirements for adoption and had all the Honduran documents that we needed to take Andrew and Sarita to the U.S. We were eager to get back to Seattle and begin our new family life there. All that remained were documents required by the U.S. Embassy to get the visas that Andrew and Sarita would need to go with us to the United States. While the legal adoption was complete through the Honduran system, Andy and Sarita were not yet U.S. citizens so the painstaking process of getting visas for them dragged on and on. Latin American administrative and legal processes are known for being long and tedious. The irony here was that we had all of our Honduras papers and legal requirements completed. Now the problem was our own embassy and getting visas for our children. It was never clear to me why this process was so difficult and took so long.

One of the great advantages of the anti-U.S. demonstrations at the embassy in Tegucigalpa was that as a result they were eager to get as many U.S. citizens back to the U.S. as quickly as possible.

*Because of this a rush was put on the visa process and within just a few days we had the papers we needed. I remember that the staff person at the embassy who we last talked to was concerned that we might feel fearful as a result of the demonstrations and thus feel a need to get out of the country. We had been there long enough that we understood the demonstrations did not make us feel afraid. But in the final meeting I did try to pretend that I was afraid when I realized that this might help us get home to Seattle faster.*

*April 21, 1988*

*The Seattle Times published the following op-ed article that I wrote during our final months in Honduras:*

*"Another heavy-handed U.S. intrusion in Honduran life"*

*"As this is written on a warm evening in the capital city, an uneasy calm prevails. In the street, the scene now includes helmeted soldiers with tear-gas canisters strapped around their necks.*

*Constitutional rights have been suspended for 15 days to let the police/military control public demonstrations.*

*Speeches and chants from distant rallies echo among the city's hills. Last night windows were broken, over 20 cars were burned, and four people were killed as more than 1,000 Hondurans demonstrated in front of the U.S. Embassy.*

*We are admonished to be cautious in moving about in the streets, because of rumors that U.S. citizens might be kidnapped as a means of revenge.*

*But isn't Honduras our staunchest ally in Central America? Isn't this the country where unprecedented amounts of U.S. military and development aid have poured in since 1981? Isn't this the place where almost any U.S. citizen is made to feel at home, to which we can testify after the cordiality we have known in our two years here?*

*Within three days a fundamental shift has taken, a fundamental shift has taken place. Why?*

*At 6 a.m. on April 5, the mansion of Ramon Matta Ballestros was surrounded by some 100 Honduran soldiers. this central figure in drug traffic between Latin America and the United States was arrested on the initiative of the commander of the security forces, under a search warrant granted by a Honduran judge.*

*Reportedly he was turned over to U.S. authorities, flown to New York via the Dominican Republic, and then taken to the federal prison in Marion, Ill. When news of the arrest was made public here, a sense of outrage filled Honduras.*

*Matta is something of a Robin Hood figure here. A poor woman told us that Matta, reportedly a billionaire, has helped the poor much more than the government has ever done.*

*Yet he has been arrested and imprisoned before, with no public outcry. Many Honduran leaders have expressed their desire to see him brought to justice.*

*The present anger has the feel of the last thorn in the camels open wound -- one more heavy-handed U.S. intrusion into Honduran life.*

*The nation's constitution states that no Honduran will be extradited when sought by another nation for crimes committed. President Jose Azcona Hoya stated last month that Matta could not be legally extradited to the United States. Now it has been done -- illegally.*

*The outrage is augmented by reports that high Honduran military officers have been involved with (and have protected) Matta in drug running, and that a former U.S. Ambassador to Honduras, John Negroponte (now second in command at the U.S. National Security Council). cut a deal with Honduran leaders on a recent visit here. Its essence was said to be "We won't blow the whistle on your military leaders if you will give Matta to us."*

*Whether this is true or not the damage is done among the people. Hondurans at all levels of life feel that their sovereignty and national dignity has been violated. A citizen has been taken out of the country in violation of his constitutional rights by the very nation that claims to be the champion of constitutional democracy in the world.*

*In 1982, Negroponte made a deal with the military strongman, Gen. Gustavo Alvarez Martinez, in which Salvadoran troops would be trained on Honduran soil under U.S. supervision. Since feeling still ran high from the 1969 war when El Salvador invaded Honduras, the move was not well-received by Hondurans, including many within the military who had fought in that war.*

*The deal was one of the factors that led to the ouster of Alvarez in March 1984 due to pressures from the military command.*

*In 1985 soon after he was elected president, Azcona said he did not know if Nicaragua contras were based on Honduran soil, but that if they were, it would be a violation of the constitution.*

*In fact, the U.S.-supported contras had been operating out of Honduras for at least two years before the election. Voices from all over the political spectrum called for their expulsion. Now, eight months after the signing of the peace agreement, contras remain in Honduras.*

*Recently, 3,000 U.S. troops were sent to Honduras eight hours after a reported request by President Azcona. Many believe that the "request" originated in Washington and that Azcona was pressured to rubber-stamp it after the troops were on their way.*

*The troops arrived without the Honduran Congress being notified, when the constitution grants only to Congress the authority to permit foreign troops on Honduran soil.*

*The Honduran Foreign Ministry, after stating that the troops had been requested to "protect Honduran lives and territorial integrity," was embarrassed when the U.S. State Department reported that the troops had been sent to support the contras.*

*The "Handbook on Honduras," published by the U.S. Embassy here, says: "The U.S. Agency for International Development supports the U.S. foreign-policy objectives of promoting democracy and fostering improvement in the standard of living to the Honduran people, especially the poor." Budget items show millions of dollars going into "strengthening democratic institutions."*

*But Honduran poverty, with U.S. hypocrisy and deeply injured sense of national pride, has led to a graphic picture of the failure of U.S. policy -- hundreds of Hondurans marching in the streets and chanting ant-U.S. slogans, in defense of a man who is one of the biggest drug lords in the hemisphere.*

## Some Closing Words

*I turned 39 while living in Central America and I am 72 as I bring these current reflections to a close. It was almost half a lifetime ago. Carl Jung once said that 39 is "the youth of old age and the old age of youth." Whatever one might say about that age that would apply to all people, I now look back at that young man who was me in the 1980s with compassion, some gentle humor and admiration. I admire his willingness to dive into the unknown on behalf of the good as best as he could discern it then and with the awareness that he had then, and I view with compassion his earnest efforts to be good and do good.*

*The work of reshaping this journal with over thirty additional years of life has given me the gift of a return visit to Central America that is no longer physically possible for me. I am very grateful. I also give thanks for the conscious and unconscious education about life on earth that I certainly experienced during my time there.*

*I smiled and my face turned red when I encountered the young man who was so pious and earnest about "doing God's will." While I edited out some of the most embarrassing passages, I also came to appreciate the honest struggle of that young man with himself and with some of the issues facing the human family in the 1980s.*

*I hope this record has shed some light and offered some relevant education for all who read it. And if it might inspire a few to go in person to meet the people of Central America or of any other place on our planet, I would be especially pleased.*

*A Honduran migrant caravan headed north for the U.S.-Mexico border.*
Photo credit: "Uma nova caravana migratória partiu de Honduras rumo aos Estados Unidos" by Johan Ordonez/AFP for Brasil de Fato, CC license 2.0. See photo credits at end of book for full details.

*In the years preceding this writing in 2020, there have been frequent caravans of Hondurans and other Central Americans traveling mostly by walking northward, toward the United States. I mourn the tragedy and hopelessness that moves them to just pick up and leave an environment that has no apparent future for them. This might move some to say that the USA's way of life is still "the last best hope of earth." Of course, it is not that simple, and the history reflected in the preceding stories say much about how our government and people have created many of the conditions that make such caravans seem necessary. The worst in us has become worse than ever as we observe children separated from parents that no one can locate and people living in cages in the midst of a pandemic. If we can find ears within us that will listen, Hondurans can become for us the teachers that our nation's soul so desperately needs. Their very suffering can offer us an awakening to our nation's capacity for compassion and justice which surely remains alive and available within us.*

*Holga: For a long time I had the same dream each night—that I had a child; and even in the dream I saw that the child was my life; and it was an idiot. And I wept and a hundred times I ran away, but each time I came back it had the same dreadful face. Until I thought, if I could kiss it, whatever n it was my own, perhaps I could rest. And I bent to its broken face, and it was horrible ... but I kissed it.*

*Quentin: Does it still come back?*

*Holga: At times. But it somehow has the virtue now ... of being mine. I think one must finally take one's life in one arms Quentin.*

from After the Fall by Arthur Miller

*"I have called you by name and you are mine...you are precious in my sight, and honored, and I love you."*

Isaiah 43:4

# ACKNOWLEDGEMENTS

More people than I can ever adequately name or remember have been important in this story and in getting it into writing. If you know your name belongs here but isn't please accept my gratitude and forgive me for my imperfect memory.

The people of Honduras, Nicaragua and Costa Rica who welcomed and patiently educated us belong at the top of the list. Many of your names appear in the story. I hope this writing does justice to your stories, dignity and courage, and especially to your hospitality and friendship.

My former wife, Kathryn Williams, was a strong partner in this journey bringing grace, compassion, commitment, political experience, and many personal and professional gifts. Kathy also gave time to read the manuscript and helped me overcome gaps in my memory.

Dr. Patricia Rumer was Latin American Secretary in the early 80s for the work of the United Church of Christ south of the border and surrounded us with support in a number of ways.

Nephew, Michael Mullins, and sister, Margaret Mullins offered support and suggestions along with the faithful support that only family members can offer.

My life is blessed with a number of good friends who are also writers and editors. Esther Elizabeth has been a dear friend, mentor, spiritual guide, and the kind of compassionate gadfly I have needed to keep writing in spite of many temptations to stop. Her influence is present in just about anything I try to write.

Laura Helper is a friend and a Friend, a Memphis Quaker who gave extravagantly of her time and offered valuable suggestions and hearty encouragement from her life as a professional editor of many books over the years.

We had many friends who came to visit us while we were in Honduras, all of whom had their own commitments to working for a more just world. Peter Shober, Barbara Cowan and friends from Chewelah, Washington, a group from University United Church of Christ, Seattle, our home church at that time, a number of other congregations and all the members of the Williams family.

Ed and Gail Crouch friends with just the right social work credentials offered the help we needed to simplify an otherwise complicated adoption ordeal. Gail and Kathleen Crouch came for a visit just when we needed one.

Nancy Hannah and Mary Ellen Smith are the ever-faithful godmothers of our children. Both of them came to visit and met Sarita before she left her native Honduras. Passing decades have only amplified the gratitude I feel.

Prof. Rex Enoch invited us to share our story with his students at the University of Memphis and would later leave his tenured position to become Director of Education at Heifer International's ranch in Arkansas. He read, and both he and Nan blessed, my manuscript and my life with 50 years of friendship.

Kathy Morefield, Ron Krom and Beth Brunton made it possible for fifteen editions of our newsletter from Honduras to be sent to a few hundred people with common concerns. I am long out of touch with you but my gratitude has endured.

Filmmakers and compañeros in Estelí, Julia Lesage and Chuck Kleinhans, interviewed the mother of the household where I lived, Silvia Diaz, there on camera and generously made it available online. https://mediaburn.org/video/home-life/

This book began as hundreds of pages of the hieroglyphic-looking markings which were my handwriting. Robin Clochard and Cameron Haramia worked generously for many hours to transform it all into beautiful, typed copy. Thank you, friends.

Our cat-loving, Ecuador-seasoned, novelist/storyteller, musician, community activist, computer wizard and long-time friend Kali Kucera brought his artistry, broad knowledge, patience and friendship to this work, holding my hand step by step in this my first effort to turn my writing into something I can call a book.

As the work came near to completion but still needed major editing, I found long-time and long-lost friend, journalist, editor and prophet of the media, Bart Preecs, in Spokane who took on the major editing of the work when the need was great. Thank you, brother.

Peter Morgan helped me overcome late waves of anxiety with words of support, especially by reminding me that I did not have to write a perfect book.

My beloved wife, Sharon Pavelda, helped in many ways as reader, patient encourager and so much more. Thank you, my love.

# NOTES AND PHOTO CREDITS

## Notes

Quote by Arthur Miller is from *Arthur Miller's Collected Plays, Vol. II*, The Viking Press, News York, NY, 1981, p. 148.

Quote by Frederick Buechner, page i, is from azquotes.com

Link for video mentioned in Chapter 2 by Julia Lesage on Family Life in Estelí, 1984, https://mediaburn.org/video/home-life/

## Photo Credits:

All the following photos are licensed under Creative Commons License BY-NC-SA 2.0 (https://creativecommons.org/licenses/by-nc-sa/2.0/)

Made in the USA
Monee, IL
26 April 2021

66665522R00213